# CAPITOL PUNISHMENT

# CAPITOL PUNISHMENT

## THE HARD TRUTH ABOUT WASHINGTON CORRUPTION
## FROM AMERICA'S MOST NOTORIOUS LOBBYIST

# JACK ABRAMOFF

 WND Books

CAPITOL PUNISHMENT
The Hard Truth About Washington Corruption From America's Most Notorious Lobbyist
by Jack Abramoff

Published by WND Books
Washington, D.C.

Copyright © 2011 Jack Abramoff

Book designed by Mark Karis

WND Books are distributed to the trade by:
Midpoint Trade Books
27 West 20th Street, Suite 1102
New York, NY 10011

WND Books are available at special discounts for bulk purchases. WND Books, Inc. also publishes books in electronic formats. For more information call (541) 474-1776 or visit www.wndbooks.com.

First Edition

ISBN 13 Digit: 978-1-936488-44-5

Library of Congress information available.

Printed in the United States of America.

10 9 8 7 6 5 4 3 2 1

# DEDICATION

This book is dedicated to the memory of my beloved mother, Jane Abramoff—may her soul be elevated in Heaven.

To my gallant and inspiring father, Frank Abramoff.

To my precious and cherished children—Levi, Alex, Daniel, Livia, and Sarah.

And to my true love, my dear wife, Pam Abramoff.

# CONTENTS

# PROLOGUE

I was scared. Real fear—the kind which paralyzes—had taken over. I was about to experience the same pain I had helped inflict on others.

As I walked into the Hart Senate Office building on Capitol Hill, I knew I was stepping into the torture chamber of American politics: the congressional hearing. Being the subject of a congressional hearing is a lot like being tossed to the lions in the Roman Coliseum. You know that, no matter what, you will soon be eaten alive.

On September 29, 2004, I was to be that lion's main course.

The air was thick with tension. Passersby gawked. My attorneys led me inside with great dignity and compassion, but to me it felt like a death march. We neared the hearing room, and encountered the one senator most responsible for this day of reckoning: Senator John McCain. He was his usual sanctimonious, preening self, the embodiment of everything I loathed in a politician. But here he was, sneering, with his foot on my throat, and the entire national press corps helping to keep it in place.

McCain's staff member directed us to a hallway outside the hearing room, and pointed. "Wait here," he said. My heart was pounding. Suddenly, the booming, self-important voices of the world's great deliberative body—the United States Senate—were audible and mordant. The grave sins of one Jack Abramoff were the topic, and there were no boundaries. On and on they droned, spewing searing accusations, including some new ones I hadn't yet heard.

Who was this villain they so contemptuously described? Had I met this Abramoff guy, I would have hated him, too.

I stood and listened to the castigation. The crowd, mainly consisting of disgruntled Native Americans, could barely contain their animosity. And then they brought me in to look that lion in the eyes. There I was, Jack Abramoff, about to be slaughtered. My attorneys and I moved in what seemed to be slow motion through the throng of cameras and the pulsating crowd. They had come for the show of the year, and they weren't going to be disappointed. The senators had stacks of my personal files at the ready. My tax returns since I was a fetus. Emails foolishly written in what seemed to be another era. For all I knew, they had my old football helmet, stained with the paint of some poor victimized linebacker I had smash-blocked in high school.

They were the Senate. They made the rules. They decided when to follow them. They kept the score, and it had already been decided—this was not going to be very pleasant.

As we crossed to the witness table, I noticed the hardened, hate-filled faces in the crowd. There was a murmur of displeasure as they laid their eyes on me. My head was pounding.

I was told to stand and be sworn in. My right arm cocked at an angle, I affirmed that I would be telling the truth. But would I really be telling the truth? Technically I would, but the only truth they would be hearing that day was a recitation of my constitutional rights. This hearing was not designed to get to the truth. It was staged to give these high-flown senators some good campaign sound bites. But I was done with helping politicians get good sound bites. Or at least that's what I thought.

My game plan was simple: don't create any problems by being stupid. Its execution was complicated, since the aim of these kinds of congressional hearings is getting you to commit perjury. I had to be disciplined. No problem, right?

I stared at the senators through the sea of paparazzi crouched on the floor between the senatorial presidium and my chair at the witness table. Most of these legislators had taken thousands of dollars from my clients and firms, and now they were sitting as impartial judges against me. Washington hypocrisy at its best.

Senator Ben Nighthorse Campbell was to be first. A Native American senator from Colorado who had switched parties years ago, he was given the choice job of heading the Indian Affairs Committee in the Senate. He was a nice guy, but didn't quite fit in with his bolo tie and folksy demeanor. He seemed to prefer riding his Harley Davidson to being a senator. We got along well in the past, particularly when I delivered campaign cash to him. But today was different. The Senator Campbell I knew was gone. In his place sat an angry man.

"Mr. Abramoff, why would you want to work for people you have contempt for?"

"Mr. Chairman," I replied, "I respect the committee's process. That's why I am here today. But I have no choice but to assert my various constitutional privileges against having to testify. I hope that sometime soon I will be able to do so in order to present all of the facts."

"Mr. Abramoff, do you refer to all your clients as morons?"

"Senator, I respectfully invoke the privileges previously stated."

"Mr. Abramoff, do you refer to your clients as monkeys?"

"Mr. Abramoff...."

"Mr. Abramoff...."

It went on and on. It didn't really matter. In my mind, I had already left the building.

How had it all come to this?

# 1

# YOU DON'T KNOW JACK!

The second question the intake officer at the Federal Correctional Institution in Cumberland asked me was whether I had a happy childhood. The first question was where I'd like my body shipped should I die there.

I found the query about my childhood to be strange. I was ensconced in a facility with life-long criminals. Did those guys have blissful upbringings? I imagined not. I, on the other hand, had a wonderful childhood.

Perhaps appropriately for someone burdened with the nickname "Casino Jack," I was born in Atlantic City, New Jersey. Of course, this was before there were any casinos. At least before there were legal ones. My grandfather was a wholesale produce broker who immigrated to the United States from Odessa, Ukraine, where his grandfather was manager of the opera house. My mother's family came to America in the last years of the nineteenth century from Grodno, which was then in Lithuania or Poland depending on what time of day it was. Mom's family included scientists, mathematicians, concert pianists, artists, and authors. Dad and his brother were the toughest street fighters in Atlantic City. I guess I got my genes from both sides.

My parents were children of the Great Depression, though they didn't resort to saving tin foil and rubber bands like some of their contemporaries. When the downturn hit, my dad's father lost all his money and then lost his health. My father went to work when he was eight years old. By the time he was sixteen, he had purchased a small luncheonette and made enough money to carry the family. When he volunteered for the Navy the next year, that luncheonette kept his parents going while he headed for the Pacific and World War II. When he returned, he dove into business and built a respectable company making miniature golf courses.

Mom was a beauty queen, and an elegant and kind person. She made sure we kids were raised right and helped us get through any difficulty. She regularly served as my lawyer and lobbyist when I would get myself into hot water with my father, who was remarkably strict and quick to mete out justice. Mom made a kid's life happier, leavening that justice with mercy and compassion.

While Mom taught me about classical music and literature, Dad taught me to fight. I remember coming home one day in tears. I must have been around six years old. Some kid slugged me, and I folded like a wet blanket. Mom was full of hugs and encouraging nods. Dad took me to the living room and gave me a boxing lesson. For this particular lesson, I was the punching bag. He made it clear I should expect the same whooping any time someone else beat me. It was the last time someone would punch me without my punching back. That is, until I became the poster child for the lobbying industry.

Our family was Republican, though my parents, like most Jews in America, grew up as FDR Democrats. By the time I was politically aware, they had made the switch to the GOP. Their conversion came from a most unlikely source: the king of golf, Arnold Palmer, who had hired my father in the late 1950s to run the miniature golf division of Arnold Palmer Enterprises. He eventually promoted him to chairman of his company.

My first political memories were from the 1960s. The America I loved was under assault from the baby boomer generation, as these newly minted leftists challenged the old order and tradition. I watched in disgust each evening as the news showed hippies attending rock concerts and radicals burning the American flag. I was at once terrified and repulsed by these sights, and, as my revulsion grew, so did my fealty to the conservative cause.

I soaked up as much as I could about conservative thought and history, but since my parents weren't as interested in politics, I often became confused. In 1968, at the age of nine, I announced my support for McCarthy for President. The only problem was that the McCarthy running for President in 1968 was Eugene, a left-wing senator from Minnesota, not the anti-communist warrior, Senator Joe McCarthy from Wisconsin, who had by then passed away. I was so confused at that age that my next political endorsement was likely to be Charlie McCarthy, a famous ventriloquist's dummy (and since my next choice was Nixon, many on the left probably wouldn't have seen a difference).

During Nixon's first term in office, NBC purchased Arnold Palmer Enterprises, and Dad became president of Diner Club Franchises, a division of the then-dominant credit card company. The new position took us from New Jersey to sunny Southern California. The summer of 1969 saw Teddy Kennedy drive his car into the water off Chappaquiddick Island, Neil Armstrong take a small step onto the moon, thousands of concert goers converge on a farm near Woodstock, New York, Muammar Gaddafi seize power in Libya, and the Abramoff family move to Beverly Hills. On the way there, I toured the country with Arnold Palmer and Dad on Palmer's new Lear Jet. I even got my first golf lessons from the great man.

It was in Beverly Hills, at Hawthorne Elementary School, that I first pursued elective office, running for president in eighth grade. There were no overarching philosophical questions for the student-voters to decide other than which candidate was more likely to bring in ice cream as an after-school snack, but it was important to me. My opponent, David Factor, was a scion of the Max Factor cosmetics fortune and a good friend. He had been at Hawthorne for years, and I was a newcomer, but the election was close.

At a flag football game the day before the vote, I dove to recover a fumble and collided with one of my teammates. I was out cold and woke up some time later in the emergency room at UCLA Medical Center. They sent me home with a bandaged head, and I fell into a two-day stupor. The election proceeded without me the next day, and the vote was a tie. Had I been there to cast my own ballot, I would have won the election.

My friends bounded to my house after dismissal and gave me the news. There would be a runoff on Monday. I was groggy and despondent. My father, as always, took charge. To lift my spirits, he had the kids organize a get together at our home that Sunday. My parents cooked hot dogs, and I was able to get out of bed to be with my friends. We jokingly decided to track all our voters to make sure no one else would be playing football and miss that Monday's re-vote.

The next day, I cautiously hobbled into school, bandaged and dizzy. George Fourgis, our civics teacher, planned to have the re-vote immediately, but first asked David and me to join him in his office. When the door shut, Mr. Fourgis turned to me and asked whether I had a party on the weekend. I said yes, that my parents organized something at our home. With great hesitation, Mr. Fourgis continued, "Well, Jack, I'm so sorry to mention this, but we have a campaign rule that limits the amount of money you can spend on your effort to fifteen dollars."

I nodded, fully aware of that restriction. In fact, I had been careful not to buy any pens or paper in making my campaign flyers for fear of spending too much money.

"I am told that your parents served hot dogs at the event. Is this true?"

I nodded again. By now, it was obvious to me that I wasn't going to be the next president of the school. My eyes welled with tears, but I tried to remain composed. I was such a little kid.

"Mr. Fourgis," I stammered, "I guess I broke the rules, and I'm sorry."

"Well," he continued, "It's up to David as to whether he wants to press the matter."

Before David could answer, I interrupted. "No. I broke the rules, and I'm going to withdraw from the race. I didn't mean to hurt anyone, but I don't want to continue. David wins."

Fourgis grabbed me and gave me a hug. I needed one. David looked like he wanted to cry as well. I am sure he would have preferred winning the presidency in the election, and not like this, but he wasn't given a choice.

"Jack, one day you will be very proud of what you did here today," said Mr. Fourgis. I admired him more than any of my teachers, and, while it stung, I trusted he was right.

My family valued tradition, at least as far as our patriotism and social mores were concerned, but Jewish faith played only a minor role in our lives. From a young age, it seemed tragic to me that our family had cut itself off from the great chain of transmission from Sinai to the present day and I foresaw that, if no Abramoff rectified this defect, it wouldn't be long before Judaism had passed out of our line completely.

This concern stayed latent for most of my youth until my father took us to see a film at the Pacific Theater on Wilshire Boulevard, a year before my bar mitzvah. As the curtain rose on the panoramic musical *Fiddler on the Roof*, I was instantly enchanted by the music and scenery. The story about the Jewish milkman from Ukraine and his struggle against iconoclastic forces of the late nineteenth century was originally written to ridicule traditional Judaism and question the sanity of those following the ancient faith. But the impact on me was precisely the opposite. By the time the curtain fell, I had decided it would be I who kept the force of assimilation at bay in our family. If I were to be a Jew, I would be an Orthodox Jew.

This was quite a proclamation for a twelve-year-old kid to make and one that didn't sit well with my family. My father had no interest in Orthodox Judaism. In fact, he viewed religious observance more as a distraction and a likely impediment to my success in the modern world. How could I possibly earn a living if I couldn't work on the Sabbath? How would I be able to attend business meetings if I couldn't eat the food? The Jews of his generation spent their lives blending in. I was making a deliberate choice to stand out. He was not pleased.

On the other hand, though, I was equally displeased with his approach, and the division in our beliefs and practices began a disagreement that has lasted decades. In order to keep the peace in our home, I had to make accommodations in my religious practice. I adopted a less strict dietary standard, didn't wear a yarmulke (our customary head covering), and tried not to separate myself from the family during the Sabbath. I knew that eventually I would be on my own, able to completely observe the faith I cherished. I wasn't thrilled about the accommodations I had to make, and at times was even despondent, but my relationship with my father was so important to me that I diligently practiced the virtue which has always eluded me in other areas: patience. And despite our disagreements on Jewish life, my father and I have remained closer than any father and son I know—both entirely convinced that, after decades of resisting, the other will finally come to his senses!

Despite my father's concern, my decision to become an orthodox Jew did the opposite of hold me back. When I reached high school, I re-entered the political arena and was elected president of our freshman class. I bounded onto the gridiron, starting a four-year football career that eventually saw me named to the West Side Los Angeles and Ocean League all-star teams. I started weight lifting at a time when few athletes focused on pumping iron, and was able to reach rarefied heights. By the time I graduated from high school, I held the record for power squatting, 560 pounds, and had become one of only two athletes to lift 2,700 pounds in four exercises.

My personal best in power lifting came one rainy day in the weight room at the high school. I put 640 pounds on the bar for an attempted power squat. None of my friends were in the room, only some junior college football players who used our facility to work out. They were immensely strong guys, regularly bench-pressing over four hundred pounds. I asked them to spot me. They must have thought I was kidding, since they started to laugh, but when I lifted the bar off the stand, the laughing stopped. I crouched into the exercise and let rip a deafening scream, as I accomplished the lift with great difficulty. The leader of their group—they called him "Chief" —gave me the best compliment he could: "You're one crazy kid, man." He had no idea how right he was.

On top of sports and school politics, I also worked at the local movie theatre, The Beverly. Like all my pursuits, I was committed to excelling at my new position. Over the course of my high school years, I worked my way up from ticket taker to theatre manager, but once I was in my new position, the owners decided to close the doors. They cut our supply of films and concessions, sending us ten-year-old re-runs and leaving me to man the sinking ship.

The rest of the staff and I were friends, and, customary of young kids, we decided to have fun in the final weeks before the theater was gone for good. Though our films were hackneyed retreads, we festooned the building with handmade posters and splashed superlatives across the marquee. We put red stanchions on the sidewalks, and positioned one of our ushers outside with flashlights to direct "the crowds." Passersby thought a premier was taking place and started to stream into the theatre. While most left once they saw we were playing old films, many loved our sense of humor, and the house was fuller than it had been when we were exhibiting the new shows. Our candy counter was bare, so we purchased snacks, popcorn, and drinks at the local supermarket, and sold them to our loyal patrons. Our fun came to an end when the owners—the General Cinema Corporation—got wind of our antics and promptly turned out the lights for good.

In my senior year of high school, I applied to three universities. Stanford rejected me; UCLA accepted me; and Brandeis, my first choice, put me on their waiting list. Brandeis was my ideal fit because it was a predominantly Jewish school celebrated for its academic prominence and its diverse student body—which included a small Orthodox population. It may have had a liberal political reputation, but I knew it would be a place where I could freely observe my religion. As I languished in limbo that summer waiting to find out if I would get in, my father's good friend and business partner, Sugar Ray Robinson, came to the house for a visit.

Sugar Ray was probably the greatest prizefighter of all time and was one of the finest men one could ever hope to meet. Having conquered the boxing world time and time again, Robinson decided to dedicate himself to helping underprivileged youths in his later years.

I had helped him in his endeavors, first by volunteering at the youth center he set up in the mid-Wilshire section of Los Angeles, and then by running a fundraiser for the group. Using Robinson's connections and my hard work, we set up the first of two celebrity basketball events at the Beverly Hills High School gym. The Los Angeles Rams football team faced off against the celebrity all stars, headed by Bill Cosby. I was in charge of everything other than securing the players, and we were able to raise approximately $20,000 for the Youth Foundation in both my sophomore and senior years.

When Sugar Ray came to visit that day, I mentioned how frustrating it was to be on the college waiting list, and how much I wished I could go to Brandeis. Trying to look on the bright side, I told him that I guessed I could put on another basketball game fundraiser at UCLA that year if I didn't get into Brandeis. I'm sure my voice didn't bear the kind of enthusiasm he was used to. He didn't say much more than his usual, "You'll be ok, little buddy."

When Sugar Ray called a few days later, I worried something was wrong—he didn't usually call me on the phone.

"Little buddy, you're all set," he said, as though that should clear up everything. But I was still in the dark.

"That school you want to go to—that Brandeis. You're in."

I thought he was just offering me his usual brand of encouragement. But sure enough, my acceptance letter arrived that week. Eventually, Sugar Ray told me what had happened. After our conversation, he picked up the phone and called the school's director of admissions, who turned out to be a huge fan of his. Sugar Ray laughed and said the guy sounded like he must have seen every one of his fights! He said, "I gave it to the guy pretty straight. I told him, 'Hey, can you let my little buddy Jackie into your school? It would mean the world to me.'" And that was it.

I was floored. Here was a man who had never gone to college, but who cared enough for me that he got me in. Sugar Ray was never intimidated by anyone, let alone highbrow academia, but the fact that he was so quickly able to find an ally and put him to work getting to the goal was a significant lesson for me—he was a great lobbyist.

After an arduous cross-country drive in August 1977 with my best friend, Phil Groves, I arrived on campus and dove right into getting settled in my dorm, Deroy, where 60's radical and Communist Party nominee Angela Davis had lived when she was a student at Brandeis.

I majored in English Literature, with the goal of becoming a lawyer, and took advantage of as many Jewish Studies courses I could find, including Hebrew language and Jewish Law. My other academic focus confused all but my mother: I minored in opera. I was the power-lifting, football playing, Orthodox Jewish, right wing Republican opera buff.

You know the type.

# 2

# RONALD REAGAN AND THE REBBE

Though I was always a conservative, my political activism in high school was confined to the student government. At Brandeis, that changed. In the student body, I met my first real communists. Their heroes were like exhibits in the dictator museum: Marx (not Groucho), Lenin, Trotsky, Mao, Stalin—Stalin! Can you imagine? It was like a big cereal bowl. Every kind of fruit, nut, and flake you could imagine was there. And I was put on the waiting list to get into this place? How did these guys get in?

The view from my window sophomore year was a gargantuan poster of Che Guevara. The daily dose of liberal and, at times, radical political activism at Brandeis, plus the fact that Jimmy Carter was president, was enough to make any conservative depressed.

On campus there was a vast array of left wing fringe groups. On the right there was only one group: the College Republicans. A fixture on hundreds of college campuses for decades, the group at Brandeis was rather typical: small and ineffectual. I signed up, but like most of their members, didn't pay much attention to them. I wanted to go to law school and that meant my time was dedicated to studying and getting good grades. I just didn't have time for the College Republicans.

At the end of my junior year at Brandeis, our campus hosted the annual convention of the statewide College Republican organization.

All the inactive members were called into service—all twenty of us. The delegates from other colleges arrived for the convention, and we Brandesians discovered something interesting: we had more delegates than the rest of the schools combined. That meant we could control the elections. We quickly caucused in some musty closet—perhaps the first time a Republican meeting room at Brandeis seemed crowded—and endeavored to choose our slate. The room went silent when our leader, Larry Copperman, asked who wanted to be state College Republican chairman. No one responded. I felt badly for Larry, a senior who dreamed of the Brandeis College Republicans winning at something—anything— so I raised my hand. That one simple movement would change my life forever.

It's not in my nature to do things half-heartedly. I could easily have been the typical state College Republican chairman, using the position to pad my resume and meet some of the party bigwigs. Instead, I dove in headfirst and resolved to build a huge organization and have real political impact.

Once elected, I made contact with Rick Endres, the executive director of the national College Republican office in Washington. He couldn't have been more helpful. Rick seemed to be looking for someone like me: a state chairman who was bound and determined to do his all to build a state organization. Since I didn't know a thing about politics, he recommended I get trained, so in the summer of 1980, I headed off to a seminar in Los Angeles run by master political strategist Morton Blackwell and Reagan Youth Director Steve Antosh. It was precisely what I needed: two straight days of political organization training. I listened to every word and took copious notes. Then I went back to Massachusetts and did something that surprised all of them: I implemented what they taught. Seemingly overnight, the College Republicans in Massachusetts became a serious political player.

When I returned to school that fall to build a new campus political organization, one of the leaders of the state Republican party provided me with a small office in a seedy building in downtown Boston. It was there that I first met Grover Norquist. From our very first meeting, I knew he was a genius. It seemed to me that Grover was able to outthink anyone on the planet. Had he set out to make money, he would have been the country's first trillionaire, but Grover was dedicated to politics.

A libertarian who worked within the Republican Party to effect change, Grover was a staunch anti-Communist and knew that the power of the state—whether in the hands of Democrats or Republicans—could be stifling for freedom. He spoke in the vernacular of a revolutionary, and this was very exciting for me. He didn't refer to political opponents as "liberals" or "Democrats." He called them "Bolsheviks," and all of us who hung on his every word followed suit. But Grover was more than a brilliant political strategist. He was a role model for us at College Republicans. With his no-holds-barred approach to politics, he exuded the confidence that our side would win the greatest political struggles in history— against the Soviets and the liberals. His fervent passion was contagious.

That Grover and I became friends at all is fairly remarkable. In many ways, we were polar opposites. I was a Jew from Beverly Hills. He was a protestant from the Boston suburbs. I studied liberal arts at Brandeis. He was a student at Harvard Business School. We agreed on most things political, but I was a bit uneasy at first with his desire to reduce the federal government to a size where he could "drag it into the bathroom and drown it in the bathtub." Grover was so hostile to the federal state that he did not trust it even with the national defense, which he felt should be outsourced to private companies. In those days, Grover had little concern with fashion, often wearing rumpled clothing. I was outgoing and extroverted—a budding politician, but Grover was reserved and quiet. At every meeting, he took notes in a small notepad. Often I would try to guess what he was writing, but I never had the nerve to ask. Had I, he would have flashed his mischievous smile—his version of "forget it"—and changed the subject. As Grover's power and prestige grew in the years to come, those jealous of his success would speculate that his jottings were most likely a list of opponents to be executed once he took power. I was never really sure.

Employing Blackwell's playbook, Grover and I sent teams of college students throughout the Bay State to canvass their campuses in search of Republican students. Once identified, our organizers would sign them up for the College Republican club, and immediately present them with a voter registration card and an absentee ballot application. The plan was to find every Republican on campus, get them registered and voting, and then have others do the same. There was no Internet, of course, so we literally went room-to-room through the dorms. Day after day, our activists were working away. I travelled the state, going from college to college, while also spearheading the canvassing of Brandeis. When the dust cleared, we had found over three hundred Republicans on our campus. I wondered how they had all snuck past the Admissions Office. Meanwhile, our state activists had created College Republican chapters at forty-two other colleges and universities, giving us a powerful statewide organization.

Since Massachusetts was not on any electoral target list for the Republicans—they had not won there since Eisenhower—we were pretty much on our own during the 1980 campaign. To have a shot at making election night interesting, we had to find every possible voter in the state and get them out. We continued to build our chapters and register new voters. We deployed our members as volunteers, manning campaign events, posting yard signs, attending rallies. The party loved having the youth involved, and the students loved the attention. None of us seriously thought we might win the state for Reagan, but we were going to give the Democrats a run for their money.

Then one day, on a street in Brookline, Massachusetts, I got my big break.

For most of the twentieth century, Brookline had been the home of the Chasidic Grand Rabbi of Boston, Rabbi Levi Yitzchok Horowitz, otherwise known as the Bostoner Rebbe. In Chasidic circles, the chief rabbinic and inspirational leader is accorded the title Rebbe, or Grand Rabbi. The present Bostoner Rebbe's grandfather had arrived on these shores in 1915 and established a dynasty which continues to thrive to this day. The Rebbe was beloved by all who knew him, and one of his particular passions was helping college students from out of town. I happened to be driving near his home when I saw the Rebbe walking outside his headquarters. I immediately got out of my car to greet him and seek his blessing, which is a custom among Orthodox Jews. In his usual majestic manner, the Rebbe was beyond gracious. He asked what I was doing, and I mentioned that I was working for Reagan's election. To my pleasant surprise, the Rebbe remarked that he was fervently praying for Reagan's victory. I boldly asked the Rebbe whether he would consider endorsing then-Governor Reagan, and to my delight, he said yes.

The last time a Bostoner Rebbe endorsed a presidential candidate was in 1928, in support of Al Smith, a Catholic who was being attacked for his religious beliefs. This time, though, the stakes were even higher, according to the Rebbe, and he was willing to do what he could. What a coup! The spiritual leader of thousands of Chasidic Jews was going to endorse our candidate.

The first call I made when I returned to my dorm was to the Reagan headquarters in Washington. I could barely speak; I was so excited. But the campaign staffer on the phone didn't share my exuberance. I asked if Governor Reagan could come to Boston to accept the Rebbe's endorsement. There was a pause and some muffled guffaws. With the debates approaching, the staffer responded that the Governor's schedule was limited. I volunteered that the Rebbe might be willing to come to Washington to meet with the Governor, but that too was rebuffed. Finally, he said they would send someone to accept the endorsement. I figured it would be Bush. Or Ford. Or Nixon. Or someone huge. Instead, they sent Maureen Reagan.

The good news was that Maureen worked tirelessly for her father's election. The bad news was that she was a leader of the pro-abortion wing of the party, and the Rebbe's endorsement was closely tied to Reagan's strong stand on family issues. She was also a feminist, and I would have to try to explain to her that the Grand Rabbi, as the leader of a Chasidic court, could not have physical contact with a woman to whom he was not married, even as much as to shake her hand. Additionally, he could not be photographed with a woman.

It was a cold and rainy October Boston day when Maureen Reagan was due to visit the Rebbe. Though I had only met him two months earlier, Grover accompanied me to this meeting. Indeed, it was rare to find one of us without the other. I cherished his sapient advice and good cheer. Whenever things seemed difficult, out came his enigmatic smile and his fortifying motto: "We're winning."

The rain abated slightly, but we were still getting wet standing on the curb awaiting Maureen Reagan's entourage. As her car approached, I glanced at Grover. The smile was replaced by a scrutinizing gaze. I expected him to pull out his note pad and record Maureen's name on the mythic list, but instead he reached to open her door and help her out of the car. A large woman, Ms. Reagan was all business.

As she emerged from the car, I introduced myself. "Ms. Reagan, I am

Jack Abramoff, the head of the local College Republican organization."

She stared right through me. I was wearing a button that featured Reagan's name in Hebrew characters, and my yarmulke was dripping with rain. "I want to just brief you on some of the particular customs of the Grand Rabbi and all Chasidic Jews. Since the Jewish laws of modesty forbid contact between a man and woman, other than those who are married, the Rebbe will be unable to shake your hand today."

She shot me an incredulous look.

"Additionally, he won't be able to be photographed with you."

She replied, "Then why am I here? If this is a political endorsement, and he won't shake my hand or take a picture, why am I here?" She brushed by me as she completed her invective, and headed up the stairs.

Despite her obvious annoyance at the situation, Maureen was a real pro. She sat with the Rebbe for almost an hour, graciously accepted his endorsement, and prepared to leave for the airport. The tension was gone and the atmosphere friendly until her male aide proffered his hand to the Rebbe's wife in thanks, setting off a minor brouhaha.

Grover and I celebrated, knowing that the Rebbe's endorsement would not only pay huge dividends in Massachusetts, but also in New York where thousands more of his followers lived. We left satisfied that we had done a good day's work. Hungry and exhausted, we headed for Reuben's Deli a few blocks away. We were both still wearing our Hebrew Reagan buttons when another opportunity presented itself. National Public Radio's show "All Things Considered" had set up shop outside the Deli to interview Jews on their electoral preferences.

They approached me first. "As a Jew," I told them, "I am voting for the Republicans this year. I love Reagan, and Carter is so anti-Israel that I can't imagine any lover of Israel voting for him."

They thanked me and looked to Grover for another interview. Now, Grover Norquist is many wonderful things, but Jewish is not one of them. Nevertheless, when asked what he, a Jew, would be doing this year, Grover didn't miss a beat: "Our people have suffered for generations and have been abused in America by the Democrats. This year, I am voting Republican. They are the only ones who treat us with respect and fully support Israel." I could barely contain my laughter, as Grover and I stumbled away like two drunken sailors.

Later that day, as we rode to yet another campaign event, I turned on NPR. They were reporting on Jewish attitudes during the election, and had chosen one Jew to speak for all of us—Grover!

The last few weeks of the campaign were spent making sure all our members voted, and manning the campaign voter turnout operations. On Election Day, 1980, I worked from before dawn until dark at a polling station in the pouring rain, encouraging voters to consider Reagan. Tired, wet, and hungry, I returned to my dorm room to change for that evening's victory party at the Copley Plaza Hotel. As I peeled off my wet clothes, I watched NBC News predict that Reagan would win in a landslide. I was thrilled, but wanted to know how we did in Massachusetts. While Reagan coasted to a smashing victory in almost every region in our state, the count was very close. In fact, it took about a week before we found out that we had won, and only by a margin of a few thousand votes. With incredible grace and kindness, the state party chairman credited us, the College Republicans, as making the difference and delivering the state. And indeed, we had.

I don't know when Grover first thought about taking our Massachusetts show on the road, but shortly after the election was over, he and I were planning my run for national chairman of College Republicans. In high school, I had lost more elections than I had won, and if you threw in my bowing out of the race for president of elementary school, my record was a pitiable one for four.

I figured the campaign for chairman of this inveterate organization would be hard fought, with a crowded field, so I approached my campaign with the greatest caution and preparation. My father stepped up to help as usual by putting together a fundraiser for me at our home in Beverly Hills. Led by prominent California developer Stanley Black, Dad's friends were more than willing to help out, and I soon had the funds to run a proper campaign. In those days, that meant traveling to as many states as possible to meet with the voters in the upcoming election: College Republican state chairmen and regional officers.

As the spring gave way to summer, the convention loomed. I had worked hard for months, and was unopposed in my campaign. It was too good to be true, I thought. After all, in the last race Frank Lavin had run unopposed the entire campaign until the night before the election. That night, as Frank slept, a group of dissatisfied state chairmen from around the nation, including future Senator Rick Santorum and future Congressman Phil English, fomented revolt. By morning, they not only had a candidate, Pennsylvania chairman Steve Gibble, but they also had the votes to win. Lavin went down to crushing defeat, and Gibble took over the organization. I wasn't going to let that happen to me.

As we rolled into Chicago, site of our national convention, my campaign workers, so ably recruited by Grover, were omnipresent. No delegate was left alone. Our group was tireless, and, in fact, the last night few of us slept at all. I certainly wasn't going to bed, not after what happened to sleepy Frank Lavin. There were non-stop meetings. I didn't crash until later the next day when I had been safely elected the new national chairman of the College Republicans. No last minute opponent had emerged.

As I awoke from my stupor, I headed to the elevator to see what the other delegates were doing and was approached by a kid who looked to be no more than fourteen years old. It was Ralph Reed, who actually turned twenty years old just two days earlier. Ralph asked if there was any way I could give him a job in Washington with the College Republicans. He told me that he was a political junkie and his lifelong goal was to work in Washington and have a political career. I loved his enthusiasm and pluck. I told him I didn't know what kind of budget we had, but if he was willing to work for almost nothing, sure. And so began a decades-long collaboration with the man whom *Time* magazine would later dub the "Right Hand of God." Ralph joined us and eventually ascended to the executive directorship of our organization. On the way, he was paid very little. So little, in fact, that he had to sleep on the couch in my apartment and eat spaghetti every night, the only meal he could put together for less than a dollar.

Though we lived like paupers, we worked like the career men we were all becoming. One of my first tasks in office was to take seriously a casual offer made by the new chairman of the Republican National Committee, Dick Richards, who had promised to fund as many training schools as the College Republicans could set up. Before long, I asked Paul Erickson, one of the very few staffers from the previous regime to continue in our office, to come up with a blueprint to change American college campuses with a dream training program for Chairman Richards to fund.

To every college Republican who contacted the national office, Paul Erickson was by far the most impressive person they had ever encountered in politics. Born and raised in South Dakota, Paul was a tall, thin raconteur, able to converse on topics ranging from congressional races to customs of the aborigines of New Zealand. In politics, and later in lobbying, there was a shorthand expression for someone who needed no coaching: "He got the joke." That meant that the person needed no explanations, no reasons and no amplifications. As soon as he heard the plan, he just seemed to get it and could immediately spring into action. No one got the joke better than Paul, so naturally he was my only choice to craft our massive training project. The result was the Fieldman Program of 1981 and 1982, the most ambitious college political training and recruitment effort since the radical leftists of the 60's launched Students for a Democratic Society.

The program consisted of five teams of four full-time student organizer-teachers, each of whom was to conquer a region of the nation: northeast, mid-atlantic, south, mid-west, and west. The mission was simple. Every weekday, two members of the team would go to one university, and the other two to another. There they would set up recruitment tables in the main thoroughfares, encouraging students to join the College Republicans. As students would sign up, they were told of an organizational meeting to be held that night on campus and encouraged to attend. At that meeting, a chapter of the College Republicans would be formed, and people would be asked to volunteer to serve as officers. Once the club was in place, the leadership and any interested member would be strongly encouraged to attend a training seminar that weekend, the Fieldman School. From there, they would be sent to canvass their school in search of every Republican, getting them to register and vote. Then they would be asked to help recruit others and spread the word. With twenty full-time organizers out in the field, starting an average of ten new chapters and recruiting approximately two thousand new members each day, and training an average of two hundred new activists each weekend, the College Republicans quickly became much more than an organization—it was a veritable political movement, a gargantuan structure which would impact elections for a generation.

Despite our success at expanding our organization, what grabbed news headlines and got us the most attention were our issue campaigns and guerilla theatre tactics. Nothing made us gag more than the previous College Republican recruitment poster. "Join the Best Party in Town" was emblazoned over a martini glass with an elephant inside. This stupid emblem did nothing if not reinforce the stereotype of country club Republicans. We trashed the martini placard and replaced it with a phrase that we felt said it all: "Join the Revolution… Join College Republicans."

We saw ourselves as revolutionaries. We disdained the political establishment—Republican or Democrat—that brought our nation low. With the exception of Reagan and a few fellow revolutionaries, we saw no hope in the standard Republican approach to politics, so we created our own. Instead of cocktail hours, our leadership organized rallies around political issues.

We thoroughly enjoyed our street theater, which was a welcome outlet for us kids who worked day and night for the cause. We organized a national petition drive to support Lech Walesa's solidarity movement in Poland, and put together a protest rally which ended with an impromptu rush on the Polish Embassy. We staged a massive demonstration outside the Soviet Embassy on 16th Street after the Soviets shot down the Korean airliner in September 1983. Most of these demonstrations were spontaneous, but we regularly scheduled the annual smashing of the Berlin Wall event in Lafayette Park across from the White House. Every August, we built a mock Berlin Wall and brought out the sledgehammers to symbolically pulverize it. It was the College Republicans equivalent of the county fair, with hearty participants doing their best to make their blow count. Little did we realize that within a decade, Berliners would be doing the same thing for real.

We didn't stop at demonstrations. Mimicking our conservative cousins across the Atlantic in the United Kingdom, we started to produce a series of provocative political posters for distribution on Capitol Hill and throughout the nation. Every mischievous idea which popped into our heads wound up on a poster. One declared, "The Soviet Union Needs You: Support a U.S. Nuclear Freeze." Another bore a picture of then-Speaker of the House, Thomas P. "Tip" O'Neill, a rather rotund individual, with a dotted line around him and scissors, with the caption:

"Cut the Fat Out of Government, Elect A Republican Congress." We were immature well beyond our years.

Our raucous activities did not escape the attention of the party bosses. Some were quite pleased with our guts and hard work. Others disdained our right wing circus and overly confident bravado. When Grover and I arrived at the Republican National Committee headquarters for the first time, we took a stroll through the various divisions well after closing hours. We were aghast to find that pictures of liberal Republicans like Rockefeller and Ford were still plastered all throughout the building, while there were hardly any pictures of Reagan. We paced the halls, Grover puffing on his ubiquitous cigarette, both of us deep in thought. These establishment Republicans, still admiring the failed liberal Republican leaders of the past, were soon to become our detractors. They were bullies to spend time attacking kids like us, but that's what they do.

My whole life I've had a hard time not attacking bullies. When I was a kid, a giant by the name of Eddie Cohen pushed into line ahead of me at the ice cream truck. Instinctively, I threw him out of line and onto the ground. He rose and beat the snot out of me. I might have learned my lesson about attacking bullies right there, but instead the opposite message took root. I would find myself siding with the underdog in almost every encounter of my life. So, when the swaggering Pooh-Bahs of the Republican National Committee looked with contempt at our fledgling efforts to revive College Republicans using conservative issues and started to make our lives uncomfortable by suggesting our organization be moved out of the headquarters, I was enraged.

Grover suggested a subtle counter attack: we would sponsor lectures in the building on important conservative issues of the day, starting with the gold standard. Promoting the return of the dollar to a gold standard is to the moderate Republican what a sprinkling of holy water is to the proverbial devil. Being new to issue politics, I didn't realize this. Being Grover, he did. We invited Jude Wanniski, one of the leading conservative, free market economists, to the RNC to give a lecture on why we should return to the gold standard. I'm not sure we could have done anything worse than that, and no one hesitated to let us know.

Because of our antics, we were denied most of the perquisites that the other Republican affiliated groups in the building were granted. On the one hand, they couldn't quite kick us out of the building, since we were training thousands of new Republicans and recruiting tens of thousands more. On the other hand, no other group (except the Young Republicans, who had already been kicked out of the building) brought them such headaches. Of course, we didn't want the perks anyway, since they mostly consisted of invitations to stuffy receptions in the RNC conference room.

Notwithstanding our penchant for riding into every ideological battle which erupted in Washington, someone on the inside must have thought we were doing good work, because in the winter of 1981, Grover and I were invited to visit with the President in the Oval Office to brief him on the political situation on America's campuses. The night before, I was scheduled to appear on Larry King's national radio show. In those pre-cable television, pre-Rush Limbaugh days, King's coast-to-coast, midnight to 3 a.m. radio show was the most influential program on the air. Being asked to appear was huge. I would be debating Bernie Friedman, the chairman of the College Democrats for the duration of the broadcast, just hours before our Reagan Oval Office meeting. I would have to finish the radio program at 3 a.m. and be at the White House by 9 a.m., but in those days I would have stayed on the radio for twenty-four straight hours and then sprint to the White House if required.

Paul Erickson and I entered the studio late that night, ready to do battle with Bernie and his executive director, Jonathan Slade. We liked Bernie and Jonathan, who were, relatively speaking, pretty conservative. Because of their indolence, the College Democrats were far from our most effective opponents on campus. Still, Bernie and I were here to go head-to-head on the air.

When Paul and I entered the main studio, King and Bernie were sharing a good laugh. As soon as he saw me, King fell quiet and became very serious. I didn't get the sense that he liked me, but I didn't really care. Like a fight referee, he gave us a briefing on the rules—no biting, no knees to the groin—and the show commenced.

For about twenty minutes, King let Bernie and me spar on a variety of issues. Defense. The Soviets. Budget cuts. Tax cuts. I noticed that Bernie had slipped, for the first time since I met him, into liberal mode, but that didn't matter. I knew these issues like I knew my own middle name, and had no problem warding off his attacks and scoring points. It got so bad, in fact, that during one of the breaks, King actually turned to Bernie to buck him up and push him back into the ring. Some impartial ref. Meanwhile, Grover was back at the office with Ralph, organizing our state chairmen and chapter leaders to call into the program. We figured we would outman Bernie and his group and fill the airwaves with our folks. We didn't realize how well it would work.

The first call came in. "Good evening, my question is for Mr. Friedman. How can you possibly defend the weak position your party has taken on opposing the Soviets and their human rights record?"

Bernie froze for a moment before he nearly shouted, "That's Grover Norquist, Jack's executive director!"

My performance was worthy of an Academy Award: "Bernie, I don't know what you're talking about!" King couldn't figure out what was going on. He was, for the first time in decades, speechless. I jumped in and answered the "question," much to Bernie's chagrin.

Another caller was on the line.

"My question is for Bernie Friedman. How can you oppose tax cuts after one of your greatest Democratic presidents, John F. Kennedy, made them the centerpiece of his economic program?"

"That's Ralph Reed, also from Jack's staff!" Bernie remonstrated with increasing anger.

I snickered quietly as King turned on his ally, "Bernie, that's ridiculous. This show is broadcast to the entire nation. How can you possibly think Jack's staff would have the first two calls?" Poor Larry King. He had no idea.

Bernie tried to regain his momentum during the final hour of the broadcast, but it was too late. Through superior preparation and unbounded aggression—traits which would come to define my political activities—we vanquished Bernie. Paul and I felt on top of the world as we burst through the studio doors into the frigid winter night. My pace was quickened by the knowledge that I would soon be seeing our hero in the Oval Office.

A few hours later, Grover met me at the Pennsylvania Avenue entrance to the White House. From there, it was only a short walk to the reception area of the West Wing. I had been to the White House before, but this was the first time I was going to the West Wing. Grover and I checked in and settled into the formal seating in the lobby area. Grover smoked a cigarette like a steam engine, billows of smoke filling the room. We sat in silent anticipation. I fidgeted with the briefing papers we had prepared for President Reagan and practiced my feeble greeting. After twenty minutes, we were invited to move to the anteroom outside the Oval Office.

I had never been, and would never again be, as nervous as I was at that moment. I could feel my sweat soaking through the shirt under my suit jacket. As we stood in the small waiting area, Grover lit a second cigarette, so that he was now holding one in each hand. I shot him a look and he quickly extinguished them both just before the door opened and we heard, "The President will see you now." The scariest words a young politico can imagine.

I felt like the cowardly lion from the *Wizard of Oz*. Only there was no long hallway to bound down, no window from which to leap. Grover and I entered the Oval Office and found ourselves face to face with our hero.

Frozen in place, I must have sounded like Jackie Gleason from *The Honeymooners*, stammering and stuttering in my timidity. Grover might have been more nonchalant, but I no longer saw Grover. I only saw Reagan. He finished writing something at the desk and rose. As always, he was in suit and tie, and he was gracious.

"Well, Jack, Grover, how are you?"

"I'm... Oh... Ah... Hmm..."

Reagan smiled, bounding over to grasp my hand. I was a deer in the headlights, oblivious to my surroundings, entirely focused on Ronald Reagan. The President did his best to help me snap out of it. He threw his arm around my shoulder and asked me what I thought of the Remington statue on the mantle behind me. "Nancy thinks I should move it over across the room, but I just don't know. What do you think, Jack?"

"Uh, yes. Yes, sir, that's a good idea. Assuming you think it's a good idea." It was a stupid answer, but it didn't matter. He knew how to put people at ease. I had calmed down and could now talk to him about what was happening on the college campuses. He related a story about how rough his relationships were with the college kids when he was governor, and I assured him it was different now. I left our papers with him, and we shook hands. Grover and I slipped out of the office, and out of the White House.

Over the next year, I was invited to a half dozen crowded receptions at the White House. So when the invitation for Sunday evening, January 31, 1982, came, I didn't think much of it. In fact, I nearly didn't go since I had plans to visit my family in Atlantic City that weekend and didn't want to rush back to Washington for just another cattle call. But the family visit ended earlier than expected, so I put on the suit I had with me (not one of my finest), and drove straight to the White House. I was hungry, and I figured if nothing else came of the evening, at least I could get some fruit at the reception.

I parked a few blocks away from the South Gate, where invitees were directed to enter. When I didn't see anyone else entering on foot, I assumed I had the wrong entrance. The guard assured me that I was at the right place, and I was walked to the East Wing entrance. The West Wing is where all the business takes place, but all the fun at the White House—the State dinners, presentations, concerts, and receptions—happens in the East Wing. Drone-like, I made my way to the foyer in front of the Blue Room, where a Marine stringed quartet was playing Vivaldi. The place was deserted. Where were all the people? Was I late? A Marine in dress uniform directed me to a door, and I entered.

As I walked into the Blue Room of the White House, I noticed that I was part of a very small crowd. Worse, the crowd included Vice President and Mrs. Bush, the secretary of state, the chief of staff, the President's counselor, and a bunch of other folks I had only seen on the news. Since the other receptions I'd been to were large, impersonal affairs—so crowded you were lucky to catch a fleeting glimpse of the President—I assumed I was in the wrong room. I turned on a dime and made a quick exit, asking the Marine where the reception for the hoi polloi was being held. He pointed back to the Blue Room. "Sir, that's the only event tonight." I was certain I didn't belong there. I was just a twenty-two year old kid. A nobody. Someone made a mistake. I asked the Marine to check the guest list. My name was on it. "Sir, in there."

I furtively slipped back into the room and found a corner in which to

hide in my shabby Herringbone suit and ragtag tie, when a woman I recognized, but couldn't quite place, approached me. "Hi Jack, how are you?"

"I'm fine. Thanks so much. How are you doing?" I had no idea who
she was. But I sure wasn't going to let on.

"It's nice to see you here. This is going to be a lot of fun, seeing a
film with the President."

A film? I was such a moron that I hadn't even read the invitation.
The evening was dinner and a movie with Ronald Reagan. I must have
died and gone to Heaven.

The woman called out to someone unseen, "Honey, come on over.
I'm over here with Jack."

Just then, the President's counselor, Edwin Meese, a hero to conservatives, walked over and shook my hand. "Hi Jack," he smiled. I opened
my mouth, but nothing came out. I had been talking to Ursula Meese,
which was stunning for two reasons. First, that the Meeses would care
to spend any time at all with me, when the room was filled with elite
Washington power players, was astounding. Second, they were able to
make this uncomfortable newcomer feel welcome just a few months after
losing their son Scott. I wanted to express my deep condolences, but I was
overcome by their graciousness and dignity, and couldn't find the words.

Next we were led to the Red Room, where four round tables of ten
were set for dinner. At the head of each table was one of the hosts of the
evening—President Reagan, the First Lady, Vice President Bush and
Mrs. Bush. My place card put me just two chairs away from Mrs. Bush.
I glanced at the menu, engraved on a card before me: hot mandrilene,
basil chicken dumplings, romano cheese bread florettes, beef and kidney
pie, mixed green salad, vacherin with passion fruit sorbet, and petit fours,
served with a Simi Zinfandel from 1978. Not only was the food not
kosher, it wasn't even close to kosher.

Non-kosher food was a problem I had faced before in my political
travels, and although my stomach rumbled, I knew just how to handle
the situation. All I had to do was to make everyone think I was eating by
cutting things up and pushing them around on my plate, all the while
quietly fading into the background so as not to draw attention to myself.
The conversation at my table was directed to Mrs. Bush. A few National
Security Council staffers were talking about the state of the Soviet Union

and matters in Poland, and I learned that the evening's movie was the documentary *Man of Iron*. This explained why I had been invited. Our Poland petition campaign must have caught someone's eye.

I chopped up and redecorated my plates through three courses before Barbara Bush caught on to my cut-and-move game. "Sorry, young man, but I notice you're not eating. Is everything OK?"

I was busted. "Thank you Mrs. Bush, I'm doing great."

"That was not my question. Why are you not eating?" Now the whole table had stopped to listen. So much for keeping a low profile.

"Well, ma'am, I keep kosher, and I'm afraid I can't eat this meal," I stammered, wishing I had stayed in Atlantic City longer and avoided this conversation. My luck would have been better at the slot machine.

"I'm so sorry. We didn't realize. You should have said something. It's not a problem at all to get you a kosher meal. I'll have them bring you one right away."

Mrs. Bush motioned to a waiter, but I stopped her as quickly as I could. "No, please. I'm not really hungry. I'm fine." The last thing I wanted was to create an even bigger commotion everyone in the room would notice.

Mrs. Bush was not only one of the most elegant and dignified ladies to occupy the White House, but she was also a mother at heart. She saw a young man without a meal, and nothing else seemed to matter to her. Those Bush kids were lucky to have such a fine mother, I thought. In the end, she arranged for me to have fruit, and I got more fruit than I could ever have hoped to consume.

When the dinner escapade was over, we moved to the family theatre to watch the film. I was relieved to be in a dark room where, I presumed, I could easily fade into the shadows. No such luck. I was placed directly in back of the President! How was I supposed to focus on a movie when my hero, Ronald Reagan, was sitting right in front of me, munching on popcorn? Just before the film started, he turned around to offer me some. I was unable to do much more than stare and mumble, "No thanks." He stared for a minute, smiled, possibly realizing that I was the same nervous train wreck who visited him a month before.

# 3

# BACKROOM BRIBERY

In the fall of 1982, I took on two new responsibilities: law school and running a political action committee, or PAC. I had wanted to be a lawyer since I was a kid, but after a year of full-time politics, I lost the fever.

Nevertheless, I promised my parents I would attend Georgetown Law Center, where I had already deferred my admission for one year to focus on my work at College Republicans. For better or worse, law school was a bore for me. While my classmates endured the most pressure filled time of their lives, I was doing things like cutting up non-kosher food and moving it around my plate at the White House. I enrolled in the evening division at Georgetown and attended class about half the time.

As much as I loved the work, my College Republicans job didn't pay much. Grover, who had served ably for a year as executive director before moving on to join Fred Balitzer and Ben Waldman at Americans for the Reagan Agenda, had been making only $12,000 per year, even with his degree from Harvard Business School. I made the same. When I couldn't make ends meet on $12,000 a year, Howard Phillips, chairman of The Conservative Caucus, hired me to do some part-time work as executive director of his PAC. Howard started his political career at Harvard College and eventually became a top official in the Nixon Administration, but what made Howard Phillips unique was a combination of unbridled kindness and unsurpassed intellect. A man whose physical appearance resembled that of a professional football offensive lineman, Howard was gracious and gregarious. To me, he was and has always been a guardian angel, appearing just when hope is dim to save the day. I was grateful to have the position with Howard's PAC, not only for the much needed funding, but because it gave me more access to Howard. From him more than anyone I would learn my political philosophy and the importance of putting principles over party. His Vision of Victory speech at the 1982 Conservative Caucus Political Action Conference in Virginia was one of the most important messages I heard as a young, aspiring politico. In this seminal address, Howard articulated a simple approach, which would focus me for the rest of my life: To attain a victory, or a goal, one must have a vision of victory. One must clearly see where one is going, and then plan to get there. Political movements without a vision for victory are doomed, as are nations, as are people. His address to the hundreds of national political activists spoke directly and powerfully to me. I would never forget it.

Inspired by Howard's oration, we redoubled our efforts at College Republicans, and soon the White House started to pay us increased attention. In February 1983, I got a call asking us to bring our members to the White House to celebrate the President's birthday with him. The fact that the invite came on a Friday, and they needed the party on that Sunday might have seemed insulting to others, but the chance to spend a few minutes with Reagan more than made up for the last-minute notice. The party was set to last all of fifteen minutes, but we had legions of students who would jump at the opportunity to meet the President, even for a few seconds.

On the morning of the birthday party, we were expecting hundreds of students to attend. My staff and I rendezvoused in our office around 8 a.m., when Randy Dwyer, our executive director, told me that a young lady by the name of Pam Alexander had come to the office at the recommendation of Ralph Reed (who by then had returned to Georgia to head that state's College Republican organization). She was looking for a job. I told Randy that this wasn't a great time for a job interview, but she was welcome to join us for the birthday party at the White House. I had space in my car, so she could ride over with me. I didn't realize it in the rush to get our members to the White House, but I had just met my future wife.

When we arrived at the White House, the lobby outside the East Room was packed with college students. My staff had made arrangements for a stunning cake, and when the President entered, his face lit up. Seeing all these kids really energized him, and instead of staying for fifteen minutes, he regaled the crowd for more than an hour with stories. I was bursting with joy at the sight of the President holding court with his young admirers, when I heard a steely command in the voice of the First Lady.

"Don't you think that's enough?" Nancy Reagan asked me, point blank.

"Sorry?" I didn't quite understand what she was telling me.

"You all are abusing the President. He's tired. He was supposed to rest. This has to end." I looked at her without quite knowing what to do or say. Was I supposed to grab the microphone from the President's hand? Was I supposed to shout, "Cut"?

Nancy Reagan didn't wait for me to respond. She rolled her eyes at me and marched up the stairs to the family quarters. I was a bit stunned, but even such an encounter couldn't possibly have ruined that day.

Chairmen of the College Republican National Committee serve two-year terms, and running for re-election is not done often. The previous two-term chairman was Karl Rove, who went on to bigger things in the years that followed, running political campaigns and eventually becoming the top White House aide to President George W. Bush. In my first two years, we had transformed College Republicans from a backwater auxiliary of the Republican National Committee to a vibrant conservative organization with followers, supporters, and members throughout the nation. But our work on campus was not done, and so when my closest confidants suggested I run for a second term, I didn't hesitate. This time, though, instead of the reserved and sagacious Grover Norquist running my campaign, I had the garrulous and lethal Ralph Reed, who had returned from college in Georgia to become the executive director at our office. Ralph was probably destined to become the executive director ever since I met him, and he spent countless hours in Grover's company preparing for the job. They paced and talked and planned and plotted. When Ralph decided to return home for school at University of Georgia, we were all surprised, but his return to Washington came about a year later. Once in place as executive director, he continued to take direction from Grover, who was no longer in the group, but maintained a strong influence.

Ralph was the natural choice to run my re-election campaign since he was bright, hardworking, and dedicated. Plus, he was like a sponge, picking up every detail about political activism he could. Unlike my first campaign, where I was unopposed, this time I had an opponent: Rob San Luis, our Texas state chairman. Ralph threw everything he had at San Luis, and more. It was one of the roughest election campaigns in College Republicans history. He had a legion of spies tracking San Luis's every move, and he distributed hundreds of packets of materials highlighting our achievements and San Luis's deficiencies. Ralph was not at all subtle. San Luis was torn to pieces in those scurrilous pamphlets. But Ralph did far more than that.

The practice in College Republicans was to run a slate of officers, since there were six national positions to fill. I avoided doing this, since I didn't wish to antagonize anyone. San Luis put a slate together, but that was probably his biggest mistake. In a move that would become emblematic of Reed's take-no-prisoners approach, my baby-faced campaign manager surreptitiously placed one of our supporters onto Rob San Luis's slate. Nothing summed up Ralph's modus operandi better than his own words: "I want to be invisible. I do guerrilla warfare. I paint my face and travel at night. You don't know it's over until you're in a body bag."

The night before the election, Ralph's time bomb exploded when this "supporter" publicly denounced Rob's slate and announced his support of my re-election. By morning, Rob's campaign was in tatters. In fact, he never had a chance since over two thirds of the state chairmen had already endorsed my re-election.

I was a bit uneasy about Ralph's reckless strategy and savage execution, but in those days—and in too many days to come—I didn't pause to consider niceties. To us, politics was war without the benefit of armed forces. "Kill or be killed" became an unspoken mantra, contrary to all I believed and was raised to believe. Drunk on the quest for what passed as power in those days, I ignored my inner voice and marched forward into my second term.

The College Republicans' relentless domination of the campus political scene may have inadvertently caused a counter attack among the professoriate, as the first inklings of the political correctness movement were stirring in the wake of the Reagan tsunami. At first, the Orwellian attributes of that movement led us to believe it would be short-lived, but the tenacity of the left should not have been underestimated. Soon, a gloomy wave of political correctness would wash over the nation, crushing free speech in its wake. In retrospect, it's very possible that the domination of the College Republicans of the early 1980s inadvertently spawned this unfortunate creed of political correctness, which has since ruled academia.

In my second term, all our efforts on hundreds of campuses, with thousands of volunteers and tens of thousands members, came to a crescendo during the campaign to re-elect Ronald Reagan in 1984. During the three years we had to prepare for that campaign, we had created one of the most effective political organizations on college campuses. Our efforts were so overwhelming, in fact, that the Democrats seemed almost absent from the discussion. Even the hard radical leftists were set back on their heels, as the majority of college students in America voiced their support for Reagan.

In the halcyon days of the Reagan re-election campaign, we did our best to make the campaign fun and that meant coming up with something witty. The most popular movie that summer, *Ghostbusters*, became an instant classic. The iconic emblem of the film was a prohibition sign cast over a friendly-looking ghost. Reagan was running against Walter Mondale, the former Vice President under Jimmy Carter. To most of the nation, Mondale was known by his nickname, Fritz. We came up with what we thought would be a clever idea for a T-shirt. I called my friend Phil Groves, the greatest cartoonist I knew, and asked him if he could draw a knock off of the *Ghostbusters* symbol with a cartoon of Mondale's visage. When it arrived a few days later, Fritzbusters was born.

Paul Erickson took it even further. He assembled four khaki overalls, tubing, and some backpacks. Now, we not only had T-shirts and buttons, bumper stickers, and posters—we actually had a group of guys who dressed up as Fritzbusters. Ratcheting it up even further, Erickson and his fellow Fritzbusters (sometimes including Phil and myself) went on tour with the Mondale campaign! Every time the Democrats held a rally, the Fritzbusters were there, ostensibly to ward off the evil spirit of Mondale. Of course, safety soon became an issue, and we decided that the Fritzbusters were more likely to survive if they attended only Reagan rallies.

Before long, we found ourselves at the Republican National Convention of 1984 in Dallas, Texas. As chairman of the College Republicans, I was allotted a speaking slot on the program. I had given plenty of speeches by then, but the audiences never numbered more than a few hundred. Mostly I spoke at college campuses, debating almost nightly the then-head of the College Democrats, Steve Girsky. Now I was given an opportunity to speak before thousands, and to be on television as well. Of course, my grand national television debut was not slotted for prime time, save in Burma or Tibet, and seen only on CSPAN, but I didn't care. This was the opportunity of a lifetime, and I intended to give a speech they would remember.

The problem was that political party conventions are not about giving speeches that people will remember. They're about obedience and towing the party line. I wasn't too good at that. In the weeks before the convention, between my debates, Fritzbusters appearances, missing summer law school classes, and tending to College Republican expansion programs, I wrote what I thought would be a barn burner of a speech.

Jesse Jackson was running for president in the 1984 Democratic primaries. While I resented his anti-Semitic remarks and hated his socialist ideology, I thought his speaking skills were brilliant. His voice had such a musical cadence that it almost didn't matter what he was saying. You listened and nodded and became entranced in the delivery. I decided to mimic his style in my speech at the convention. I figured it would be noticed and get a few laughs. But the words I chose were quite serious.

I arrived in Dallas on the Sunday before the opening of the convention to practice my speech. When I reached the communications trailer just outside the arena, I was greeted by the speech committee, a veritable brigade of lawyers who explained that the podium would be fixed, but the platform adjacent to the podium, on which we would stand, would rise or fall depending on the height of the speaker. They also told me that any speaker who created a problem would be lowered, presumably into the abyss. They weren't joking. They wanted a smooth show. Uniformity. That was the byword of this and every other convention. These guys were the uniformity police.

They showed me how the teleprompters worked and bid me to practice my speech. As I started, they stopped me and told me that they had made a few edits, and that the new speech was on the teleprompter. I was stunned. I was never told anyone had the power to change my speech. I tried to argue, but these guys had neither the time nor the inclination to joust with me. After a few minutes, they informed me that they would cancel my appearance if I didn't give their speech. I stewed for a few seconds, but then agreed to their demands and practiced their stupid speech, which went something like, "Dear delegates, young people love the Republican Party and Ronald Reagan and think you're all swell and really neato." Trite and insipid drivel. Nothing more. Nothing less. I wasn't going to give this speech. But I played along, and once they believed I could do it with all the sincerity they felt it deserved, I got to leave the trailer and catch up with my parents, who had come to Dallas to hear my speech.

When my parents heard what happened, they were disappointed. They knew how much it meant to me to speak at the convention, but they also knew how I loathed the suits who were forcing me to spew treacle into the camera. I told them what I had in mind. I figured they would try to talk me out of it, but they only smiled and told me to go for it, so go for it I did.

The next day, Frank Fahrenkopf, chairman of the party, introduced me as I strode to the podium. "And from Beverly Hills, the chairman of the College Republicans, Jack Abramoff, to address the convention." I could see through the cracks between the teleprompters that the California and Texas delegations in the front were milling about, undoubtedly figuring they were about to hear another hackneyed discourse.

My speech and the revision from the suits started the same way: "Fellow Republicans, I come before you today representing American students—the future of our Republican party." That's where the texts diverged. I gripped the podium with my tightest clench, and waited for the bottom to drop out. Literally. I spent the night before memorizing my speech, and I had my index cards up my sleeve for good measure. I was going to give my speech, come what may.

"Today, our party readies itself to mount the wave of the future," I intoned. "Will we ride that wave to glory, or will it send us crashing ashore? If we're the party of tax cuts, and not the party of 'ifs' and 'buts,' then we're riding our wave. If we're liberating students from Grenada, and not bowing down to a Cuban dictator, we're riding our wave."

As I pounded out these fighting words, I noticed a stirring in the delegates below. The California and Texas Republicans were cheering and pointing. They couldn't believe it. Someone was speaking like a conservative. I ended the speech to a hail of applause and turned to make my way off the stage. Fahrenkopf, not knowing what transpired the night before, smiled and nodded. Then I saw the suits.

The main suit shouted my way, "You are NEVER going to speak at another Republican National Convention! Do you hear me?" I laughed and blew right by him. So what? I wasn't going to be head of College Republicans in 1988, and it wasn't likely that this guy would run another convention either.

I marched out of the arena smack dab into a Fritzbusters rally. Hundreds of kids were singing the theme song and clapping. That's what it was all about anyway.

The election was a blow out. Reagan smashed Fritz, and the campuses went for the Gipper. Our job was done, and it was time to consider who would take over the organization once my term ended that spring. In the midst of my deliberations, I received a phone call from Jeffrey Bell, a conservative leader who had run for U.S. Senate in New Jersey in 1978, and lost to Bill Bradley. Bell was a top advisor to Lewis Lehrman, former chairman of Rite Aid Drugstores, who was now chairman of President Reagan's grassroots lobbying organization Citizens for America. He offered me the position of executive director. They needed someone to revive the organization and turn it into the leading conservative group in Washington. They also needed to win some victories on Capitol Hill for the President, and Bell thought I was the man to do it. He had been following my career, he said, and I came highly recommended from Howard Phillips. I was immediately intrigued and accepted the position.

Ending my chairmanship of the College Republicans early, I handed the reins to my co-chairman, Ted Higgins, and, at the relatively young age of 26, started my new job at Citizens for America in late January 1985. Somehow, I convinced Grover to join me as the field director. Until that point, he was working to build Americans for the Reagan Agenda, a group dedicated to organizing Americans to support the President's initiatives. As field director, Grover would be spared any managerial responsibilities at

Citizens for America and could focus on his greatest strengths: recruitment and organizing. We immediately set about building the organization at the grassroots level. After a few months, our efforts were showing results. In many ways, our activities at this group were similar to those of College Republicans. We worked day and night and spent many hours motivating members and their staff to become active in supporting the President's legislative agenda. There were differences, too. Instead of our ramshackle College Republican rooms and paltry stipends, we had plush offices and decent salaries. Plus, we had all the staff support work-a-holics like us needed. With ample resources at our disposal, we were able to build the organization into a powerhouse. The White House was pleased, and my meetings with the President always included a kind word and an expression of gratitude. We were given the major lobbying assignments, including aid to the Contras in Nicaragua, the MX Missile, and Tax Reform.

In the spring of 1985, we were given the assignment of getting the votes together to fund the MX Missile. President Reagan referred to this massive missile as the "Peacekeeper," and it was, in the sense that no one on the other side would dare start a war knowing MX missiles might be heading their way in response. As usual, the Democrats opposed America building the missile system, with Senator Teddy Kennedy leading the charge. They were consistent in trying to stop Reagan's attempts to rebuild the military, and the MX Missile battle was one of the most difficult campaigns we faced. It was also where I got my first lesson in Washington corruption.

Our mission at the grassroots lobby was to line up votes. We worked for weeks, directing citizens to communicate their support to Congress. We were doing everything we could, but we were still short six votes of victory. We continued to pound Congressmen with phone calls and radio ads, but no one was budging. At that time, pugnacious Pat Buchanan was President Reagan's Communications Director, and our point person in the White House for this effort. He wanted results not excuses, but we just couldn't get the votes.

Then, in the middle of the battle, I received a phone call from a Democratic Congressman from Corpus Christi, Texas named Albert Bustamante, who asked me to come to his office immediately to discuss the MX Missile vote. A twenty-six year old go-getter, I was in a cab before I even hung up the phone.

I got out of the taxi and bounded down the hallowed hallways of the congressional office building. My shoes clicked on the marble floors as I rushed to the stately offices of the representative. In those days, I was still in awe every time I entered the congressional buildings. As soon as I entered Congressman Bustamante's suite of offices, I was whisked into his private chamber. Like most representatives, his walls were adorned with self-congratulatory pictures and countless plaques extolling his greatness. Most Americans visiting these offices would feel like they had entered the inner sanctum of power because most don't realize that there are over 400 such sanctums on Capitol Hill.

Bustamante got right to the point. "Mr. Abramoff, by my count, you are six votes short on the MX Missile in the House. I have thirteen votes for you, but I need something in return."

I was shocked. Thirteen votes? We would win right there. Did he want me to vacuum the floor or shine his shoes? I would gladly have done either.

"Yes, sir, what can I do for you?"

"The Defense Department is planning to place a new naval base in the Gulf of Mexico, and I want it for my district. I hear they are looking at Florida instead. If I get the base, you get the votes. If I don't, you don't. The votes are from the Hispanic Caucus, and they are solidly in my control. What do you say?"

I couldn't believe what I was hearing. I thought this only happened in the movies. I stammered, "Uh, well, sir, I'll have to call the White House." What else could I say? I was just trying to buy myself some time.

He would grant me no such luck. "Fine, call them right now."

I picked up the phone and dialed Buchanan. "Pat, I'm here with Congressman Bustamante, and he'll get us thirteen votes if he gets a naval base in Corpus Christi. What do I tell him?"

There was a short pause. "Hold on, Jack," Pat replied. Would they actually consider this? How could they? Was this legal?

A few minutes later, a different White House staffer came on the line: "OK, tell him he has the base." I kept asking myself whether this was really happening. What a naïve question. Of course it was happening. It happened all the time. It just hadn't happened to me. Bustamante, who would later go to prison for similar antics, was impassive when I told him he'd get the base. He knew all along he'd get the base. The only one unsure about any of this was me. I left his office feeling dirtier than I had ever felt in politics before. Unfortunately, I would soon become used to it.

My tenure at Citizens for America quickly became rocky, as Grover and I implemented our usual playbook of recruitment, activism, and conservative ideology. Some of the staff from the previous regime disliked our new, brash style, and resented what they considered to be "juvenile political activities" such as voter registration, rallies on issues, and activist projects like petitions. They began to undermine Grover and me with the powerful Republican donors on the organization's board of directors. Eventually, the board made Lehrman miserable about it, and the clock started to run.

In the early spring of 1985, Jack Wheeler, a good friend and brilliant conservative icon, approached me. Jack was known as the Indiana Jones of the right, since he was the only man who had lived and fought with each of the anti-Soviet freedom fighter groups across the globe.

"Each year, the Soviets gather their various terrorist groups under the auspices of the PLO," Wheeler began. "They share stories. They share strategies. They share tactics. These meetings are invaluable to them, since they all share a common enemy, the West. We have anti-Soviet resistance groups fighting the same enemy in at least six countries: Angola, Nicaragua, Afghanistan, Laos, Cambodia, and Mozambique. What we need is an annual meeting of these groups, so they can share stories, strategies, and tactics. They are all fighting the same force, the Soviets. Our guys just don't know each other. I have lived and fought with each group, and they all believe they are alone."

I knew that Jack was the formulator of what would eventually become the Reagan Doctrine—a strategy or active resistance adopted by the Administration to defeat the Soviet Empire. Through this doctrine, the United States aided a number of anti-communist guerrilla movements, including those on Jack's list. A meeting where all of these minds could collectively come together would be historical, and I wanted to be a part of it. Organizing it, though, would be a logistical nightmare and cost a fortune. But I thought I could make it happen. Lehrman was a patriot, and the whole point of his organization was to change history and make things like this a reality. I told Jack that I would ask Lehrman to consider funding the meeting.

Lehrman, as I anticipated, was more than willing to help. We funneled Wheeler approximately $50,000 to start, and set about resolving the first and most problematic issue: location. Where on earth could we hold a meeting of the five or six people at the top of the Soviet death list? America? No, too many chances for them to wipe out the entire group, and make it look like a drug deal gone bad. Israel? Sure, they'd be secure, but the politics would be problematic, and the Israelis didn't like to fan flames. Taiwan? Probably OK, but might be tough to get them there.

Wheeler came back with a creative suggestion: Free Angola. By this he meant the territory which was held by Jonas Savimbi and the UNITA resistance movement. "Jamba, his provisional capital, is quite nice. We can be safe there, since the South Africans maintain a defense perimeter that covers Jamba. That's where we should go." And with that, it was decided.

The next step was the press. The cause of these freedom fighters would be greatly advanced by the exposure, and it was only natural the media would want to cover such a historical proceeding. We held off sharing the location for obvious safety purposes, but, like most things, word got out. Arnaud deBorchgrave, then-editor in chief of the *Washington Times*, told me he figured out where we were going when his intelligence connections reported that the Soviets had moved a few of their helicopters within range of Jamba, probably "to make sure they could wipe you out." Arnaud loved to be melodramatic. Nevertheless, I started to lose sleep. Arnaud could be histrionic, but my neck was on the line.

At the end of May, we made our way to South Africa. From there, we took a private plane to Angola. Most of the invitees would travel that Saturday to Jamba, but since I couldn't travel on the Sabbath, I left a day earlier. Adolfo Calero, the head of the Nicaraguan Contras, agreed to travel with me in advance of the rest of the group.

Our Dakota plane, a relic from the days of the Red Baron, no doubt, felt like it was going to come apart in the air. There were no seats, only metal benches surrounding the perimeter of the interior. There was also no cabin pressure, and no heat. It was a miserable three-hour flight from Jan Smuts Airport in Johannesburg. Calero, the former manager of the Coca Cola bottling plant in Managua, Nicaragua, made light of the rough flight and the abrupt thud of a landing. As the door opened, rifles were thrust into the cabin. When the greeting party decided we were not, in fact, Soviets, they took us on flat bed trucks on the three-hour ride to Jamba. These trucks made the airplane seem like a Posturepedic mattress by comparison.

After a long, grueling trip, we were shown our huts and allowed to unwind. The beds were made from straw. That evening, I said my prayers and hurriedly ate a Sabbath meal alone. After that, Savimbi invited Calero and me to a gathering of his people, where Calero spoke from the heart to the massed crowd. It seemed to go over well, though I couldn't understand a word. He spoke in Spanish. They spoke Portuguese. Nonetheless, a connection was made. The next morning, I stepped out of my hut and saw there were hundreds of people lining the roads to the encampment, as if a parade were about to commence. I asked the guard what was happening. He said they were awaiting the arrival of the important guests. No one was slated to arrive until evening, but these poor people stood there all day. Finally, around 9 p.m., the trucks arrived bearing a group of exhausted freedom fighters, media, and Citizens for America staff. An emotional and expressive man, Jack Wheeler was clearly in heaven. He had waited for this day, and he was going to relish it.

The crowd on the road had swelled beyond measure. Their cheers pierced the stillness of the African night. Finally, the participants and the media convened in the small conference center. Savimbi took the podium. The media filmed and recorded. For forty-five minutes he delivered an oration entirely in Portuguese. No translator. On and on he went. The media started to simmer. The other participants' heads bobbed, exhausted from the trip. And then he commenced another speech, in English. Another forty-five minutes.

After Savimbi, it was Lehrman's turn to speak. Not known as a brief orator, he went on for about thirty minutes. Each of his phrases were, in turn, translated into Portuguese, stretching out the agony all the more. He presented the freedom fighters with framed copies of the Declaration of Independence, and delivered the most important message of the conference, the letter from President Reagan.

Getting this letter had turned out to be tougher than we thought. Future Congressman Dana Rohrabacher was one of the few conservative heroes to survive the many ideological purges conducted by the moderate Republicans who took control of the Reagan White House and someone

I counted on from the moment we met. He was Reagan's favorite speech-writer and had been with Reagan since the 1960s, even before his first gubernatorial campaign. I didn't have a chance to meet Dana until I joined Citizens for America, but once we connected, we became life-long friends. Dana was fearless, but also very wise, and he was deeply involved in organizing the meeting of the anti-communist resistance leaders and knew that a letter from Ronald Reagan would be the highlight of the conference. Dana worked for weeks to get such a letter, thwarted at every turn by the disloyal and politically moderate White House staff. Dana was near giving up when, one night at his desk he received a phone call. It was the president calling to thank Dana for a brilliant speech he had written. Dana jumped on the opportunity and popped the question: would the President agree to address these brave fighters as they convened for the first time, at risk to their lives? Reagan responded with a resounding yes, and we had our letter.

Lehrman read the letter to the assembled group, and there wasn't a dry eye in the house. Dana's brilliance was evident in the draft, as Reagan wrote to these freedom fighters that "your cause is our cause." The group seemed to rise in their seats when that line was read. It was late—almost 1 a.m.—and everyone was tired, but the words of Ronald Reagan meant the world to this group.

Despite the late hour, we had three more speakers to go. Adolfo Calero gave us a break and spoke for no more than three minutes, translating his own brief greeting in English into Spanish, thereby giving the intrepid translator a break. Next up was Gholam Warduk, one of the leaders of the Afghani resistance. Warduk had been in London when he got the call asking him to come to Angola. Jack Wheeler had travelled to Peshawer, Pakistan to escort several leaders of the Afghan resistance movement to the meeting, but they were arrested on the plane, and only Jack escaped. He quickly found Warduk and redirected him to the meeting.

Warduk looked like he came from central casting. He had a flowing beard and wore the standard issue turban and robes of the region. He brought his son to translate, but his progeny lacked the appearance of the Afghan fighter. He wore a cheap, ill-fitting suit, no doubt purchased from a thrift shop. Warduk took the podium and launched into a harangue in his native Pashto language. After what seemed to be several minutes of blustery bellowing, he paused to allow his milquetoast offspring to trans-late: "Good evening, it's nice to be here." The overly tired assembly froze. Some were having a hard time quashing giggles. The senior Warduk roared again for at least several minutes. His son offered no more than four words as interpretation. This continued over and again. Later I discovered that his son couldn't remember what his father was saying, so he just made up whatever came to his feeble mind. Fortunately, this comedy act didn't last too long. But it was getting very late, and it wasn't very amusing.

The final presentation was from Pa Kao Her, the leader of the Laotian resistance group. I asked his translator to please have him move as quickly as possible, since the hour was late. After receiving the nods you get from people who absolutely don't understand a word you've said or don't care, they took the podium. Pa Kao proceeded to give a detailed geography lesson about Laos, including descriptions of estuaries and bogs. It was a command performance, though it had little or nothing to do with the conference. Or perhaps his translator was just a more creative version of young Warduk and decided to make up a different speech. Who knew? Who cared? We were all relieved when he stepped down and we could retire to our straw beds. The conference began the next morning.

We sat in meetings for two days, and then ended the conference with the signing of the accord. Lehrman and I left ahead of the participants on a Lear jet he had chartered to take us to Johannesburg. As our plane lifted off, I was confident the ride home would find Lehrman praising the con-ference and our efforts. We had changed history. But instead, he seemed upset. When I reminded him that the next week would be consumed with media interviews, he snapped into a non sequitur. He wanted me to fire Grover Norquist. I was shocked by this request. While we flew in luxury across Africa, Grover continued to work himself silly on the ground in Jamba. He had done an amazing job building the organization. But Lehrman complained that our recruitment efforts were too aggressive and that our confident, defiant attacks on the left were overdone and, that our staff was engaged in too many ideological campaigns. And that we were spending too much money. These were the rants of the establishment Republicans on our board. In the face of our greatest triumph, Lehrman was attacking all that made the organization powerful. I refused to fire Grover, and when Lehrman threatened to do it himself, I agreed, figuring my assent would buy some time. I hoped that I could at least get Grover some severance pay to ease the blow, but I knew that his days, and mine, were numbered.

A few weeks later, Lehrman came to Washington to complain about how the organization was being run. That was rich considering the group was now viewed as the premiere conservative activist group in the nation, the membership had been quadrupled, and we had just pulled off an historic event in Africa. The Administration was delighted with our lobbying, and the President had told numerous people how grateful he was for our efforts. But Lehrman was under a different influence. He wanted to take away my control of the group's finances, while leaving me in charge of the programs.

I was twenty-six, and already one of the highest paid activists in Washington that year, making over $150,000. I had one of the most powerful groups in the land at my disposal, and all of official Washington was at my door. Senators called me for favors. The President was in my debt. I should have kept my cool and accepted his wish to make that cosmetic change. But I didn't. I was impetuous, and I quit. Lehrman told me to be out by 5 p.m. that night, and I had my staff call the movers.

I was exhausted. I had spent the last five years of my life in intense political battles. The infighting had drained me. I turned down other political job offers, including from my kind and good friend Howard Phillips to return and run the PAC again, and decided I needed a total break from politics, at least for a while.

I decided to join my father in his real estate development business while I finished law school. Dad was the best. He was always there to help, whatever I needed. But I could not get myself excited about real estate. I was someone driven by passions, and they were not ignited by real estate. Politics gave voice to my soul and allowed me to fight for a greater good. Real estate was formulaic and staid. In my political life I met some of the most interesting people on the planet, such as Grover Norquist, Howard Phillips, Dana Rohrabacher and, of course, Ronald Reagan. Who was I likely to encounter in a real estate transaction? A county tax recorder? I knew it was not for me, but, for a while, I had to give it a try. I knew I needed a break from Washington politics, but I also knew that real estate wouldn't satisfy me. I had to find another kind of excitement.

# 4

# WHAT'S WRONG WITH THIS PICTURE?

Ronald Reagan started out in movies and then made his way into politics. I went in the opposite direction. Though I grew up on the doorstep of Hollywood, and had always loved films, the business of making them wasn't attractive to me. After college, I had politics in my veins and once I ignited the passion for that blood sport, I couldn't conceive of any other pursuit, let alone movie making. Law school helped change that.

For three years, Georgetown felt like an extracurricular activity. I was focused on my work at College Republicans and Citizens for America. In my last year, I ran myself ragged working on real estate development with my father and trying to launch some other business opportunities, including an ill-fated effort to bring American racquetball to Israel, but nothing seemed to compare to politics. As a result, I had failed to attend a law seminar course I needed to graduate, and was now faced with finding another one to fill in that gap.

The only seminar that seemed remotely interesting to me was Entertainment Law taught by Professor Richard Gordon, a former associate dean of the school and one of its top contracts law instructors. Unfortunately for me, the class was one of the first to fill up, and there was a substantial waiting list to get in. But I hadn't spent years in politics for nothing. I would find my way into that seminar no matter what it took.

I had images of John Houseman from The Paper Chase swimming

in my head as I strode into Professor Gordon's office. Stacks of books lay haphazard on every possible surface. Paintings and tapestries were strewn about with no apparent pattern. Persian carpets covered both the walls and the floor. The strains of Chopin's Second Piano Concerto emanated from his radio. The lighting was somber and dignified. Gordon's stentorian voice greeted me as I entered, "What can I do for you, young man?"

"Sir, I was hoping to enroll in your Entertainment Law Seminar this spring."

"Yes, you and half of the student body. The class is quite full, and I am only considering last year students."

"I am a last year student."

"And I am only considering those who are hoping for a career in entertainment."

I was in politics. That's entertaining. "That's me, sir. I am the very model of an entertainment industry-bound student, sir." I was hoping he would catch my allusion to Gilbert and Sullivan. He did.

"Not funny, young man. It's not likely, but you can check back with me periodically, and we'll see. Goodbye."

That was all I needed. "Thank you so much, Professor Gordon. You'll not regret it."

"Regret what?" he retorted. "Letting you check back with me? I already do."

As I left his office, I was already calculating how I could get myself into that class. I devised every excuse to be in constant contact with Gordon, using each communication to further my bid. I did my research and found out that not only was he a conservative, but he was a religious Catholic, and he loved opera. We were made for each other!

I called him and dropped by his office almost daily for a week. I plied him with offers to meet the nation's leading conservatives. I invited him to the opera. I got my friend Ben Waldman, who worked for the Reagan administration and had dining privileges at the West Wing of the White House, to get him an invitation to eat there daily. If none of this had worked, I would have made a serious effort to have the Pope call on my behalf. Fortunately, my full press was effective, and I got my spot in the seminar.

Week after week, Gordon introduced the class to his former students who returned as guest lecturers. Each had attained immense success in the entertainment industry. The filmmakers were the most impressive. As I sat listening to their stories, I was transfixed. Politics was the joining of statescraft and business. Filmmaking was the intersection of stagecraft and business. As the weeks passed, I realized that both spoke to the depths of my soul. I entered Professor Gordon's class looking for an enjoyable way to fulfill the seminar requirement at Georgetown Law, and I left it wanting to be a movie producer.

For better or worse, I soon got my chance to try. A month into the semester, the cherry trees bloomed around town, and I received a call from one of my former College Republican state chairmen. A friend of his, Mark Richards, was making a documentary about the resistance to the Soviet and Cuban occupation of Angola, and he wanted to ask me some questions about my experiences there.

When we met, his first question was about the lodging situation in Jamba. "You'll be sleeping on straw," I told him. "And not the good straw, like in Rumpelstiltskin. If I were you, I would bring my own food, water, and air."

"Seriously, is it that bad?"

"Worse."

I spent about fifteen minutes regaling him with horror stories about the logistics of Jamba and then asked why he was doing a documentary at all. He stared blankly at me as I suggested he use his funds to make a low budget action movie about the Soviet and Cuban occupation. Most people won't see a documentary, but they will see an action picture. Richards said he knew nothing about making a feature film, and truthfully I didn't either, but that had never stopped me before. I offered to put something together for him and, if he liked it, we could use his funding and make an action film. After all, how hard could it be to make a movie? I would soon find out.

Taking a leap into the world of film wasn't the only major move I was making, though. I started to date Pam Alexander, the beautiful blonde Georgian who attended Reagan's birthday party. Pam had moved to the Washington area to live with her grandfather in Alexandria, Virginia. By the time we started to date, she had moved in with Rabbi Avrom Landesman and his family, and was attending our synagogue. For me,

Pam was ideal: an elegant beauty who shared my conservative politics and orthodox Jewish religious orientation. Most importantly, though, she had a sense of humor, which served her quite well on our first date: to a shooting range. Pam's uncanny skill with a .357 Magnum left me wondering whether the action hero in the film I was crafting for Richards would beat her in a duel.

After a few weeks hard work, I had written the movie plot I wanted Richards to make. It went something like this: A Soviet Special Forces officer is sent to a fictional African nation to destroy its anti-Soviet resistance movement. The officer fakes a defection to the rebel side and, once accepted, attempts to kill their leader. Things go awry when the rebel chief senses something is wrong and foils the plot, leaving the officer at the mercy of his Soviet handlers who don't appreciate his failure. The officer escapes from his former bosses and flees into the African bush where he collapses, only to be rescued by a tribe of bushmen. After healing his body, they heal his soul, and he becomes a man of peace. This new Elysium is shattered when the Soviets and their allies kill most of the bushmen, sending the hero on a mission of revenge.

It seemed to me I had a winning formula for a successful action adventure film. I contacted Richards again, but his interest had passed. Mine, however, hadn't. I wanted to make a feature film.

Using the knowledge I gleaned in the seminar, I pushed the project through the early stages of development. When I ran out of resources and experience, I called my brother, Bob, who had recently worked for Warner Bros. Television. Bob laughed nervously when I told him I wanted to make a movie, probably because he knew I would ask him to join me in the adventure. He reminded me that there were thousands of accomplished producers out there who couldn't get their films financed and made. What made me think I had a chance to do one? I didn't quite have an answer for him, but it didn't matter to me. I was determined to make it work.

We needed help from someone with real experience. Bob offered to discuss the idea with another pair of brothers, Greg and Gary Foster. Greg was one of Bob's high school classmates and worked for MGM. Gary had followed their father, David, into the film business and was already a successful producer. The Foster boys saw immediately that we had the right ingredients for a blockbuster film and agreed to join us.

Next, we needed money to get the screenplay written. Once again, my dear friend Howard Phillips came to the rescue. He connected us to Robert Hall, a retired physician-turned-investor who owned a vineyard on the Cape of South Africa. Robert was excited about the movie and invested the funds we needed to hire Arne Olsen to write our script. Olsen was close to the Fosters, but had previously not penned a produced film. We went with him out of trust for the Fosters. He seemed to understand our goals and wrote a competent screenplay.

The summer of 1986 was a momentous time in my life. I graduated from law school in June, married Pam in July, and had my work cut out in my new career as a filmmaker—starting with finding the right title for our future film. Since I learned my public relations skills through politics, I engaged one of the top polling companies to help us choose a title and discern the market for this project. We made a list of possible titles, and *Red Scorpion* prevailed. Not only did the poll reveal our film's title, it proved that our target demographic—men fifteen to thirty-five— were 85 percent more likely to see a film called *Red Scorpion* without any additional information than they were to see a film by any other name we had considered.

Aside from the title, the lead actor is one of the most important elements of a movie. For *Red Scorpion*, I wanted Dolph Lundgren, who played Ivan Drago, the mammoth Soviet boxer pitted against Rocky Balboa in *Rocky IV*, and was now starring in *Masters of the Universe*. The box office superstars of the '80s—Schwarzenegger, Sylvester Stallone, and Chuck Norris—weren't getting any younger. We thought Dolph was the future. The Foster brothers had a relationship with Dolph's agent, and soon we had a letter from him agreeing to star in the film if the screenplay was consistent with the synopsis. That letter was worth Dolph's considerable weight in gold.

In a political campaign, one produces posters, buttons, and bumper stickers for the candidate's supporters. Not knowing any better, I contracted with graphic artists to create a poster and logo for the movie, which we could use on buttons and bumper stickers. I'm not certain what we thought we were going to do with these buttons and bumper stickers, but we printed them any way.

Three times a year, independent motion picture producers have an opportunity to offer their productions to distributors from around the world. These markets are held in Los Angeles in the winter, Cannes in the spring, and Milan in the fall. In mid-September, while I was busy securing financing for the film, Bob took Paul Erickson with him to Milan to test out distributor interest at MIFED, the International Film and Multimedia Market. In the old days, Paul had convinced the Republican National chairman, Dick Richards, to fund the largest political training and recruitment program in the history of college campuses, and he had successfully hypnotized most of Washington's official media to afford us national press during the College Republican years. No one was better to parachute into a crisis than Erickson. In fact, skydiving was one of his passions. So, without any hotel reservations, without any idea as to how the MIFED market was organized, and with absolutely no experience in film sales, Paul and Bob headed to Milan.

Normally when a producer attends these film markets, he is armed with the film he is going to sell. At worst, he'll have a product reel, which will include several completed scenes. No one would consider trying to sell a film that didn't even have a screenplay. Our intrepid salesmen arrived in Milan with nothing but posters, buttons, bumper stickers, and the letter from Dolph Lundgren's agent. Since they didn't even have a booth or office at the market, they unfurled a *Red Scorpion* poster and tacked it to the wall at the convention hall. Under this they placed a card table. Almost instantly, several distributors approached. "How much for this film?" "When will it be ready for distribution?" We agreed in advance of the trip that Paul and Bob would make no deals while in Milan, only listen and learn. Fortunately, they stuck to the agreement. More distributors saw the poster and came to meet them. A line started forming. A crowd massed. "Have you sold Central America yet?" "I represent Germany, and would like to make a bid."

Soon, they found out why our poster had generated so much interest. When Stallone made *Rocky IV*, he was too busy with his next movie to do the usual worldwide publicity tour. Instead, Dolph was sent to hundreds of cities to promote the film, creating a large following. He was a kickboxing champion in Europe and gave demonstrations that thrilled the crowds. The distributors agreed with us: Dolph Lundgren was going to be the next big action star, and they wanted to buy his films. So when they saw his massive visage on the *Red Scorpion* poster, they assumed that this would be his next action blockbuster. Though they were confused by the lack of a product reel, much less a completed film, distributors from every international territory still tried to get Bob and Paul to sell them theatrical rights. The frustration-fed bids rose and rose, but none were accepted.

Bob collected business cards and developed relationships with these distributors, while Paul was doing his own distribution—of *Red Scorpion* buttons to every attractive girl he saw. He knew how to play the Hollywood producer title better than any casting couch veteran. Suddenly, hundreds of beautiful women traversed the market wearing our unique buttons. After our success with these trinkets, at future film markets, every production produced buttons, but that year ours were the only ones in town. The bumper stickers never quite caught on.

By the end of their time at MIFED, Bob and Paul had over 250 offers from distributors. Representatives from several major studios—including Warner Bros. and MGM—watched this circus carefully. Everyone was talking about *Red Scorpion*, a movie without any filmed scenes, without even a screenplay. And all this success without so much as a booth at the event. In years to come, MIFED established the "*Red Scorpion* Rule": no one was allowed to tack up their posters on a wall without first purchasing office space at the market.

In the meantime, I had been in South Africa trying to find funding for the film. The government of South Africa had recently created a special tax credit to spur growth in their motion picture industry. Peter Gower and Allan Rosenzweig of Intertax, a South African tax advisory and investment company, were intrigued with the film industry and, after a few positive phone conversations, invited me to Johannesburg to discuss funding for our film. While Paul and Bob were in Milan, I secured the entire budget of our film through the tax credit and agreed to the single term it demanded: to film the movie in southern Africa.

When the idea of filming in Africa became a requirement, the Fosters started to do their homework. They visited with Sidney Pollack, director of *Out of Africa*, to get advice. Pollack told them to film *Red Scorpion* in Mexico and avoid Africa like the plague, which might very well be one of the things they would encounter should they choose to ignore his counsel.

His experience in Kenya couldn't have been worse. But with the prospect of full funding derived from the tax credit, I wasn't willing to go any other route. Whatever problems we might encounter, we would deal with them.

The Intertax financing required a distribution agreement and a completion bond. The distribution agreement would assure that the film was marketed throughout the world, which would generate the promotional expenses needed for the tax credit. A completion bond was an insurance policy guaranteeing the timely completion of the film, on budget. If the film were not on time or budget, the bond company would have the option of completing the film or refunding the financier's capital.

When we convened in Los Angeles to sort through the MIFED experience, a number of non-studio distributors were making aggressive contact with us to secure rights to the film, including a doughty company based in L.A. called Shapiro Glickenhaus. But we wanted to work with a major studio. We estimated our production budget to be approximately $6 million. MGM offered $2 million. We passed. Lorimar, a major television production company, famous for the hit show "Dallas," was just starting to produce feature films. They offered us a "negative pick up," meaning they would guarantee a payment of $6 million upon delivery of a complete negative of the picture which met the pre-agreed creative standards. This deal would secure the Intertax money, and enable the picture to move forward. While we were negotiating with Lorimar, however, we maintained contact with Warner Bros. They, too, were interested in the film, but had yet to make an offer. They asked that we keep them informed on our progress with Lorimar and that if anything went wrong we come to them.

Soon enough, something went wrong. Lorimar, assuming we had no other offers from major distributors, drew up their contracts with a $4 million offer, rather than the agreed-upon $6 million. Bad move. We walked away and called Warner Bros. They offered us the $6 million, with the caveat that we wouldn't film in South Africa or Namibia. In those days, South Africa was subject to international sanctions and condemnation due to its racist political system of apartheid. We agreed to this exclusionary provision. Since we planned to film in Swaziland, which was completely independent of South Africa, we didn't see a problem. *Red Scorpion* was finally a reality—though inevitably, not the kind we hoped for.

What followed was one disaster after another. Duwayne Dunham, our first director, quit when we refused to add a high tech scene that would have pushed the budget over $7 million. I asked the Fosters to intervene, but they thought the scene was vital to the story and resisted my efforts to keep the budget under control. A power struggle ensued over this issue, but there was no choice: we couldn't afford the new scene. So, the Fosters decided to join Dunham in exiting the film. Only six months into the project, Bob and I were left with a gaping hole in the creative side of the endeavor, and a studio none too pleased that their approved director had walked.

On Warner Bros.' insistence, we hired Joseph Zito who had recently directed *Missing in Action* and *Invasion U.S.A.* with Chuck Norris, as well as one of the Friday the 13th films. We met Zito and found him to be affable and charming. Too charming. Zito was a master manipulator, who made it fun to obey his will. It was not fun for long. Almost immediately, Zito and I travelled to Swaziland to commence pre-production. To replace the Fosters, Zito recommended a string of producers. Being inexperienced, I didn't realize the worst thing one could do was to allow the director to choose the producer. The producer has to keep the director under control, or the picture will soon be drained of funds. Once I hired his choice for producer, it was all downhill from there.

But despite the road bumps and conflicts to come, we were soon ready to commence principal photography, the part of filmmaking where the picture is actually filmed. Pam was home in Maryland, pregnant with our first child, and I was busily working away in Swaziland with the rest of the crew. She was due on September 15, 1987, and I had planned to come home on the thirteenth. Dolph Lundgren had just arrived in Swaziland, and filming was to commence the next week. All seemed to be in order, until the night before I was to depart for Washington. As I sat with a few of the crew members over dinner, I noticed our production manager, David Anderson, with his head in his hands across the room, like he had just heard the worst news of his life. I approached David to see what was wrong.

"Jack, I didn't know when to tell you, but the government told me today that they held a secret cabinet meeting last night and removed our permits to film. We have to leave the country."

Removed our permit to film? We had built a mock Soviet air base and spent millions of dollars in this nation. For eight weeks, I had been paying salaries, hotel costs, and per diems for our crew as they prepared for filming. Now, in an instant, we had lost our permits?

My first call wasn't to the government, or to Warner Bros., or to the investors, or to the completion bond company. My first call was to Pam. "Hi Sweetie. How are you? Good. Good. I have a bit of a problem. It might be difficult for me to fly home tomorrow. It seems our permit to film has been revoked, and I have to find out what is happening. The entire project lies in the balance. Are you able to hold on a bit longer?" I kicked myself as soon as the words came out. Was I an idiot? Did I think she could keep the baby in by force?

Fortunately, I married better than I deserved.

"Honey, you take care of that problem. I'll be fine. If we can wait, we will. If not, I'll tell you all about it."

It would kill me to miss the birth of my first child, but what could I do? Everything we had was tied up in this project. Failure was not an option; I stayed.

The next morning, I headed to the office of the Minister of Trade and Industry, who had originally convinced us to locate in Swaziland. The film had a major impact on their economy. The film was their economy. But he couldn't tell me clearly why they were removing us, and recommended that I visit with the Defense Minister. I found that an odd suggestion. What did a Defense Minister have to do with a film project?

The next day, I got an appointment with Defense Minister Dlamini. I had already informed the cast and crew of our difficulties and asked them to be patient. Most of the supporting cast had not yet arrived in the country, but Zito was working with Dolph on the first segments to be recorded while I scurried about trying to undo this expulsion edict. Minister Dlamini received me graciously, but was adamant that we had to leave the country. He wouldn't reveal the reason for our eviction, and recommended that I seek an audience with Prime Minister Dlamimi. Did they all have the same name, I wondered?

"I am confident you can see the Prime Minister within the next few weeks," Minister Dlamini proclaimed with pride.

I did my best to stay calm. I had a baby coming any minute on the other side of the world and over two hundred people on my payroll waiting for me to sort this out. "Mr. Minister, if there is any way to get me in to see the Prime Minister sooner, I would be most grateful."

He responded, "Yes, we are very happy you are here, enjoying our wonderful weather. Perhaps you can come back and see me again some time?"

I felt like I was in a bad episode of "The Twilight Zone."

"OK, Minister, thanks. Great to meet you."

I called the Minister of Trade again, and he somehow managed to get me a meeting with the Prime Minister the next day. The Prime Minister explained that my permit had been revoked once it was discovered that the coup d'état in Algeria was carried out by soldiers posing as a motion picture company. When their fake filming commenced, they took over the palace.

I was flabbergasted. The coup in Algeria had taken place in the 1960s. Had the news just arrived, decades later? Couldn't this have been discussed before we built a mock Soviet base and spent half the budget of our film?

"Mr. Abramoff," the Prime Minister suggested, "How about if you just take a rest and come back to film in three to four months? By then, everything should be fine."

He obviously had no clue about filmmaking.

"Mr. Prime Minister, if I cancel filming, I lose my crew and actors. Once I lose them, the production is finished. If we cannot film here now, we are sunk."

"I am very sorry, my friend."

And with that comment, our experience in Swaziland came to an end. Head bowed, I returned home just in time for the birth of my beloved son Levi on September 25. It seemed that Pam was the only one in our family who could complete a project.

In early October, I headed back to southern Africa to find a new filming location. With the Warner Bros.' prohibition on filming in South Africa or Namibia, and all our funding in the southern African rand currency, our only options were Zimbabwe, Botswana, and Lesotho. Zimbabwe was impossible, since *Red Scorpion* was anti-Communist, and Zimbabwe was ruled by the Marxist dictator Robert Mugabe. Botswana was ruled out since, for whatever reason, most of the foreigners in the country were being detained and held for questioning. So we were left with Lesotho.

If I were a contestant on Jeopardy, and asked to name the country with the highest average elevation in the world, I would answer, "What is Tibet?" And I would be wrong. The answer is Lesotho. Pronounced Le-soo-too, this nation, like Swaziland, was a member of the British Commonwealth. Unlike Swaziland, it was entirely surrounded by South Africa. The cast and crew had been relocated to Johannesburg and were in a holding pattern. Dolph was refining his shooting skills and martial arts capabilities, and the rest of the crew alternated between set design, production, planning, and sloth.

When I arrived in the capital city of Maseru, I was struck by how un-African the surroundings were. It looked like Switzerland with no buildings. The Africans wore heavy wool cloaks to protect against the winter weather. There were no trees, no bush, no animals. My backyard in Maryland looked more like Africa. If we were to make the film there, we were going to have to bring in everything, including sand.

The bigger problem, though, was that after seven weeks of promising to approve the production for filming, the cabinet of Lesotho never came through. Our options were gone. We could either film this movie in Namibia and hope for the best, or we could pack up and go home.

The completion bond company president Lawrence Vanger and I were invited to a late meeting on a stormy Johannesburg night at the Intertax offices. Vanger was faced with a dilemma. If he allowed the production to proceed in Namibia, Intertax would provide the funds needed to complete the film, but we would be in violation of the Warner Bros. agreement. If the production shut down, the film would not be completed, and the completion bond company would have to pay out all money already spent. Vanger looked like he was going to faint; he needed the Intertax financing to complete the film, but losing Warners would put him and his company at risk. The only way out was for the film to be completed and for another distributor to take over, in the event Warner Bros. put the production in default.

Warner Bros. was contacted about our move to Namibia. Their executive in charge of the production told us to go ahead, but "keep it quiet," as if that's possible with a war film. While we were able to keep it quiet for a few weeks, the explosions eventually came, and they weren't from the pyrotechnics department. On January 8, 1988, the *New York Times* not only revealed we were filming in Namibia, but also asserted that the production was merely a South African government project, aided by the South African army, starring South African army soldiers! The absurd lies rankled us, but the crushing blow was the denial by Warner Bros.: "In California, a spokesman for Warner Bros., Rob Friedman, said the company had had no involvement with the film. 'Warner Bros. declined to be involved even before they decided to shoot in Namibia,' he said."

And I thought Washington politicians were liars!

We had no time to grumble about Warner Bros. We finished filming the movie, and began to look for a new distributor. We finally signed with Shapiro Glickenhaus, the company which had evidenced so much interest early on. They were thrilled to get the film and paid us $8 million for just the foreign rights, going far beyond the $6 million Warner had agreed to pay for world rights... before they forgot they were involved.

This would have been reason to celebrate if Zito hadn't insisted on keeping everyone out of the editing process. While we had a completed film, the result was an inferior product. When we were finally able to view the work, Dolph and I asked for numerous changes to improve the picture, but these suggestions fell on deaf ears. Shapiro Glickenhaus was rushing the film into the theatres, and there was no time to correct the multitude of errors and flaws.

*Red Scorpion* did smashing business in markets where the audience spoke little English. It opened in the United States in 1,200 theatres. Shapiro Glickenhaus also took domestic U.S. distribution, planning to build a new distribution company in the wake of the release of the film. It was a complete flop.

The *Red Scorpion* experience should have left a foul taste in my mouth about filmmaking. But instead, I was more convinced than ever that it was a robust business. What truly excited me, though, was the notion that tax credit financing could propel film projects from conception to reality. The tax credit Intertax used for *Red Scorpion* soon evaporated, but I was already spanning the globe to find its first cousin. I found it in several nations, including Canada, Luxembourg, and Malaysia, but launching projects in these territories proved to be an arduous task, and one which cost fortunes of resources and time.

Sequels are the magic elixir of movie making. Producers will make a sequel to anything, because the brand is already known in the marketplace, whether it stinks or not. So I shouldn't have been surprised when I was approached by August Entertainment to produce a sequel to *Red Scorpion*. The first film was horrendous, but had done serious business in the overseas markets. In fact, it had broken records in a number of Asian cities.

Gregory Cascante, the head of August, had connections with Canadian producers and would set us up to film in Canada, where we could avail ourselves of the Canadian tax credit financing for film production, and the project could move quickly, or so I was told. Although Dolph Lundgren was too expensive to use again (and probably not interested in a sequel to a film he thought was poorly done), the distributors felt we could sell the film based on the *Red Scorpion* title alone, so I crafted a story which could take place in Vancouver or the Pacific Northwest.

The plot line revolved around one of the most fascinating relics of the Middle Ages, the Spear of Destiny. This artifact was allegedly the spear thrust by the Roman centurion Longinus into the body of Jesus on the cross. According to Christian scripture, water and blood flowed from the piercing and that miracle caused Longinus to convert to Christianity. The spear gained special status and was passed from ruler to ruler throughout European history. Finally, the relic purported to be the spear wound up in the treasure house of the Hapsburg Palace in Vienna. The young Adolph Hitler was fascinated by the spear, and all icons and relics of antiquity. One of his biographers contended that he would sit for hours in Vienna staring at the spear. The legend grew from the time of Charlemagne that he who held the spear could attain power. When the Nazis annexed Austria, one of the first acts of the SS was to bring the spear to Hitler, where it remained until the day he died. After that, it was returned to the Hapsburg Palace. That much is true.

In *Red Scorpion 2*, the sequel, a neo-Nazi movement rises in the Pacific Northwest. They are in possession of an ancient prophecy:

When one and one is one
And the Eagle rises
The Scorpion will wield the Spear
And the Earth will be reborn in Fire

The Nazi group steals the Spear of Destiny from the Hapsburg Palace and obtains a nuclear weapon from the former Soviet Union (the fire with which the Earth will be reborn). They set out to find the Scorpion—the *Red Scorpion*, of course—who will wield the spear and ignite a nuclear holocaust which will bring them to power.

After much wrangling over minor copyright issues, we made the film. But like its original, the trail from story to film was full of potholes, and *Red Scorpion 2: The Spear of Destiny* turned out to be even worse than Zito's cinematic flop.

For almost eight years, I tried to set up motion picture projects in far flung lands. Sometimes I succeeded, but more often than not the only thing I got for my trouble was more trouble.

After being away from my family for my third trip of more than six weeks' duration, I knew it couldn't continue. I was thirty five years old by then, we had five small children at home, and Pam was raising them by herself. She was an amazing mother, but I wanted to be part of it, too. It wasn't as if I was making films that were going to save Western Civilization. Nor was it the case that I was making a fortune.

Something had to give.

# 5

# K STREET CONFIDENTIAL

Throughout my years making films, I kept my hand in the political pot, sponsoring fundraisers and helping friends connect to the conservative movement in Washington. I cheered on the Republicans in 1994, as they surged to take Congress for the first time in a generation. While filmmaking sparked my creativity, my inability to have consistent success depleted my finances and sapped my energy. I had a few friends in Hollywood, but since I never moved there, I did not make the kinds of connections one needs to join the upper echelon of that community, which would ensure success in the movie business. Plus, deep down, I knew part of me would always be married to Washington and that politics was my true calling.

One of my close friends during that period was Rabbi Daniel Lapin, a brilliant former South African who was quickly becoming an intellectual force among conservatives. In the 1990s, Dana Rohrabacher, now a congressman, organized a series of luncheons in the Capitol where Rabbi Lapin explained the biblical foundations of conservative philosophy to Republican members of Congress. At one of these luncheons, I met the man who would become one of the cornerstones of my career—Tom Delay.

What struck me about Tom in our first meeting was how sincerely religious he was, and how intensely interested he seemed in Rabbi Lapin's observations. Tom had a strong working knowledge of the Bible, which struck Rabbi Lapin and me as unusual for a member of Congress. The lunch didn't last more than an hour, and Tom and I didn't have a chance for any small talk, but from the way he spoke about his core beliefs and how they empowered his political activism, I hoped he was destined for a larger role, maybe even the leadership of the party. It was several years later, however, before that potential would blossom, and in the interim, I had very little contact with the congressman from Houston.

The election of 1994 brought about a sea change in the American political landscape, and I felt the urge to dive back into the waters I'd left behind. My parents came to visit that fall, and my father strongly urged me to return to politics. He knew how frustrated I was making films, and he thought I was wasting years of experience and contacts in Washington. I listened passively to him, knowing he was right but not knowing quite what to do about it. The election provided a solution.

The day after the Republicans swept the congressional elections, my good friend Ralph Nurnberger, a Democratic lobbyist, called me. He was head of a small, boutique lobbying firm on K Street that mainly employed Democrats. He knew that with the new Republican tide, he needed to hire a Republican lobbyist. Was I interested in joining his firm?

I wasn't a lobbyist. I was a movie producer. Not a good one, but a movie producer nevertheless. What did I know about lobbying?

Ralph reminded me that we met when I was heading Reagan's grass-roots lobby and that I would be a natural for the job. That was true, but I still couldn't see myself becoming a lobbyist. Lobbyists were those evil corporate pukes who disdained ideologues like me. They were the guys in the $2,000 suits who sucked the lifeblood out of our nation. Why would I ever become one of those guys? I set it on the backburner, and didn't see the attraction.

That Sabbath, as usual, I attended services at our synagogue. After services, our neighbor and fellow congregant, Jonathan Blank, approached me. He was a Republican and wanted to share his glee over the triumph in that week's elections. We were congratulating each other on the amazing turn of events when I told him about my interesting encounter that week with Ralph. I was laughing as I recounted the meeting, but Jonathan had a mischievous look on his face. When I finished, he asked if I would ever seriously consider being a lobbyist... like him. I had no idea that he was a lobbyist—I thought he was an attorney.

Jonathan explained that he was both an attorney and a lobbyist, and that if I ever wanted to join a firm, it should be his: Preston Gates Ellis and Rouvelas Meeds. Jonathan could see my skepticism, and he asked if I even knew what lobbyists did.

"Suck money out of the taxpayer? Impose regulations on small business? Undermine America?"

He laughed. Their firm, whose senior partner was Bill Gates' father, primarily represented Microsoft. Their job was to keep the government off the company's back. This was starting to sound appealing. I liked the idea of getting the government off Microsoft's back. I liked the idea of getting the government off everyone's back. Maybe this could work. Maybe this was the job which would keep me home, with Pam and the kids.

When I came to his office two weeks later, Jonathan introduced me to one of the senior partner of the firm, Emanuel Rouvelas. Manny had been the chief of staff of some congressional committee eons ago, and seemed to be a thoughtful and gracious man. As Jonathan left the two of us to chat, he stopped to say, "Manny, Jack is the most conservative person I have ever met." I wasn't sure if he meant that as a compliment, or as a warning, and Manny and I exchanged uncomfortable smiles as we started to discuss my background, but just then Jonathan poked his head back in the room again with a postscript.

"Actually, his wife is the most conservative person I ever met, but he's second."

I burst into laughter and so did Manny. That's when I knew I could get along fine there.

We talked about the role of lobbying and lobbyists in the American political system. My preconceived notion that lobbyists were two-headed hydras was diminished. I spent the next few hours meeting the other partners and found them likeable. They were mainly Democrats, though there were a few Republicans as well. To me, it seemed clear why they needed me. The new regime in Congress was not only Republican—it was conservative Republican—and most lobbyists, including Preston Gates' Republican lobbyists, didn't know how to speak their lingo. I did. Many of the representatives in power and their staff had come through our Fieldman Schools and College Republican clubs in the 1980s. They had attended our rallies, read our books, studied at our schools, or joined our clubs. Clearly I would be an asset.

My last meeting of the day was the most important to me. Lloyd Meeds was a liberal former member of Congress from the firm's home state of Washington. Lloyd was a short, stout man who wore suspenders. He was incredibly personable, still retaining the charm that returned him to the Congress election after election. Lloyd's office was in a private alcove of the firm. After a few moments of small talk, Lloyd popped the question: "If the firm had a client with demands which went against your philosophy, do you feel you could still work hard for that client?"

I stared at Lloyd, wishing I could evade this question, but I couldn't.

"If a client was pushing something against my beliefs, I couldn't help them at all. In fact, I would probably oppose them."

Oh well, I thought to myself, there goes the lobbyist job.

Lloyd looked me in the eye, and leaned into me. "Are you saying that you wouldn't do it, even if it meant the firm would lose that business? Even if the firm demanded you do it? Even if we promise you more money?"

"I couldn't do it for all the money in the world."

"You're sure?" He sounded like he was giving me a chance to dig myself out of a hole.

"I'm sure."

Lloyd's face beamed with a huge smile. "Then, as far as I'm concerned, you're hired! I've been waiting for someone like me to show up here for more years than I can count. We might not agree on the issues, but I respect you for sticking by your guns."

Lloyd Meeds might have been short in stature, but from that moment on, he was a giant in my eyes. To start, I was offered $150,000, a modest salary by lobbying industry standards, and told I could begin with the firm at the New Year. I accepted and even reported a few weeks early, without pay, so I could learn the computer system and find out more about this lobbying thing.

My first few weeks at Preston Gates found me making the rounds in the office. I learned what every professional was doing, or at least what they wanted me to think they were doing. As I went from office to office, I was constantly bothered by the inefficiencies and lack of aggressiveness at the firm. At first, the firm focused me on their two main practices: maritime and Microsoft. The maritime practice came from Manny's background in the Congress. We worked on arcane issues related to where a shipping vessel could be based, what routes it could take, and other mind-numbing conundrums. Though I was stupefied by all of this, I tried to find creative ways to make the issue interesting and, more importantly, exciting to conservatives on the Hill. One of the most vital things a lobbyist can do when working an issue is to ignite the passion of congressmen and their staff. Few issues required as much creative flexibility as maritime did.

Most people hire lobbyists because they want to stop the government from doing something that will harm their business. When it came to Microsoft, Preston Gates was focused on keeping the government off the company's back. As a conservative, I could understand and support such a mission. Microsoft wasn't and isn't alone in trying to keep free of the federal bureaucracy. Almost every industry in the nation has the same interest, as do many states and territories. Even foreign powers sometimes feel the need to come to Washington to keep U.S. federal government actions from impeding their economies.

But playing defense against the aggressive government isn't the only reason people hire lobbyists. Some use the government to get a competitive advantage. Forcing your competition to be over-regulated is an age-old method of getting a leg up in business. Plus, legions come with their hand out for federal funds. Generations of supplicants—individuals, unions, and corporations alike—have brought this nation to a state of economic catastrophe that could very well lead to our demise.

The firm was so close to Microsoft that they sometimes operated like symbiotic organisms, nurturing each other. The revolving door between the firm and Microsoft was constantly in motion. The head of legal affairs at the company had come from the firm. Attorneys at the firm had worked at Microsoft. But this cozy connection wasn't evident in the day-to-day working relationship, at least not in the lobbying area.

There seemed to be a constant tension in the Washington office of the firm about Microsoft, in part because of the personality of the attorney who headed the representation. Bruce Heiman was an intelligent and cautious attorney who had previously worked for the late Senator Patrick

Moynihan, an iconic liberal Senator from New York. Having been with Preston Gates for years, he was chosen to lead the lobbying for this important client. While I liked Bruce immensely, he always seemed extremely nervous about the Microsoft relationship, bordering on paranoid. Since most of the firm's revenue was derived from that company, it made sense. The haughtiness and arrogance of the Microsoft employees toward folks in the Washington office was sickening, and certainly not how Bill Gates himself treated us. When he was being briefed in advance of a senate hearing, Gates was kind and unassuming. His underlings were not, and this served to unnerve Bruce.

After a few months of dealing with these software grandees, I, too, was at the edge. My job was to assess whether Microsoft could find allies on the right to help them combat the assault Washington was directing at them. At that point in the company's development, they had been thwarted from purchasing Intuit, makers of the popular software Quicken. The anti-trust crowd was just about to unleash hell on the company, and they were trying to determine how they should approach the political landscape. Naturally, I was a strong advocate of Microsoft aligning itself with free market activists and others on the right. While the conservative base might not appreciate the cultural liberalism of the company, or its history of supporting candidates on the left, getting the government off one's back played right to the sweet spot of most right-leaning groups. I forcefully advocated that Microsoft shift the focus of their contributions from environmental and population control organizations to free market and traditional conservative groups. This didn't go over well. I guess it was bad enough for the Rulers of Redmond that they had to deal with mere groundlings in the Washington office of Preston Gates, but now they had to deal with a Neanderthal conservative to boot? Perhaps this was understandable. There were no Jack Abramoff's or Howard Phillips's sharing wine and brie with the elite techies in Seattle. They didn't know what to make of conservatives, and they were liberals. It was inconceivable that conservatives were their ultimate saviors. Today, Google is experiencing the same betrayal. Their liberal leadership finds their company under assault from the Obama administration the same way that Microsoft's progressives woke one day to find the Clinton gang had them in their gun sights.

In 1995, when Microsoft needed access to the House Republican

Leadership, conservatives were there to help. When the company started to feel the Clinton administration's pressure on the issue of software program encryption export, it was Majority Whip Tom DeLay who came to the rescue. I recall enjoying the awkward meeting between DeLay and the Microsoft bigwigs about this and other key issues. DeLay expressed his general support for their positions and reminded them that it was likely to be the Republicans who would defend the freedom they required to develop their company. He made a soft appeal for political contributions from the company, reminding them that, were the Republicans to lose the majority, the very Members of Congress who supported the Clinton administration attacks on Microsoft would then be free to dismantle their software company.

One of the Microsoft executives firmly brushed off his solicitation, prompting DeLay to deliver a stern message. When he was a freshman in Congress, he told them he approached Walmart for a campaign contribution. The government affairs director of Walmart told him that Walmart didn't like to "sully their hands" with political involvement. Staring intently at the Microsoft executives, DeLay continued: "A year later, that government affairs rep was in my office asking me to intervene to get an exit built from the federal highway adjacent to a new Walmart store. I told him I didn't want to sully my hands with such a task. You know what? They didn't get their ramp. You know what else? They will never get that ramp."

DeLay smiled, without taking his eyes off the quivering executives. As we would often say in the lobbying business: They finally got the joke. A $100,000 check was soon delivered to the Republican Congressional Committee, and Microsoft's relationship with the American right commenced. Fortunately for Microsoft, they couldn't have asked for better teammates. At my suggestion, they soon engaged Grover Norquist to advise them. Though I stayed in periodic contact with Grover in the years since Citizens for America, while I was traveling the globe trying to make films, he was building from scratch the organization which would one day become the most powerful group in the conservative movement: Americans for Tax Reform, or ATR. Founded on the simple notion that taxes needed to be cut, not raised, Grover put to work his years of experience and political skill to create a group which would single-handedly stop any inclination on the part of Republicans to join Democrats in trying to raise taxes. Grover authored a pledge which virtually every Republican signed, a vow that they would never vote to raise taxes. Eventually, Americans for Tax Reform would be seen as the leading free market group in the nation, and the undisputed head of the conservative movement. Based on his well-deserved reputation, Grover was instantly hired by Microsoft as they attempted to encourage Republicans to support their legislative agenda. They also spread their contributions to most of the other conservative groups I had been suggesting and, in doing so, they built a strong cadre to defend their company and freedom in the tech world. The Republicans were doing what they would have done anyway, but now they were getting resources to retain power and control of the Congress. I was proud of this since it was one of the main reasons I landed on K Street, the lobbyists' domain.

While I supported Microsoft's mission, it was harder and harder to justify the hours I was spending on this client. For all the help they were providing conservative groups, they were still imperious and supercilious. I wanted to get away from these guys, and the feeling was mutual. So, after a few terse and frigid meetings with the Microsoft government affairs personnel, I was able to bow out of further work for this client. Somehow, I figured they'd find a way to survive the loss, and in any event, they were unalterably on a course to support the conservative movement, for their own benefit. Mission accomplished.

By the time I had been at Preston Gates for a few months, I was hooked on the challenge of the work, but not making the kind of money I desired. I was still being paid a rather modest salary, and my clients were interesting, but low paying. Even had I been paid a percentage of the revenue I generated for the firm, my pay would have been paltry. I had to find a way to build a more substantial and lucrative client base, or I'd find myself back in the entertainment world. Soon, my father would present one of the greatest opportunities that would ever come my way.

The Commonwealth of the Northern Mariana Islands—or CNMI— was a U.S. territory in the Western Pacific. Consisting of thirteen islands, three of which were inhabited, the Marianas had voluntarily joined the United States in the 1970s. In exchange for ceding control over their islands and the vast seabed in their territorial waters, the CNMI negotiated a covenant with the United States which granted them two key economic concessions. In order to develop a self-sustaining economy, the CNMI was granted authority over their immigration and minimum wage. The ability to grant a quick visa to potential Asian tourists and workers was essential if they were to compete with Hawaii and other holiday destinations. Since the CNMI was part of the Asian economy, paying American minimum wage rates would have crushed any opportunity to develop a manufacturing base. So the wise leaders of the Marianas, realizing they were affording the United States with an incredible opportunity to have a forward position in the Western Pacific, held out for these two essential concessions. The United States, realizing that the trade was a good one, said yes.

It took more than a decade for the economic incentives to work for the CNMI, but once manufacturers and entrepreneurs discovered these two advantages, industries started on the islands. After a number of false starts, the garment industry took hold. By the mid 1990s, garments manufactured in the CNMI were streaming into the U.S. mainland. Since the CNMI was a U.S. territory, the garments could bear the "Made in the USA" label, which so many producers coveted. This didn't sit well with the U.S. garment makers' unions and their allies. Instead of the media lauding the incredible success of the Pacific Islanders and the fact that, thanks to tourism and garment manufacturing, they were not constantly begging for congressional appropriations, a campaign of vilification commenced.

The CNMI was accused of being a slave colony, of systematically abusing foreign workers, of running an island-wide brothel. The *Washington Post* led all media outlets with vitriolic attacks on the Marianas. As is often the case with the Potomac Two-Step, these articles were followed by congressional action. Indignant statesmen in the Congress vowed to put an end to this island abuse. Hearings were held, and legislation was introduced to eliminate the lifeline which kept the CNMI from returning to the abject poverty they knew before the covenant. Of course, there was no talk of returning the islands' territory to them.

One day my father called me and reminded me that a few years earlier he had tried to set up a casino resort in Northern Marianas. He had just received a call from Randy Fennell, his attorney from the islands, who told him that Governor Froilan Tenorio was looking for a lobbyist. Dad asked me if I thought I could help them. I wasn't sure, but I knew this was a big break, so I answered with my usual reply, "Absolutely, I can!" The Governor was coming to D.C., and Randy would get us a meeting with him.

In mid-May 1995, the CNMI landing party entered the hostile nation's capital looking for a lobbyist. They met with all the top firms in town, including Preston Gates. By the time our meeting took place, the Governor was busy doing something else, and we were left to meet with his chief of staff and cousin, Brenda Tenorio, and a few of her employees. We had a pleasant lunch at the famous Maison Blanche restaurant, where I pitched our capacities.

"I think we can beat this back, Ms. Tenorio. The notion that the United States should be destroying the economy of the CNMI by limiting its free market is anathema to conservatives, and this new Congress is conservative. I think we need a full effort to educate people about what is really going on in the CNMI—assuming the abuse stories are false—and we are the firm to get this done. Few other K Street firms understand conservatives and what makes them tick. I do, since I not only come out of that movement myself, but I helped to train many of the congressmen and staff when they were College Republicans."

Brenda stared at me for a few moments. It seemed like an eternity.

"Are you saying we can beat the effort to take away our minimum wage and immigration control?"

"Yes, that is exactly what I am saying."

More stares. Now her staff was exchanging glances. What did I say? Wasn't that their goal?

Brenda explained that every other firm they had met with in Washington had said there was no way to win this fight and suggested that they compromise and negotiate a gradual, phased in elimination of the incentives.

I jumped on this.

"Can you live without the incentives?"

"No," she answered, "but there is no point to losing them in a week, if we can lose them in a few years."

"You don't have to lose them at all."

I could tell by her expression that she wanted this lunch to be over.

No sense in sitting with a madman. My own colleagues were looking at me in disbelief. But I kept at it.

"My recommendation to you is this. If you are going to lose, lose on your own. Don't pay a lobbying firm—even this one—to help you lose. That's crazy. If you fight, fight to win. If you are going to give up, you can do that for free."

With that, we ended our meeting. I was fairly sure I had made a mistake and lost the pitch, but I couldn't be in a business where the goal was losing as slowly as possible.

Within a week, I read that the Northern Marianas had signed with the prestigious firm Verner Liipfert. They had a former governor of Hawaii at their firm, and clients tend to be impressed by former bigwigs. They hire the firm where the big name sits, giving themselves cover in the event something goes wrong, a built-in excuse: "I hired the best—it's not my fault." But hiring the former bigwig doesn't always work, not when your life is at stake.

Within a month, the U.S. Senate passed the bill to strip the CNMI of their control of immigration and minimum wage. The vote was unanimous. So much for the former governor of Hawaii. The Marianas were now headed over the cliff. There wasn't going to be a transition of a few years. They were going to lose their incentives immediately. The bill was also wending its way through the House.

A couple of days later, I received a letter in the mail. It was from Governor Tenorio. After rattling on for a page, he got to the point: we were hired. Brenda Tenorio would be in touch, and we could start our campaign to stop this take over. I guess I wasn't so crazy, after all.

I sent an email to the firm announcing our engagement and within an hour, Lloyd Meeds was at my door. He knew I would need help with this representation, and his years of experience dealing with labor issues in Congress would be invaluable to me. The fact that he had impeccable liberal credentials didn't hurt either, since it was quickly becoming clear that this representation would become an ideological fight. I was thrilled to have him by my side. Lloyd knew that our first order of business needed to be visiting the islands to see for ourselves whether the corruption reported in the media was fact or fiction. In the meantime, we had to make sure the takeover bill didn't move.

Lloyd called his friend Don Young, the chairman of the House Resources Committee, where this bill would have to pass first, and asked him to give us some time. Next, it was my turn to talk to friends in the House Leadership in case the bill's proponents tried to make an end run around Don Young by attaching the bill to the appropriations bills.

In order to secure the Republican House Leadership on this issue, I first visited with Ed Buckham, the chief of staff for Tom DeLay, who was now Majority Whip of the Congress. Ed was a very thin man about my age. In fact, he was so thin that I often wondered whether he was ill. Many months later, it was discovered that he was, in fact, very ill, and this caused him eventually to leave the position he held with DeLay. I met Buckham through another DeLay staffer, April Lassiter, who had also attended those luncheons with Rabbi Lapin and was keen to connect the committed Baptist Buckham with her two new Orthodox Jewish friends.

In late 1994, when I first joined Preston Gates, Ed Buckham was managing DeLay's campaign to become the Majority Whip of the House. I offered to contact every Congressman I knew to push DeLay's candidacy. I remembered meeting DeLay from our lunch with Rabbi Lapin, and thought he would be a superb leader for the Republican Party. DeLay won in a landslide, and Buckham and I soon became close friends. I would spend hours with him in his office in the Capitol building discussing the Bible and politics. Ed had the demeanor of a country preacher, but he was smart and sly as a fox. He had many years experience in politics, and knew how to apply pressure when kindness was not an option. He was generally a good judge of character, and always seemed to have DeLay's best interests at heart.

When I approached Ed about the Marianas, it was an easy sell. He immediately grasped the free market issues at stake and said he didn't think Tom would disagree, though I would have to present it myself. Tom had a reputation for being a tough guy, and, by then, I had already seen him in action a few times, including with Microsoft, where he'd let a few zingers fly about their liberal culture and contribution record. What might he say about the Marianas? Ed set a meeting for me with Tom later that day, and I entered his office with more than a little trepidation.

I presented my spiel to him, and he listened carefully. Then he started: "Jack, are you sure they are not doing the things they are being accused of?"

"I'm not sure, since I have yet to go there, but I am going within the month and will find out. If they are, I am not going to represent them. The issue is not whether there is any abuse in the CNMI. There might be. There is abuse two blocks from this building in Washington, D.C. The issue to me, and I hope to you, is whether it's systemic and whether the government there is doing all it can to stop it. If they are, then there is no reason to destroy their economy."

"I couldn't agree more. No bill is going to move in the next week or so, and then we are recessed for the summer. Let me know what you find."

We shook hands, and I proceeded to the next member of the leadership: the Speaker of the House, Newt Gingrich.

I first met Newt Gingrich when I was national chairman of the College Republicans. In October 1983, President Reagan sent our armed forces to liberate the island of Grenada from a Marxist military coup and free the American students who were there attending medical college. One year later, Reagan was running for re-election, and we decided to celebrate the one year anniversary of this liberation by reuniting those students and sending them to speak at college campuses across the nation. We called it Student Liberation Day. Several members of Congress joined our efforts, but none as fervently as former college professor Newt Gingrich, then a relatively unknown member of Congress. I did not maintain a relationship with Newt in the years that followed, but Grover did. Newt recognized Grover's brilliance and brought him into his inner circle. Grover's continued advice and assistance were invaluable to me as I got my footing in the lobbying industry. So, when I needed to meet with Newt, I called my friend. He made a call, and I got the meeting.

I had only a few minutes with Newt in the Speaker's office, but I figured that should suffice. I was wrong. His tendency to wander was a bit unnerving, as he never seemed to be able to sit still or focus for more than a few minutes. Finally, when I told him about the Marianas, his response stunned me. He suggested we make the Marianas and the other American Pacific territories—Guam and American Samoa—part of Hawaii. "That way," he said, "they can all have a congressman and be a real part of the United States."

Was he not listening at all, or did I somehow say something to lead him to such a conclusion? Later on, I'd come to realize this was classic

Newt. As soon as he heard an issue, he would quickly decide what to do—even without the benefit of all the information—and that was the end of the discussion. I tried feebly to bring us back to the real issues at hand, but he was having none of it.

He continued, ignoring me, "Yes, part of Hawaii. That would be great. That would solve their problems. Super… Jack, you take care." The meeting was over.

Though the meeting with Newt was something of a disaster, I would soon learn he had little to do with the movement of legislation through the House. That was Tom and Dick Armey, the Majority Leader of the Congress. What I was only then coming to appreciate was that the leadership of the Congress has a division of labor, and that the Majority Leader and Whip control the legislative processes far more than the Speaker, who is often the public face of the Congress. This was a suitable arrangement since Newt loved the public stage far more than Tom DeLay or Dick Armey.

Armey, like Newt, was a former professor, but that's where their similarity ended. Armey was thoughtful and focused. He was also careful and modest in his recommendations. It wasn't likely that he would propose the CNMI join Hawaii. But I hadn't seen him for almost twenty years, since he was running for Congress in Dallas in 1984, and I was national chairman of College Republicans, going door-to-door to encourage his constituents to vote for him. I needed a way to get him involved with the Marianas.

At this time, it was becoming clear that there was plenty of work to be done for our clients with the conservatives running the Congress, and I was given the green light to hire another conservative at the firm. I chose Dennis Stephens, a former staff member of Armey's congressional office, who later served as legislative assistant for Congressmen Joe Barton (R-TX) and Roger Wicker (R-MS). Dennis would lobby the Armey folks for us, while I worked with DeLay and others. After about a week of meetings, we had put an effective block in place to stop the legislation which would have hurt the CNMI. I rendezvoused with Lloyd who did the same with House Resources Committee Chairman Young. The House was secure, for now. The only issue was whether the main senator sponsoring the offending bill, Frank Murkowski of Alaska, would try to sneak the language through the approval process by attaching it to another piece of legislation. The favorite bill for such a move would have been the Interior Appropriations Bill, which funded all territorial operations and supervision. Under normal circumstances, it would be an easy thing for a senator to add such an arcane issue to such a bill and push it through quietly, but our firm was on guard against this through the rest of the pre-summer recess session and, in any event, the appropriations bills were slated for the fall Congressional schedule.

A few weeks later, Washington was in hibernation. Nothing gets done in August in Washington, D.C. Most members and staff, at least those who mattered, were out of town. The oppressive heat stifled any thoughts of work.

Taking advantage of the down time, Lloyd and I travelled to the CNMI. From the moment we landed in Saipan—the largest island of the CNMI—it was clear the Island had been inundated with federal officials, mostly meter-maid-like citation writers from the Occupational Safety and Health Administration. The Congressional takeover issues were the topic of almost every conversation virtually everywhere we turned. Even our taxi cab driver knew the most intricate details of the legislative process. Minutes after leaving the airport, he turned to Lloyd and me to ask if we were from the government. When we said no, he asked, "So, do you think the senate takeover bill will be inserted into the Interior Appropriations Bill during the conference session?" We had never encountered this level of engagement on a political matter by the general public.

We met Governor Tenorio and his staff the morning after we landed. Brenda warned us that the Governor was very blunt and pulled no punches. He was the most conscientious governor they ever had and an ideal leader for the fight for their survival. Froilan Tenorio did not disappoint. A tall man with a bold shock of white hair, he spoke haltingly with a thick island accent, but he made it very clear to us that they had to win this fight no matter what. We peppered him with tough questions about the accusations and he answered all to our satisfaction. Then he rented us a car so we could tour the island ourselves.

With a map in hand, and only forty-five square miles of territory to cover, we visited a dozen or more factories over the next few days. Each time we went to a factory, Lloyd sprang into action. He looked like a government inspector, and I am sure that most of them thought that's what he was. I was his junior assistant. He would check the lighting and the temperatures, review the shift hours, speak with the workers and supervisors, demand to see the workers' housing and cafeterias, check the doors, sample the upholstery of their work station chairs. He was a man on a mission. At times he was so thorough, I suspected that he was determined to find something wrong, so we would have to forego this representation. When we finished with the garment factories, Lloyd started in on the hotels. Were they mistreating their staff? What did they pay their employees? What hours were they working? Where did the staff live? What did they do on their off hours?

Next, Lloyd insisted on meeting all government officials charged with enforcing laws related to the garment industry or hotels. He reviewed the codes and met with those who enforced them. He demanded to know details about the various raids conducted by the Labor and Immigration Department. He met with the Attorney General of the island. He met with the police. With the church leaders. With everyone on the island but our original cab driver.

In all these meetings, I was second fiddle. I sat and watched the master at work.

While the accusations confronting the Northern Marianas would lead a casual observer to believe Saipan was a virtual gulag, the truth was quite the opposite. We had expected to see widespread worker abuse and governmental indifference. Instead, we found that most workers were treated quite decently. They were provided with an attractive salary, by Asian standards, clean and safe housing, nutritious meals, and health care. Considering there was a huge waiting list to get one of the positions in Saipan, the system looked eminently defensible.

But there were some problems. The biggest issue we discovered was that the recruitment agencies in China sending workers to the islands was charging onerous fees of the candidates. The CNMI government was pressing the Chinese government to crack down on this practice, and we were told that several of the more egregious offenders were barred from doing business with the CNMI companies. Additionally, there were reports of some individual abuse of workers by supervisors. Such venal behavior occurs in most places in the world and there is no realistic way to stop it all, other than by making it illegal and then enforcing those laws.

After meeting with the CNMI Department of Labor and witnessing government raids of abusive factories, we determined that the local authorities were serious about preventing mistreatment of the workers. They even hired outside consultants to train private sector and governmental supervisors in human resource management more akin to that in practice on the mainland than throughout Asia. In short, the CNMI we discovered was far from the slave colony portrayed in the *Washington Post*. With Lloyd's stamp of approval, I had no qualms at all about vigorously defending the Marianas in Washington.

When we were finished, I needed a vacation, but sixty-eight-year-old Lloyd Meeds was ready for more. On the flight home, he gave me a preview of what he was going to tell the firm: "Not only can we accept this client, but we must do so. They have been horribly maligned, and, if we can save them, then we should. That is not to say that there is no abuse of workers on the island, but the government is doing all it can to stop it, and there is far less abuse there than in most major U.S. cities." As far as he was concerned, we needed to move full steam ahead.

That was all I needed to hear.

During World War II, one of the most important Pacific battles occurred in Saipan. The Japanese held the island and fought furiously to rebuff the American forces. Once it was clear that the United States would prevail, the Japanese Emperor Hirohito instructed his soldiers—and the thousands of Japanese women and children who also resided on the island—to take their own lives rather than submit to the depredations of the Americans. Over twenty thousand took their lives, many leaping over the craggy hilltops later dubbed "Suicide Cliff" and "Bonzai Cliff." When the Congress returned from the summer recess of 1995, the second Battle of Saipan commenced. The stakes in this battle may not have been so ominous, but losing would have dire consequences.

At first, the coalition of labor unions and liberal activists moving the takeover legislation did not realize that the CNMI had joined the fight. There was no opposition to the takeover legislation passing the Senate, and there were no rebuttals of the accusations in the press. Of course, at that point, the anti-CNMI forces had no idea we had frozen their bill in the House, either. As we feared, they tried to add the takeover legislation as a "rider" onto the Interior Appropriations Bill. This is a common maneuver when one wants to move a piece of legislation. To get a bill on the fast track, you find a "moving train," another bill which is likely to pass, and then get the desired language inserted or attached.

Murkowski was a formidable foe. He was the chairman of the powerful Senate Environment and Public Works Committee, and not someone other Senators wished to perturb. We were in a firefight as soon as the Congress returned, but were able to meet with scores of Republican senators and representatives and secure enough opposition to stop Murkowski's amendment.

Fortunately, at this point, Murkowski was not personally engaged in the matter. The entire effort to smash the CNMI came from his staff director, Jim Beirne. Like many of the mainlanders who felt they knew better than the islanders, Beirne had a patrician and patronizing attitude toward the CNMI. As one of his allies proclaimed: "Those brown people don't know what's good for them." This racist and degrading comment was emblematic of the approach adopted by both the self-appointed administrators of island policy in Washington and the media. They were committed adversaries, but they weren't expecting the fight we gave them.

As the first term of the 104th United States Congress came to a close at the end of 1995, the Marianas survived the Murkowski bill and still retained local control over immigration and minimum wage, but the battle lines were drawn. We had spent the fall meeting with every congressman we could and lining up strong support from free market conservative groups. The takeover had become a cause célèbre on both the right and the left. The smooth path to the takeover of the Marianas had been blocked by a small army of determined conservatives, and the issue had become partisan. Normally lobbyists don't want their clients to rely on one party or the other. They want bipartisan support to rule the day. But in our case, there was little hope that Democrats would break with one of their top union supporters, the garment workers, so we made a conscious decision to focus on conservative support, and forget about the left.

The counterattack on the CNMI was swift, harsh, and sustained. No one could believe that we had stopped Murkowski's takeover bill, and our opponents were out for blood. Since the unions and their supporters could hardly reveal that their main hostility toward the Marianas had to do with union authority and control, they redoubled their accusations of abuse. The stories peeled off the presses with great speed and portrayed the CNMI in the worst light possible. I watched this assault and worried that these new attacks would be far more effective than the last ones which we had just defeated. We armed our lobbyists with materials showing that the accusations were false, but the difficulty in combating abuse allegations of any kind—let alone those purportedly taking place halfway around the world—made it very difficult to gain traction. We had to do more.

Then it hit me. Why were Lloyd and I so adamant in our support of the Marianas? Why did we, even more than our other lobbyists, take this so personally? Because we had been there. We had seen with our own eyes that these accusations were overblown and political. And we resented the lies. We needed to make sure that as many people as possible saw what we had seen. We couldn't bring the CNMI to Washington, so we had to bring Washington to the CNMI.

For the next few years, our firm became a travel agency. We organized trips to the Marianas for every Congressman and staff member who would go. Since the CNMI was not exactly just down the street, and required a full day of travel just to get there, we had to work hard to get people on the planes. But when we were done, over 150 members and staff touched down on Saipan and got to see the place for themselves. Since the congressional ban on representatives accepting gifts, including travel, did not include governmental bodies, the CNMI was able to pay for all these trips. They never spent their money more wisely.

The travelers to the islands were politically diverse. We sent Democrats as well as Republicans. By the dozens, the travelers would branch out to replicate Lloyd's island inspection. They met with government officials and supporters of the economic boom on the islands, as well as with the opposition. While we didn't want to pummel the visitors with too many meetings, there was a lot to see and learn. So, in addition to viewing the factories and worker housing, they met with scores of folks on the islands—from factory workers to government officials to church leaders to retired statesiders— many of whom seemed to be waiting to give speeches. Some were boring, and some riveting, but in the end the travelers got a good sense of what was going on in the CNMI.

The media pounced on the CNMI congressional travelers for visiting an exotic locale during their legislative recesses, accusing them of going on a pleasure junket. I was panicked that we would have no takers for future trips and that the past visitors would flee from the media attacks, and might even resort to attacking the CNMI as a way to deflect the assault. Neither could have been further from the truth.

Our travelers became fulltime supporters of the CNMI, resenting the media for their constant attacks. While the attacks on the Republican visitors' recreational activities were ceaseless, there was no mention at all of similar beach visits by those hostile members and staff who were attacking the CNMI. I personally witnessed Congressman George Miller and his staff enjoying a gambol at the beach, as did some of the media covering the island. But since Miller was the main opponent of the Marianas in Congress, his rendition of Beach Blanket Bingo drew nary a mention. Only the local newspaper, owned by Willie Tan, one of the top garment manufacturers, published revealing photos of Miller's surf and sand inspection. These photos were promptly ignored by the very media outlets working overtime to impugn the islands' reputation.

With scores of Congressmen and staff coming to the CNMI, our lobbyists were regularly on site to facilitate their travel needs and offer information and camaraderie. Of course, these trips were not all hard work. The Marianas are exotic and beautiful, not to mention equipped with golf, the favorite pastime of Congressmen and lobbyists alike.

Consider: if you're trying to influence someone from the Congress, why meet them in their stuffy, overcrowded office, where the noise and distractions are constantly in climax, when you could meet at a pastoral, posh country club where the only interruptions are from a waiter offering Courvoisier and a fine cigar, or a caddy offering a five iron for your next shot? In an office, the lobbyist will have to make his case in a few minutes and pray that the staff or representative is paying attention. On the golf course, you have four hours to make your case, as you indulge the decision maker with all manner of luxury. Now you see why Congress loves golf. To most lobbyists, a game of golf is just another day at the office. We were no different. Golf was a centerpiece of our lobbying efforts.

Fortunately for me, several of my staff members were avid golfers, which generally meant that I sent them for golf meetings. I hadn't picked up a club since I was ten years old. But in 1996, I found myself back on the course when Governor Tenorio insisted we play together during one of my many trips to Saipan. When the governor decided, one Friday afternoon, that I play with him that next Monday, I tried to convince him that he wouldn't enjoy playing with me. I hadn't played for over twenty-five years, and frankly I wasn't a huge fan of the sport. He didn't take no for an answer.

The date was set for 9 a.m. on a Monday at Kingfisher Golf Club in Saipan, and I only had the weekend to prepare. The legislators of Saipan played golf every day. They would convene their legislative session in the morning and be out on the links by mid afternoon. The golfers of Saipan were reputed to be among the best. I panicked and called my father as I hurried to find the golf supply store I recalled seeing next to the local supermarket. "Dad, the governor invited me to play golf on Monday."

Dad waited for a punch line, but when none arrived he replied, "Tell him you can't."

"I tried that. Didn't work. I have no choice. What do I do?"

"Can you flee the island?" I wasn't sure he was joking. "Jack, you can't play golf. You run the risk of losing your client. No one wants to play with a hacker, not even another hacker." He paused and took pity on his son.

"Ok, just dress the part and stay out of the way. If you hit the ball badly twice on a hole, pick it up and just keep moving. Don't delay the governor at all. Oh, and don't beat your client at golf, no matter what. I say this to you knowing it's impossible, but just in case, you best hear it. You may survive, but I wouldn't place money on it."

With those fine words of encouragement, I entered the store and proceeded to buy golf shoes. I needed to dress the part, as Dad said. When I asked the salesman what else a golfer would wear, he smiled and probed why I would ask such an inane question. I told him I had to play golf on Monday and hadn't played since I was a boy. I needed to purchase some books so I could read about how to play golf. His quizzical look tempted me to explain that the Jewish Sabbath was about to start and reading was the only thing I could do, but I refrained from that discussion. After loading me up on golf paraphernalia, he asked whether I had clubs. Of course I didn't, and the price tag on the clubs was steep. Seeing my hesitation, he offered to lend me a set. I was elated. While I was at it, I scheduled a lesson for Sunday.

I read about golf during the Sabbath, and when the Sabbath ended that night, I took a club in hand and practiced a swing in the hotel room. After nicking the ceiling a few too many times, I decided to wait for the course.

Sunday morning I arrived at Kingfisher. The course was stunning. The luscious green of the fairways was juxtaposed against the deep blue of the ocean just off the course. The layout was daunting. How could I possibly handle this pressure with my client? I had no choice.

I waited for my trusted instructor. And waited. And waited. He was a no show. After two hours, I took matters into my own hands and purchased a small bucket of balls to try my luck at the driving range. Slowly I was able to regain the feeling of my youthful swing, though the path of the ball resembled a banana, not an arrow. After hitting golf balls for an hour, I got up the nerve to try the course. I figured that at least I'd be familiar with my surroundings the next day. As I drove around the course, swatting the little white ball in every possible direction, I started to feel like I might pull this off.

The next morning, I got to the course at 6 a.m., hoping to get in some more practice before the governor showed up. But there was already a car in the parking lot. The governor's car.

"Jack, what are you doing here at this hour?" he asked me.

"Governor, I'm here to learn how to play golf, so I don't make you hate me today!" I replied.

He laughed and continued working on some documents. I headed to the range. At the appointed hour, I returned to find the governor and the other members of our foursome: one of the major business figures on the island and the Speaker of the House. Well, I thought to myself, if I am going to lose the client, I might as well go down in flames!

As we pulled to the first tee, the others noticed my golf bag. It contained the newest set of Calloway clubs then available. I didn't know Calloway clubs from Cab Calloway music, but the reaction of my fellow golfers educated me quickly. "Wow, you must be a great golfer to have Calloways," they said in unison.

At the first tee, I prayed for a good game. I slowly moved the club and then thrashed into the ball with all my strength. Somehow, I was able to strike it squarely, and the ball flew over 220 yards down the center of the fairway. I was still in shock when the abuse started. "Ah, you said you didn't know how to play? What do you call that?"

Fortunately for my reputation as a non-golfer, there were more opportunities than that one lucky swing. I hacked and slashed all day, and my companions were generous and friendly. I wouldn't lose my client, but I would gain a bad habit: playing golf like an addict.

As we finished that round, the governor asked me to add up the scorecard. I had already added mine in my head, and reached the total of 102. His totaled 105. I had broken the most important rule of all by beating my client at golf. To wiggle out of the difficulty, I told the governor his score. He was delighted in this horrible total. After he asked mine, I told him I was already well over 100 in my head, and asked if I could stop counting. He laughed and reminded me that it would take years before I could play as well as he did. So much for the vaunted Saipan golfers.

The real benefit of the congressional trips was only apparent once the representatives and staff had returned. From the end of the first trip to the Marianas during Easter recess of 1996, we had a permanent cadre on Capitol Hill ready to stop any attacks on the CNMI. Spread throughout the Congress, the former travelers not only took up the cudgels of the Marianas, and vigorously defended it, but also served as an early warning system for our firm. Whenever any representative or staff launched an anti-CNMI attack, one of the travelers would detect it early, inform us, and then usually take the lead in the counter assault.

In addition to the travelers, we had a number of Members of Congress who, even in advance of their eventual trips to the CNMI, understood the issues at stake in the larger ideological scheme, and assisted our efforts. Chief among these was my good friend Congressman Dana Rohrabacher. Dana immediately understood the situation, as he has always understood the philosophical battle lines, as well as the political stakes in legislative maneuvering. Though he would eventually visit the islands, Dana did not wait to see for himself what was going on. There were enough people he trusted who had seen the situation on the ground with their own eyes, and Dana realized why the unions and their followers were attacking.

The unions were not alone in their assault. The sword and shield in their strike against the CNMI was inside the Clinton administration. The Office of Insular Affairs, or OIA, is the division of the Department of the Interior which is responsible for the insular areas of the United States. These territories include the Marianas, Guam, and American Samoa in the Pacific, as well as Puerto Rico and the American Virgin Islands in the Caribbean. The OIA's mission was to support the economic growth and independence of the territories. That may have been what they were trying to do in the other four territories, but in the CNMI, they were out for destruction.

It was from the OIA staff—especially their communications officer, David North, and the head of their office, Allen Stayman—that the most stinging assaults on both the CNMI and our firm came. They correctly calculated that the effort to take over the Marianas was failing because we were in the way. So they launched an assault on the firm—and on me personally—right where they knew it would hurt, in the main newspaper of the firm's home office, Seattle.

Accusing me of everything short of war crimes, their disingenuous reporters concocted story after story about how the CNMI representation was impairing the otherwise stellar reputation that Preston Gates enjoyed. I was the skunk at the garden party, and the CNMI was a blight on the hallowed traditions of Seattle's most prestigious firm. These attacks did me no favors.

The staff at the OIA went beyond reason in their quest to strip the CNMI of its economic advantages. Ultimately, their zealous efforts to destroy the Marianas would eventually lead them to break the law.

# 6

# NEW TERRITORY

In the midst of our brutal slugfest over the Marianas, another life-changing connection was made. Marc Levin, a long-time family friend and a brilliant securities attorney, put me in touch with his companion, Nell Rogers. Nell was the head of planning for the Mississippi Band of Choctaw Indians, and they needed a lobbyist.

As Nell explained in our first phone call in October 1995, the new Republican Congress was attempting to place a 30 percent UBIT—Unrelated Business Income Tax—on Indian tribal gaming revenues. The tax, which would have drained tens of billions of dollars from tribal government budgets over a decade—was inserted into the Budget Reconciliation Bill, up for a vote that next week, and they were trying to fight it. Marc had told her I was a Republican lobbyist, and she wanted to know if I might be able to help.

I had not yet heard about this, but I told Nell that if in fact the Republicans were trying to pass such a bill, it violated their pledge not to raise taxes, and I would organize conservatives to oppose it. After doing my research, I couldn't believe what was happening. Nell was right. What in the world were my fellow Republicans doing? We were opposed to taxes, right?

I called Grover Norquist at home to discuss the matter. With his group, Americans for Tax Reform, Grover had pioneered the most effective bar to new taxation in a generation, a pledge which every Republican Member of Congress who ever wanted to climb the leadership ladder signed. The pledge was simple and direct, committing signatories to "oppose any and all efforts to increase the marginal income tax rates for individuals and businesses" and to "oppose any net reduction or elimination of deductions and credits, unless matched dollar for dollar by further reducing tax rates." Grover, brilliant as always, was able to keep the Republicans who signed it from the temptation of raising taxes. George H. W. Bush signed it, and when he broke that pledge—and his "read my lips" affirmation of it—he went down to a humiliating defeat. Grover agreed that a tax on the Indians, while not an increase in the marginal rates, was still a tax, and that anyone who supported the bill would be in violation of his pledge on taxes. This gave me my strategy—I would fight the tax from the right.

The next day, I was scheduled to speak with the chief of the tribe, Philip Martin. I told him that I had researched the matter and believed we could attack this as an unfair tax and win. I ran through my basic strategy with the Chief. Since the vote on the Budget Reconciliation was in two days, there was no real way to beat this in the House, at least not yet. We needed to plan for a fight in the conference committee where the House and Senate normally came together to work out the differences between their legislative acts. Once a bill passes one of the legislative bodies, the leadership names the conference committee. In the case of important bills, the leadership will stay active in the process to make sure that the provisions they desire are not lost in the conference compromises. Once the conference committee issues a unified bill, it returns to both chambers for ratification before it is sent to the president for signature. My strategy would be aimed at the conference. To win, we would attack the provision as a tax increase, activate the tax groups, build a hard Senate position opposing the provision, and work the House Leadership to push the conference to accede to the Senate position.

The Chief liked what he heard, but wanted to know why conservatives would go for this. They had never been allies of the tribes in the past. "Chief," I answered, "I have not been a lobbyist long, but few understand how a conservative thinks better than I do—because I am a conservative. I come from the same place they do. I am them. And I can tell you, Chief, that when most conservatives hear the word 'tribe,' we think of socialism and Russell Means. I have been in politics off and on for a long time, and I don't ever remember meeting a Native American at any Republican function. That's the problem, Chief. Conservatives think the tribes are Democrats."

"Well, they should come down here and see our tribe. That couldn't be further from the truth."

"Precisely. But they don't know that. They don't have much regard for tribes, but that cannot be our focus right now. Our focus is that this is a tax increase. That's how we win this. We can start building bridges between the tribes and conservatives tomorrow. Today we have to stop this tax."

"Whoa, there, Jack. One thing at a time. I should tell you that our tribe hires a lot of firms, and each of them does something different for us. Let's get through this first fight before we see if there is more for us to do together."

This was fair enough. Next, I knew, would come the big question of our fee schedule. Since I was still new at this business, I wasn't sure how to price our services. The Marianas were paying our hourly rates, but other clients paid a fixed fee. While some lobbyists charged their clients $10,000 a month, at that point we were billing at least $20,000. Larry Latourette, the managing partner of the firm, was at the Washington Redskins game against the Detroit Lions that day, so he couldn't join me on the call.

"Just tell them I'm going to the Redskins game, and we'll sort out the fees on Monday," he told me the day before.

I bristled. "Larry, I can't use the word Redskins with an Indian chief! It's offensive!"

Larry made a crack about how liberal I was becoming, a low blow predicated on the unfair assumption that conservatives were racist. I had met just as many racist liberals as racist conservatives, but liberals always seemed to escape that charge. I let it go, and focused instead on practicing how not to say the word Redskins. "My managing partner is at the football game," I said to myself in the mirror. "My managing partner is at the football game. Football game. Football game…"

Of course, when Chief Martin asked about our fees that day, the first thing out of my mouth was, "Well, Chief, I need to include our managing partner in this discussion, and he's at the Redskins game and …"

Silence on the other end of the phone. I didn't know what to say, but I was sure I'd blown it in that one moment. Finally, the chief helped take my foot out of my mouth, and said, "OK, Jack, let me know when you can. Please get this bill stopped."

With that, we were hired.

We sprang into action the next day. Dennis Stephens and I were still the only movement conservatives at Preston Gates, so we had to do most of the lifting with the House leadership and conservative members. The moderates at the firm worked on the Senate Republicans, and the others filled in where needed. I needed more conservative lobbyists, but didn't have time to find them. We had to make do with what we had. The team and I worked relentlessly to implement the plan I outlined for the Chief, and almost immediately we were making headway.

When I approached Ed Buckham about getting Congressman Tom DeLay to support our position, he was skeptical. "Tom hates gambling," he averred.

"I understand, but this is not about gambling. This is about taxes. This is a tax increase and, worse, if we Republicans tax only the tribes, and no one else, we leave ourselves open to an accusation of racism. None of us wants that."

Buckham conceded the point and promised to raise it with DeLay, although, again, I would have to make the pitch directly. From the time I started as a lobbyist, I pressed everyone I knew—especially my clients—to contribute to Tom DeLay. I believed in him and wanted to see him succeed. Most people assumed DeLay put a strong arm on me to motivate me to raise funds for him and his organizations. Not true. The entire time I was a lobbyist, Tom DeLay never once asked me for a contribution, let alone strong-armed me. He didn't have to. I did it because I believed in him, and because when I needed help, he and his staff were there.

Moreover, I believed that it was part of my job as a Republican lobbyist to raise money for our team. In fact, I deeply resented Republicans who made their way to K Street because of their Republican credentials, and felt that they owed no obligation to sustain the Republican majority, or to help conservative groups.

My first meeting with DeLay about Indian tribes took place in his beautifully appointed Majority Whip Office in the Capitol Building.

As I started to discuss the plight of the tribes, I couldn't help but notice that most of the paintings on DeLay's wall were classic George Catlin masterpieces depicting Native Americans. That had to be a good sign. Tom listened intently to my presentation and agreed that it was wrong to tax the tribes.

Still, he stressed, he was diametrically opposed to gambling; however, taxation was not the way he wanted to eliminate the vice. Always interested in a conversation about religion, Tom asked me what Judaism had to say on the subject. I explained that, in Judaism, gambling is certainly not encouraged, but it is not strictly forbidden, as it was in his Baptist faith. The main focus of Jewish law on gambling revolves around the disqualification of the habitual or professional gambler from being a witness in court. I explained that putting yourself into one of the categories of individuals excluded from testimony was akin to destroying your reputation in the community. Still, Jews were not forbidden from gambling. Although our conversation certainly didn't change his views on the subject, Tom agreed that the provision was a tax and promised to get it out of the Budget Reconciliation conference committee report.

We were making tremendous progress. But our efforts could not be limited to DeLay. Lobbyists who relied on one representative to save their client—even one as powerful as DeLay—were likely to be defeated. I was still learning about lobbying at this point, but I was quickly figuring out how the game was played. In order to secure a victory, not only did I need a solid strategy which I could implement, I also needed to figure out my opponents' moves. As my career evolved, we formed teams in our offices to work on behalf of our clients. These teams would be charged with replicating our opponents' battle plans, and then devising countervailing tactics. For each move we assumed our opposition would make—or which we would make were we in their place—we would have at least three countermeasures. As I entered the fight to remove the tax on tribal gaming, though, I did not have the resources to plan out my opponents' moves and counter them. I could only stick to our game plan and hope for the best.

With Grover's affirmation that the tax on Indian gaming was a violation of the Americans for Tax Reform pledge, we started contacting key Republicans on the Hill to notify them that they were about to raise taxes. While ATR's main focus is on taxes, and the group has expanded the pledge to include almost every office holder in the nation, Grover was busy with other conservative movement building activities as well. One of the sources of his immense influence in Washington is the meeting which takes place in his office each Wednesday. Crammed into the ATR conference room each week are the leaders of every major conservative organization, along with the leadership of the House and Senate Republicans, various other Congressional leaders, key Administration figures (when the Administration is Republican), and representatives of conservative media. Grover presides over this group and sets the agenda. When this powerful group decides to act, almost nothing can stop them. Grover has since set up copycat meetings in almost every state capital in the nation. Whenever we were lobbying on a conservative issue, Dennis or I would bring it to Grover's meeting. We brought the tax on Indian gaming before the group immediately. The response was mixed, as we expected. The social conservative groups who abhor gaming were opposed to our position, with many of them delighted that a special tax might impede the growth of the tribal casinos. Others understood our point that, whether one likes the activity or not, a "sin" tax will, one day, come back to bite them, once their favored activity was declared a sin. Opposition notwithstanding, Grover helped us build a consensus against the tax, and another piece of our strategy to defeat the bill was in place. Grover sided with our efforts because he believed the Congress was applying a tax. He helped us because he believed we were right. That did not stop me, however, from encouraging my clients to help his organization. A strong ATR would mean a strong force against taxation, including taxation on Indians. I was delighted that Chief Martin and Nell Rogers understood this and quickly became major contributors to ATR, as had so many other citizens and companies across the nation who wanted to reduce federal taxation.

With several conservative groups backing us, and ATR's support against the tax, we moved back to the leadership of the Congress. Dennis secured support from Majority Leader Dick Armey's office. Tax reduction was a major issue in his office. They were not going to support a tax increase no matter what. With DeLay's support, and now Armey, we had two-thirds of the House leadership backing our position. Next we would aim for the Speaker. Notwithstanding my bizarre meeting with him about the CNMI, I felt that the Speaker's support on this tax issue was important. Thanks again to Grover, I secured a few minutes with Newt Gingrich. I mentioned that we had an anomaly in the Budget Reconciliation Act, and that we were proposing taxing Indian tribes. I assumed Newt would react like DeLay and Armey. I was wrong.

"Yes, I know about that tax. You know what? I was flying last week and sitting right there, in first class, was an Indian. Where do you think they're getting that kind of money? They need to be taxed like everyone else."

I couldn't believe my ears. "Newt, what? You're kidding, right?"

He wasn't kidding. He felt that the tribes had a sweetheart deal with their untaxed casinos. It wasn't fair.

I wanted to ask him whether he thought it was fair that the Indian nations made treaties with our country and had every one of them broken, often accompanied by mass slaughter of that tribe? Was it fair that we made agreements with the Indian nations and later decided that the land we gave them was too valuable, so we moved them to swamps and bogs? Was any of that fair? But, I kept quiet. There's no sense arguing with Newt Gingrich. He is always right.

My next move was getting the Senate solidified in their position against the provision so they would not accept the tribal gaming tax in the final bill. Since most of the Republicans in the Senate were not movement conservatives, Dennis and I could avail ourselves of the rest of the Preston team, and they performed marvelously. We organized a letter to be signed by Senate conference members stating that they would not under any circumstance accede to the House position. We passed the letter to DeLay and Armey and they notified their House conferees that this tax increase had to go.

When the conference convened, Buckham made sure he was in the room for all discussions, and he provided me a play-by-play recap of the action every chance he got.

When the tribal tax came up, Bill Archer, the Texas Republican who chaired the Ways and Means Committee in the House, and the original author of the anti-tribal provision, pushed hard for its inclusion. The issue went back and forth until DeLay demanded its removal and put an end to the discussion.

We won.

I called Nell and told her we were in the clear. She was ecstatic. I mentioned how crucial DeLay had been to our success, and suggested that the tribe consider making contributions to those Members who supported our position. It was the only decent thing to do, I thought, and it didn't take any convincing on my part. "Jack," Nell told me, "send me the names and addresses of the committees to which we should give. We would be delighted."

DeLay's tenacity in removing the gaming tax saved the tribes tens of billions of dollars over the years. As a lobbyist, I thought it only natural and right that my clients should reward those members who saved them such substantial sums with generous contributions. This quid pro quo became one of the hallmarks of our lobbying efforts. Because of a loophole in the campaign finance laws, the tribes were categorized as individuals as far as giving contributions, but they were also considered to be political action committees, in the sense that they were not constrained by the limits on total giving which bound individuals. Since the tribes I represented lived and died by what the Congress did to and for them, and since they had comparatively unlimited funds, we were in the position to deliver millions of dollars in legal political contributions, and did. While the impact of campaign funds on legislation is often overplayed by organizations vying to limit those funds, there is no question that contributions have a significant impact on the process—and that impact is not positive. What I did not consider then, and never considered until I was sitting in prison, was that contributions from parties with an interest in legislation are really nothing but bribes. Sure, it's legal for the most part. Sure, everyone in Washington does it. Sure, it's the way the system works. It's one of Washington's dirty little secrets—but it's bribery just the same.

The early, grateful contributions by the tribes soon led to contributions designed to create gratitude on the part of the member. These were leavened with all manner of perquisites, sponsored by my clients, and administered by my staff and me. Golf, elaborate meals, tickets to sporting events—any favor a representative or staff needed, we were there to provide. Why? To create a relationship that would help get our clients' messages to decision makers quickly.

None of this seemed in any way wrong to me, or to any of us. Even the ethics officers at the law firms I served didn't see this issue as I do now.

We spent our days looking for loopholes, and when we couldn't find one, we just did what we had to do anyway. The rules were not being enforced, certainly not against the lobbyists. Only the representatives and staff really had to pay attention, or so I reasoned. I was never more wrong in my life.

What is most shameful for me, in retrospect, was that I was in the middle of it. Every night, and most mornings, I took time to study the Torah and our other holy books. My studies started when I was a boy and have continued to this day. I spent a good deal of time studying the laws of bribery as laid down clearly in Scripture, and explicated in the Talmud. I knew that one is not permitted to provide any gratuity to a judge, and that the cases brought in the Talmudic tracts are incredibly strict. If a litigant even helps a judge from stumbling in the street, he is not permitted to bring his case in that judge's court. But I didn't make the connection. I didn't see that legislators are, in effect, judges. Maybe I didn't want to see it.

Our victory in the Choctaw tax fight was a turning point in my career. Chief Martin liked my aggressive nature and the fact that we were winning. I loved working with Nell and the tribe, since they were the perfect clients. They trusted us to get them to their goal, and when we earned that trust time and again, they rewarded us by doing what we suggested. My first year as a lobbyist ended in triumph. We had removed the tax on Indian gaming. We prevented the takeover of the CNMI's economy. My clients were paying healthy fees. Conservative groups and candidates were benefitting from my efforts. By the end of the year, Manny doubled my salary to $300,000. Many in my position might have eased up and taken stock, but not me. I never saw a finish line that didn't resemble a starting point. My clients accounted for a small percentage of Preston Gates' revenue, but I wanted my group to be the dominant focus of the firm.

The first key to successful lobbying is to present the client's position well. Detailed, solid arguments are essential to persuading Congress to adopt the client's position. Most lobbying firms excel in preparing support for their position, and we were no exception. But when I joined Preston Gates, we innovated.

Since the Republican majority was a philosophically conservative majority, I pressed the firm to mine each of their policy positions to find those aspects that would be consistent with conservative ideology. I knew that most conservative Members of Congress couldn't resist a philosophically conservative approach, because I couldn't resist it. Until additional conservatives could join the firm, I was the grand arbiter of which vestiges of our representations were acceptable to conservative ears. When there was nothing about the client's position that was conservative, I would push them in that direction—often to the dismay of the client's primary lobbyist. It usually worked. Throughout my lobbying career, I found that having some philosophical bent to the representation was what encouraged me to take on a client. I was convinced that transforming the usually mundane lobbyist's patter from childish begging to the more elevated realm of philosophical discourse would ennoble interactions with Capitol Hill. I believe that the reason our efforts enjoyed so much success was that our activities were based in the belief system and rhetoric of the conservative movement.

Of course, having the best arguments and presentations is essential, but arguments not heard by anyone are irrelevant. Many times lobbyists had better arguments than we did. Our clients were not perfect, after all. But since it was we who had the meetings with the decision makers, and not they, we won. We had access, the second key to winning lobbying. How did we get this access? By hiring people who already had access of their own.

Each month my client group expanded, as did the revenue we brought to the firm. As I entered my second year at Preston Gates in 1996, I realized that we didn't have enough staff to ensure victory for our clients. It was time to staff up, but the kinds of hires I wanted to make were not the usual Preston Gates types. Like most law firms, Preston Gates was used to hiring lawyers. But like most Washington law firms with a "governmental affairs practice," hiring non-lawyer lobbyists was essential. Not everyone with access to Capitol Hill had taken the bar exam. Many never even attended law school.

After Dennis Stephens and myself, we hired the firm's third non-attorney lobbyist, Pat Pizzella. Pat was a long-time Republican political operative, and a stalwart member of the Reagan administration. Smart, likeable, clever, and hard working, Pat was a perfect addition to the quickly emerging "Team Abramoff." Our team eventually included some of the greatest minds in the policy business, many of whom went on to head important governmental agencies or think tanks, as well as some of the roughest, toughest street smart killers who ever walked the halls of well-healed law firms. It was like the cast of American Chopper was working at the corporate offices of Rolls Royce.

Todd Boulanger was not one of my hires, and a more unlikely candidate for a law firm would have been hard to find. A Gulf War veteran with gel spiked hair, tattoos, and the mouth of a marine master sergeant, Todd left his job with Senator Bob Smith of New Hampshire when the Senator bolted from the GOP to make an independent run for the Presidency. Todd was a loyal Republican and didn't abide by disloyalty in others.

Working as a research assistant at the firm when he first came to my attention, Todd was a straight talker, a solid strategist, and hard worker. Of course, it didn't hurt that he had the right connections among the staff on the Hill.

When I realized what a huge asset this seemingly out-of-place guy was, I started assembling a collection of Todd Boulangers: Capitol Hill staff who were well connected and could play hardball when needed. After a few months at Preston Gates, it became clear that the best hires from Capitol Hill were the staff, not the members. With some exceptions such as Congressman Dana Rohrabacher—members were generally lazy. The Congressional staff were the only ones who really got things done.

The word lobbyist is usually hurled as a slur. Its provenance is questionable. Most people in the industry and in academia attribute the name to those mendicants pacing the lobby of the Willard Hotel in Washington, D.C. during the time President Ulysses S. Grant was residing there. They paced the lobby, hence, they were "lobbyists." Others note that the term comes from the lobbies off the chamber of Parliament in London where petitioners waited for their representatives. Either way, the term has evolved into an insult or punch line. The scandal which brought me to prison certainly didn't help.

A lobbyist is really nothing more or less than an advocate. In the same way that an attorney will represent a client before a judge, a lobbyist will represent a client before a non-judicial decision maker. Like the lawyer, a lobbyist must present a cogent case with great effect. Unlike those operating within the rules of civil or criminal procedure, however, the lobbyist has many more ways to influence a decision. Some of these are legal and some illegal. Some lobbyists operate in what they convince themselves is a gray area: not illegal, but probably not something you want to see on the front page of the *New York Times*. In a system where there are dozens of decision makers—not all of whom operate with the highest ethical standards—there is plenty of room for corruption. When the corruption becomes the norm, as it often does, it can pierce the very fabric of our democracy.

Luckily, most lobbyists don't enter the profession with a fanatical, win-at-all-costs attitude, as I did. They don't even do the work they need to do to win for a client, let alone the questionable activities in which some of us engaged to ensure that our clients never lost a fight. In fact, deep down, many lobbyists don't really care if their client wins or loses. The typical successful lobbyist might have a dozen clients, paying approximately $5,000 to $10,000 per month. He might even work hard for them, winning some efforts and losing others. He might lose a few clients one year, but he'll gain a few more the next year. Life is very comfortable. At the end of the year, Mr. or Ms. Lobbyist will take home around $300,000. Not bad for someone who was previously making just under $100,000 on Capitol Hill. And especially not bad when one considers that the medium income in the United States is less than $50,000.

Americans are rightfully upset and concerned about the special interests operating in our nation's capital. What is wrong is the assumption that the problem is limited to the huge sums of money required to run for office. Sure, that's a problem, but it's not the only problem. It's not even the main problem.

Most lobbyist contacts with Congress at least start with propriety. But once the lobbyist sees the need to have a strong relationship with a particular representative's office, the urge to "enhance" their dealings becomes powerful—especially knowing that almost every other lobbyist has the same urge and acts on it.

Enhancing one's relationship with a congressional office can involve a myriad of tactics. Some lobbyists bring fresh donuts to congressional offices in the morning or sandwiches at lunchtime. Some buy the representatives and staff meals at posh restaurants. Some offer tickets to sporting events and concerts. Some sponsor the representatives and staff when they wish to play golf at one of the prestigious golf courses dotting the Washington area. Some arrange overseas trips or visits to resorts. Some raise campaign funds. I did all of the above and more. But these were not the most decisive method in lining up Congressional support. Lavishing gifts on members and staff might attract public wrath, but if a lobbyist wants to control a Congressional office almost completely, it can be done without anyone ever knowing about it—through the hiring process.

Once I found a congressional office that was vital to our clients—usually because they were incredibly helpful and supportive—I would often become close to the chief of staff of the office. In almost every congressional office, the chief of staff is the center of power. Nothing gets done without the direct or indirect action on his or her part. After a number of meetings with them, possibly including meals or rounds of golf, I would say a few magic words: "When you are done working for the Congressman, you should come work for me at my firm."

With that, assuming the staffer had any interest in leaving Capitol Hill for K Street—and almost 90 percent of them do, I would own him and, consequently, that entire office. No rules had been broken, at least not yet. No one even knew what was happening, but suddenly, every move that staffer made, he made with his future at my firm in mind. His paycheck may have been signed by the Congress, but he was already working for me, influencing his office for my clients' best interests. It was a perfect—and perfectly corrupt—arrangement. I hired as many of these staffers as I could, and in return I gained increasing influence on the Hill. But I was not alone in this method, and it continues today, unabated by reform campaigns or public ire at the Congress.

My new hires at Preston Gates thrived in legislative firefights, and they were impeccably organized. Once a client hired us, we would designate a team leader who would be responsible for organizing every effort we made for our clients. The frenetic pace of our business required these team leaders to be tireless and relentless. As my staff grew and the clients expanded, each of our lobbyists would have dozens of assignments. The team leaders would have to stay on them to make sure nothing was left undone. Each team met at least once a week, and in the heat of legislative battle, they would meet daily.

My inspiration for this organizational tactic originated in the early days of representing the Choctaws. As soon as we were hired, Nell Rogers asked me to attend the weekly Washington lobbyists' meeting dedicated to stopping the Indian Gaming tax. I dutifully attended the first few sessions, but it quickly became obvious the entire room included only Democrat lobbyists who knew nothing about what was going on in the Republican Congress and had nothing to offer. When I realized these lobbyists were taking the inside information I was bringing to the meeting, repackaging it, and relaying it to their clients as if they had created it, I stopped going.

While putting competing and often hostile lobbyists in the same room served no purpose, the dynamic of a team effort was exciting to me. And, if the meetings were comprised of only lobbyists who worked for the same firm, they could be quite effective. So I scheduled internal meetings for our lobbyists at Preston Gates where we could share information and strategies. Almost immediately, it paid off. Longtime Preston Gates attorneys and new non-lawyer hires would interact, and the ideas would flow. Few things benefitted my clients more than having their lobbyists sit together once a week to brainstorm and plan.

As our lobbying efforts became more intricate, involved, and sophisticated, it was no longer possible to win every fight with arguments and access alone. We needed to plan ahead, to have better strategy than our opponents. No longer could our team leaders merely hand out assignments for position papers and lobbying meetings. They had to war game.

Our team meetings became three-dimensional chessboards. We would craft our initial strategy for battle. Then we would put ourselves in our opponents' shoes. What would they do in response? Usually, three or four grand counter strategies would emerge. The team would then counter the counter strategies. On and on it would go until we had uncovered all possible strategic threats and had come up with solutions. We were always better prepared than our opponents. When an opponent launched an offensive against our clients, we didn't worry. We already thought of it, and had a response.

The hectic pace we kept was more than most firms could comprehend. Whenever we made a lateral hire from another firm, that poor newbie's head would spin as he tried to keep up with the frenzied pace of the office. Joining our team was like learning to sprint a marathon. There was no stopping. No leisurely jogs.

Being a lobbyist at any hard charging K Street firm requires a lot: having contacts and meeting with Members of Congress and their staff, as well as the Administration; researching and writing papers advocating your client's position; gathering intelligence on threats to or opportunities for your clients; drafting and editing legislative language to attain your client's goals; preparing your clients for congressional hearings; tracking votes on client legislation; and preparing a counter effort in the event any of this fails. That's in addition to making hundreds of phone calls, attending scores of fundraising events, sending thousands of emails, traveling with members or staff on fact finding missions, and a dozen other such things. That's not to say that most lobbyists do all these things, but they should. The life of a good, hard working lobbyist is fast paced and borders on the insane. When you add a hyper-type A, workaholic boss like me to the mix, the insanity becomes the unimaginable. Our team required full commitment, and constant and instant availability. There were always crises, and we could never fail our clients.

The only time my staff got a break from my relentless drive was from dusk on Friday afternoon until dark on Saturday night. During those precious twenty-five hours of the Jewish Sabbath, they were free of me and my torrent of emails and phone calls. I didn't work on the Sabbath. I didn't use any electrical or communication devices on that day. But every other day, I sent emails at all hours of the day and night. I was addicted to my Blackberry, and this addiction would later come back to haunt me as my nearly one million emails sent from it and my computer would be used to destroy me. But, in those days, my thumbs tapped out a never-ending stream of messages on my "Crackberry" from golf courses, airports, cabs, and even racquetball courts. New hires were probably most unsettled by the emails they got from me at 3:00 a.m., but once they got used to my workaholic style, they came to see that there was no better place on earth to have a job.

# 7

# MILLION DOLLAR BET

As I busied myself building my lobbying practice, there were rumblings on Capitol Hill. The Republican caucus, so united in their ten-point 1994 Pledge to America, started to develop fissures. The stresses were in the chain of command and along ideological lines. Gingrich was the prophet who brought the Republicans to the promised land of congressional majority, but he was proving to be ill suited as a speaker of the house. Conservatives never trusted him, and many representatives found him to be incredibly arrogant and haughty. When eventually he was forced out of office, few Republican members mourned his exit.

Perhaps the most turbulent period for the former speaker took place in the summer of 1997, when a handful of recently elected congressmen staged an aborted coup. That coup attempt would reshape the leadership dynamic among the Republicans.

In February of that year, Russian Prime Minister Viktor Chernomyrdin was planning to visit Washington, D.C. My Russian energy client, headed by Alexander Koulakovsky, asked us to schedule the Prime Minister for meetings with the Republican caucus on Capitol Hill. An official meeting with Gingrich and the senate leadership was already slated, but the Russians wanted to meet DeLay. They were fascinated by this Texan political agitator. In their minds, he was a throwback to the days of the cowboys. DeLay was far more sophisticated than that, but the media conveyed the most negative image they could conjure, which to liberals is the American cowboy. Of course, DeLay was in good company, since the preeminent American political cowboy was Ronald Reagan.

After Chernomyrdin finished the meeting with Gingrich and the other Congressional leaders, I led him to DeLay's suite in the Capitol. The Prime Minister was absolutely giddy as Majority Whip DeLay unfurled a huge bullwhip and explained, facetiously of course, that he used it on recalcitrant congressmen. He even presented the whip to Chernomyrdin, who probably returned to Russia and did use it on his political caucus. At the conclusion of the meeting, Chernomyrdin invited DeLay to come to Russia to see the progress they were making. DeLay elicited a nervous chuckle from his Russian guest when he noted that the last time he was there, he was busy smuggling Bibles to dissidents in the old Soviet Union and helping sneak out a Jewish family caught in that evil empire. With an invitation from the Prime Minister, and Alexander's close relationship, we were tasked with organizing DeLay's trip. Since a trip to Russia would involve a huge logistical undertaking, it was decided that Ed Buckham would make a preliminary visit to Moscow to sort out the details. That preparatory visit indirectly helped set in motion the coup against Gingrich.

While Ed was in Moscow, a small group of disgruntled members, including future television host Joe Scarborough and future Senator Lindsey Graham, met clandestinely, first with Majority Leader Dick Armey and then with Majority Whip DeLay. The plan was for the other members of the leadership—including not only DeLay and Armey, but also Conference Chairman John Boehner and Congressman Bill Paxton—to present Newt with a fait accompli: resign or be removed by parliamentary procedure. The desire to get rid of Newt stemmed as much from his perceived lack of fealty to the conservative cause as from his ham-handed fumbling of the government shutdown. The predominant feeling at the time was that, with Newt continuing to lead the party, the Republicans were doomed to lose the Congress in the next election. This group wanted to prevent that and turn the speakership over to a more stable conservative. According to several of the members present, Armey committed to support their plan. DeLay did more than offer support. Without Buckham there to stop him, he committed to lead the mutineers to the House floor himself, if Gingrich did not abdicate.

As majority leader and second in command, Armey presumed he would ascend to the speaker's office, but when he discovered that DeLay intended for Paxton—a bright, young Congressman from New York who was immensely popular among the members for his folksy manner and strategic capabilities—to be Speaker, he withdrew his support from the insurrection. At that point, all hell broke loose as many of the plotters pretended they never heard of the effort, and others became almost violent in their support. Graham was said to have lunged at Armey during the Republican caucus meeting called to sort out this matter. Buckham returned from Russia to find his boss' career teetering on the edge and immediately put his staff into a crisis mode to deal with the questions coming in from almost one hundred Republican members. I spent most of that next day in the DeLay office offering my support and assistance. The staff was divided on whether Tom should admit his role in the plot, or mimic Armey and deny he was ever involved. By mid afternoon, word came to us that Tom refused to lie and was going to admit his involvement in the coup. A meeting was slated for the next night of the entire Republican caucus, where the collaborators would be exposed and punished.

I was as depressed as any of the staff. Tom was my friend, and I respected his move against Gingrich. I would likely have done the same if I were in his position. I certainly did similar things in my past, including endorsing a libertarian opponent to liberal Republican Senator Charles Percy while I was national chairman of the College Republicans. That almost cost me my job as College Republican chairman and all of us concluded that Gingrich would make Tom pay for his rebellion with his position.

Gingrich was a huge liability to the party, with his arrogant demeanor. He was one of the most unpopular politicians in America. Replacing him with Paxton would have boosted Republican prospects immensely. Further, Gingrich was constantly suppressing conservative initiatives. He had to go, and Tom was right to try it—or so we thought. The problem with a failed coup is that, in most places, the plotters are executed. Thus, both Tom's staff and mine were convinced that Gingrich would demand Tom's resignation and that his career was over. It was to be a calamity for conservatives, as Tom was the movement's most reliable friend in the Republican leadership. On a business level, it was equally disastrous for me. DeLay was our champion on almost every issue of importance to my clients. Losing him would be a major setback.

Tom made it clear he was going to take responsibility for his actions, but he was not going to resign. The people in his Houston Congressional district elected him, not Gingrich. If they wanted him out, so be it, but they would have to wait for the next election to send that message. As for his position as Majority Whip, if the caucus wanted him out, they could relieve him of that position whenever they chose, but Gingrich had no plenipotentiary power to do so. In fact, Tom had come to his leadership position against the wishes of Newt from the start.

I realized that, with the Speaker and likely dozens of other members pressuring him to resign, Tom would become a pariah. He could count on support of very close friends, but that would be it. He would be persona non grata among the lobbyists, who only cared about power. That meant it would be immensely difficult for him to raise funds. I felt I had to do something to help, so I took to the phone, calling each of my clients. After giving them an update on what was happening, I asked that they send every dollar they could to Tom and the groups in his political network. Almost immediately, hundreds of thousands of dollars started flowing from my clients to prop up DeLay. They appreciated Tom and wanted to do what they could.

As I worked the phones, I received a call from Alexander Koulakovsky's top colleague, Marina Nevskaya. She deduced the trouble for Tom resulted from Ed's trip to Russia, and Alexander wanted to help. I thanked her, but told her it wasn't legal for foreign citizens to contribute to political campaigns or political action committees (PACs).

"We'll have to think of something," was her reply, and I didn't think much more about it.

The following day seemed like it might be the last of Tom DeLay's political career. His staff was despondent. I entered the Majority Whip's suite of offices after he had already departed for the members' caucus meeting. I was ushered into Tom's private office, where Ed sat with Tom's wife Christine. I had known Christine to be Tom's pillar of strength and the backbone of his faith and conservative beliefs. When I entered the room, she had been praying and crying. We sat silently waiting for his return. After about an hour, Tom returned to his office. He had a serene look on his face, though he was clearly fatigued. After kissing Christine and hugging Ed and me, he said it was in the hands of the Lord whether he would survive this. He had been honest and told the caucus what he did and why. His fellow members were rather stunned by his actions and his honesty, but offered no immediate reaction. In truth, most of them probably agreed with what Tom and the others tried to do.

Tom asked the rest of his staff to join us in his office and he offered a prayer. The atmosphere reminded me of a losing candidate's post election gathering. There was a air of resignation about, but there was also a sense of spiritual serenity, as if Tom had done what was right and now the matter was in God's hands. After a few moments, Paxon and his wife, Congresswoman Susan Molinari, joined us. Unlike Tom, Paxon was not elected to the leadership, he served at the pleasure of Gingrich, and he was about to lose his position. The hopeless mood was broken, however, when Congressman Ray LaHood entered the room. LaHood was a leader of the moderate Republicans and an opponent of DeLay's on almost every issue. Later he would actually join the cabinet of Barack Obama, one of the most liberal men ever elected as president of the United States.

LaHood's presence was a bit of a shock, and the room immediately fell silent as he spoke: "Tom, I want to tell you that I completely disagreed with your actions against the Speaker, but I came to tell you how much I admire and respect you for your honesty." DeLay nodded and tried to smile.

One by one, scores of representatives entered Tom's office bearing a similar message. Ed and I looked at each other. This wasn't what either of us expected. Instead of being booted from the House Republican caucus, DeLay had gained admirers. Instead of removing his greatest critic, Gingrich had inadvertently provided him a podium to display true character to the members. Newt further empowered DeLay by letting him stay around without a fight. From that moment on, Tom's influence grew. Eventually he would control the entire caucus and Newt would be out of Congress.

Still, the Russians were worried that the advance recognizance trip had caused DeLay real harm and that, worse, his trip to Moscow might be cancelled. Alexander and Marina were counting on Tom's visit, as they did not wish to disappoint their prime minister. They had nothing to fear. Later that summer, I joined the DeLay entourage for the flight to Russia.

The trip to Moscow involved non-stop meetings for Tom and his staff. I attended his appointment with President Boris Yeltsin's chief of staff, but otherwise stayed out of the limelight. Chernomyrdin received his American friend with great enthusiasm, and Alexander reveled in the amity between the two leaders, his friends.

At the end of five grueling days of meetings, our hosts scheduled us to play a round of golf, not something one would associate with a trip to the former Soviet Union. The premier course in Russia at the time was the Moscow Country Club, a Meridien resort course designed by the world famous golf architect Robert Trent Jones. Alexander, anticipating an opportunity to join DeLay in a game of golf, spent most of that year studying the game and even set up a golf simulation environment in one of his warehouses. When we arrived at the course, the foursome set to play included DeLay, Alexander, Ed Buckham, and me. Immediately, Alexander took charge. He arranged that Ed and Tom would be a team, that he and I would be a team, and that we would be betting on this match.

Tom started to laugh, since Alexander had never played golf, and I wasn't exactly the student Arnold Palmer had hoped for. Alexander insisted though, and it was decided that our team would be granted four extra strokes per hole to make up the likely differential in scores.

At the first hole, Alexander, a burly and powerful man, announced we would be betting one dollar on this hole. He then took a mighty wallop at his golf ball, but it only traveled a few yards down the course. I sliced my ball into the thick rough and watched Buckham follow me there. DeLay fought back a smile as he powered his ball long and straight toward the hole. Things didn't improve for Alexander and me as we hacked our way around the course, and Ed and Tom won the dollar.

On the tee box of the second hole, Alexander proclaimed the bet would be for ten dollars. DeLay shrugged, and let loose another booming drive. The rest of us less so. Alexander's shots improved, but not by much. Another hole was lost. Now Tom and Ed were eleven dollars richer.

The wagers increased with each hole, but Tom and Ed dominated. Alexander seemed to improve with each hole, but we were woefully outmanned. A one-time Houston club champion, DeLay was just too skillful for us to have a chance. On the tee box for the sixth hole, the unflappable Alexander announced the bet was to be increased to one hundred dollars. My gulp must have been loud because Alexander leaned over and whispered that I shouldn't worry about these losses. He would cover them. Just play and relax. But I guess I was too relaxed, since we lost that hole, too.

When Alexander declared that the stakes on hole seven would be one thousand dollars, DeLay stopped smiling and shot me a look. I shrugged and tried to smile, but my pained expression left no doubt that I was clueless as to Alexander's actions. One of the classic scams in golf is where a superior golfer "sandbags," or plays badly for a number of holes, only to pour it on when the betting starts to get serious. I had no doubt this crossed DeLay's mind, but he teed it up and ripped a blazing drive down the fairway, almost driving his ball onto the green on the relatively short par four hole. Not taking any chances, DeLay birdied the hole. Buckham wasn't far behind with a bogey, but for the first time, Alexander put together two solid strikes and was within twenty yards of the green. His next shot, however, landed in the sand trap, and it took him two more swings to get out of the bunker. On the green, he fared no better, three putting to finish the hole in nine strokes. My bogey of five strokes meant another lost hole, and Tom and Ed winning one thousand dollars. The tension was palpable as we mounted the climb to the next tee box.

"One million dollars," Alexander announced with a proud smile. DeLay started to object, but Alexander cut him off.

"Tom, we play. No questions," he said in his broken English.

DeLay teed up the ball and aimed at the green on this tricky par three hole, which was playing at approximately 140 yards over a ravine to the front of the green, and 160 yards to the hole. Striking his ball well, he landed on the green within twenty feet of the flag. Ed hit his best shot of the day and was also on the green. My shot landed in the rough just off the green. Alexander carefully teed up his ball and thrashed at it with all his might. His ball sailed through the air and landed on the green, but the forward momentum carried it into the rough. DeLay looked panic-stricken. One million dollars wasn't a normal golf bet, and not one which Tom could pay. Now, all of a sudden, Alexander was playing well. Tom was expressionless, but Ed looked as though his head was going to explode. I envisioned the end of my lobbying practice, but Alexander's face was radiant as we strode toward the green. After catching a glimpse at my ashen face, Alexander winked and flashed a toothy smile. I couldn't believe what was happening.

On the green DeLay missed his birdie, but Buckham sank his. Their combined score was a five. Alexander and I needed a combined score of eight to win the hole—and end my lobbying career. Alexander chipped his ball barely onto the green, and proceeded to three putt again. I had to chip and putt to win the hole. My chip was played as well as I could, and my ball was only two feet from the cup. If I made this putt, Tom DeLay and Ed Buckham would owe us one million dollars and I would have to seek asylum in Russia.

As I moved toward the ball, Alexander intercepted me and whispered, "Jack, you will miss." I figured he wanted me to miss, resulting in a tie where no one owed anything. I putted the ball one foot past the left side of the hole and could see that Tom and Ed were breathing again. As I circled the cup to position myself for the tying putt, again Alexander approached: "Jack, you will miss again."

I stared at my client and friend in disbelief. What was he doing? If I missed, Alexander would owe one million dollars—because I certainly wasn't going to be paying. He nodded to reaffirm his command. I settled over the ball and missed the putt. Tom and Ed were aghast. None of us knew what was happening. And then Alexander filled us in.

"Tom, you are a strong leader and a good friend. I admire you and wanted to help you when you were in trouble recently because of the coup, but Jack told us we cannot give money to you because we are not Americans. So, I decided I would not give you money. I would lose the money to you legally in a bet. So, I spent months learning to play golf and bet you. You won, and I shall pay my debt. Use the money how you want. It's yours."

Tom froze for a moment and then burst into laughter.

"You're a great friend, and very clever, but I can't accept a million dollars from you like this. Your desire to help me is more meaningful than you can know, but this approach violates the law, or at least the spirit of the law, and I can't accept. Of course, it almost didn't matter anyway, since I nearly had a fatal heart attack when I saw your ball land on the green. From now on, we're not betting more than one dollar."

As we walked to the next hole, Ed sidled up to me. "If he's serious about wanting to help, there is a way Alexander can give money."

A year later, in 1998, Buckham's organization, the U.S. Family Network, received its largest contribution.

That year proved to be a tumultuous one for the Republicans in the House. After a stinging defeat in the mid-term elections, Gingrich announced he would step down as speaker. DeLay led the Republicans to impeach Clinton and, at the end of the year, Gingrich's replacement, Congressman Bob Livingston, also stepped down after disclosures of marital infidelity.

With Majority Leader Armey still unpopular with the Republican caucus because of his prevarication about his role in the coup, when the Republicans were gathering to reorganize their leadership at the end of 1998, DeLay stood ready to assume the speakership and run the House of Representatives. His credibility with the caucus was at an all time high. Conservatives were happy to see one of their number in leadership— especially one who broke the infamous rule propounded by journalist M. Stanton Evans: once one of ours (a conservative) rises in power, he ceases to be one of ours.

I was thrilled Tom would ascend to such heights. Visions of DeLay wielding the gavel before the House chamber danced in my head. Plus, with DeLay as speaker, my clients would surely benefit from my access to this seat of power. But it wasn't to be.

Ed called me at home after the Sabbath ended on the weekend after Livingston stepped aside. Tom wasn't going to run for speaker. While he had the votes to win, the media would have launched a debilitating assault, putting him into the spotlight and foiling the Republican agenda in Congress. Dennis Hastert would become speaker. I was skeptical.

"Of course the media will attack Tom and the Republicans, but do you really think they'll attack less if Denny is speaker? Ed, this makes no sense."

Buckham hesitated and then revealed the real reason behind Tom's refusal to take the top position. Tom and Christine made it a practice to adopt foster children and raise them. Most of their charitable work revolved around foster children, and unlike many celebrities aiding good causes, they practiced what they preached. The DeLays had just adopted a new child and Tom feared that, by becoming speaker, he wouldn't be able to give that child the family he deserved. As I listened to Buckham's words, I realized that DeLay, this man I so admired, wasn't even the same species as most Washington politicos. He was a real mentsch.

In a few days, I would find out more. After the dust settled, I had a chance to see Tom in his office. I mentioned that Ed had shared the real reason for his declining the speakership with me. Tom tried to change the subject, but I pressed.

"Tom, the media attack you incessantly. They claim you gave up the speakership because you knew you are extreme and divisive. Can't we leak out this information, about the real reason, so they can see you as you really are?"

Tom smiled and shook his head. "If this reason comes out, our new child will grow up thinking he denied me the chance to be speaker. It will hurt him. Let's just let it pass."

And so, with quiet humility, Tom DeLay endured yet another series of assaults on his character and status. I always wondered why Tom would allow the press and establishment to attack him with impunity. It was as if they didn't matter and he didn't care. They would later inflict horrific and politically fatal blows on this faithful and dedicated man and, as I too would discover in the course of my own fall from grace, few of his erstwhile "friends" would be there to defend him.

# 8

# POLITICAL GOLF

Governor Froilan Tenorio was a tireless public servant in the Marianas. When he wasn't rushing to every backwater villa to recruit possible business opportunities for the CNMI, he was broadcasting his support for conservative political issues. Since he was a Democrat, this made for great fodder on Capitol Hill. The Democrats, virtually all of whom were supportive of the federal takeover, reviled him, but the Republicans loved him. In the span of a few months, Governor Tenorio proclaimed that the CNMI would cut taxes to a 10 percent flat rate and that they were going to initiate a school voucher program. Our travelers ate this up. The conservative groups in Washington had found a new hero in this Democratic governor of our least populated territory. But as much as his friends loved him, they were also constantly caught off guard by his idiosyncratic behavior. His public pronouncements were blunt and, sometimes, very odd. One day he would advise the young ladies of Saipan to marry only rich guys. Another day he would proclaim it ethical for a sitting governor to take loans from a felon. Froilan was a source of unending wonder to us, but on matters of principle and personal clashes, he was unbending. No issue provided a better intersection of these two areas than whether the Marianas should be awarded a delegate to the U.S. Congress.

Every territory controlled by the United States had a delegate to the Congress, except the Marianas. The Resident Representative in Washington of the CNMI, Juan Babauta, focused almost entirely on getting the Congress to approve upgrading his position to that of Delegate, but with little success. Babauta was the archetype Pacific islander emissary to Washington, D.C. His natural shyness, coupled with his truckling and unctuous demeanor left him invisible to almost all of official Washington. A favorite of the patrician and pedantic bureaucrats bent on destroying the islands' economy, because he never opposed their nefarious aims, and even gave comfort to those attacking the Marinas with public assertions of their proper intentions, Babauta quickly became Froilan's favorite target. With every visiting delegation to the islands, Froilan would immediately focus on what he called the wasteful and selfish attempts by Babauta to gain delegate status, even at the expense of the U.S. taxpayer. Froilan commanded us to ensure that Babauta's delegate bill would be defeated. Since we resented Babauta undercutting our lobbying efforts with public calls for a federal takeover of the Marianas, and since the bill would have cost the Congress an additional one million dollars, we had no problem stopping this.

Froilan's side battles and peculiarities eventually caught up with him in the next election. He was a campaign manager's nightmare, and when he drew a re-election challenge from his uncle, former governor Pedro P. Tenorio (known as Teno), he was in trouble. Froilan was too busy governing and didn't seem to care that running for office and running that office were two different things.

I found myself on Saipan during the final days of the hard fought 1997 Gubernatorial elections. Both camps were confident of victory, but a storm was brewing—literally and figuratively. The night after the election, super typhoon Keith, with winds gusting to 100 miles per hour, buffeted the islands. The election commission had to work without power. All guests were confined to the hotel, and most of the islands' residents braced for the worst.

As the winds whipped to a frenzy, I foolishly tried to get a peek outside. The hotel strongly warned guests to draw curtains and take position in the bathtub, but I had never witnessed a super typhoon before and was too curious to stay in the bathroom. I yanked the sliding door to the balcony open, and, in a split second, I felt the most powerful blast of my life. My body was being sucked out the door, but my grip on the portal saved me. My glasses were not so lucky, flying away into the eye of the storm faster than a speeding bullet.

By morning, the islands were shorn of all vegetation, and some real damage was felt on Rota, the southern-most island of the chain. But the damage we felt was more severe: When Typhoon Keith settled down, Typhoon Froilan was washed out to sea.

Worse still, at a time when the federal government was accelerating their assault on the islands, the voters had replaced Froilan, the governor we lovingly called "the lion of the Pacific," with a docile and almost pusillanimous Teno.

It was during the transition between the Froilan and Teno administrations, in December 1997, that we planned a trip to the CNMI for the most important visitor of all: Majority Leader Tom DeLay. This would be the first time a senior member of the House had come to the islands, and the excitement was palpable among the locals.

DeLay was the greatest champion the CNMI had in Washington, and he was certainly its most powerful advocate. Working with Majority Leader Armey's office, his staff had foiled every attempt to impale the Marianas economy, because he believed the CNMI was unfairly attacked and that, ultimately, this battle was merely one battle in the larger war between the free market and socialism. Upon his arrival, Tom was greeted as a hero. He toured the factories, spoke with workers, and attended briefings and inspections.

As part of the ongoing assault against the islands in the media, ABC News' investigative program "20/20" sent a camera crew to get compromising footage of Tom during this trip, but they weren't having much luck. One evening, the camera crew showed up at a reception the Chamber of Commerce was hosting for Tom. They filmed from a conspicuous distance, perched behind some bushes, so the footage would look like they had been kept out of the event. Tom walked over to them and told them to come out and film in the open. He had nothing to hide. They refused.

The next day, after a marathon of morning briefings, we decided to take a break and play golf. A large group descended on the Lao Lao Bay East Golf Course, one of the more beautiful and challenging golf courses on the island. Designed by champion golfer Greg Norman, the course's stunning views were more than matched by the difficulty of the layout. Teno, former CNMI Speaker of the House and future Governor Ben Fitial, and I would play with Tom, and the rest of the entourage would pair up as best they could. Again, "20/20" camera crews hovered at enough of a distance to make it seem like they were being kept off the course.

Ben was one of the leaders who helped shape the covenant that we fought so vigorously to defend. He was also a boon companion to all the travelers who visited the islands. Having retired from politics to work for Willie Tan's companies, Ben was one of the most affable and knowledge-able representatives the CNMI had. Plus, he was a great golfer. In fact, Ben made the annual pilgrimage to Houston to play in the DeLay Foundation for Kids golf tournament, always winning some prize for his golf skills.

As is tradition, when four players set out on the course, a friendly $5 bet was proposed. We would play as teams based on our ability, and the teams would share the same golf cart. In order to calibrate the strokes to even out the teams, we all declared our handicaps. I remember hearing Ben's and worrying. He was a skilled golfer, but had claimed a high handicap. Having played with Ben before, Tom knew better and did a double take when he heard it. Tom was a stickler for golf etiquette and rules, and pumping your handicap was just not acceptable. People normally stretched the truth to win a golf bet, but we only had $5 riding on this, so Ben's declaration confused me as well. As we rode to the first hole, I popped the question, "Brother Ben, are you sure you gave the right handicap?" We always called each other brother, and we meant it.

"My brother, of course I did… for this occasion."

I was panicked. All we needed was Ben giving a high handicap and winning the measly $5 bet, angering DeLay and putting the entire support network on Capitol Hill at risk.

"This occasion? What do you mean?"

"My brother, what is more important here? That we give the right handicaps, or that Teno and DeLay spend the day in the same golf cart getting to know each other? If I'd given my handicap properly, Tom would be on your team, not Teno's. The combination of your real handicap and his would be equal to the combination of my real handicap and Teno's. Sure, we'd have an accurate golf game, but Teno wouldn't be able to bond with DeLay. Understand?"

Did I ever. Ben wasn't a skilled politician for nothing. I beamed. Until the first hole, that is.

After hitting a straight but short drive, Ben hit his next ball just off the front of the green. DeLay was on the green in two shots and putting for birdie from a distance. Teno and I were hacking away and out of the hole. Ben waited while Tom made his first put, which stopped a few inches past the hole for an easy par. Ben calmly approached his ball with his sand wedge, and promptly chipped his ball into the hole! Only a real pro could make that shot. Ben said he was lucky, but DeLay looked suspicious.

The second hole at Lao Lao Bay is a hard par five with a zigzagging, "dog leg" (or bent) fairway, leading to a green protected by sand traps. Ben teed off first, hitting his usual straight but short drive. I hit second, walloping my ball down the middle of the fairway. DeLay outdrove me, and Teno sliced into trouble. Ben's second hit was solid and put him in position to reach the green on his third try. My next attempt sailed out of bounds, taking me out of play. Teno was never in play. Tom hit a long iron well past Ben's ball, and a mere sand wedge for the green. As Ben stepped up to play his next ball, he winked at me. I looked to make sure Tom hadn't seen it. What was he up to now?

With his smooth swing, Ben hit his ball right at the flagstick on the green. The ball nestled about two feet from the hole, positioning Ben for another birdie. That would be two birdies in two holes. If one ever needed proof that he submitted too high a handicap, we were all about to get it. DeLay looked upset, not that he might lose, but that he was playing golf with someone who didn't honestly declare his handicap. About a year later, when Tom was driving the impeachment of President Clinton, he told me that he loathed the adultery, but the dishonesty was what impelled him to take action. "A man who cheats at golf is going to be a cheater in most things," he said more than once to me.

As Ben stood over his birdie putt, I held my breath. When the ball hit the bottom of the hole, I started seeing visions of a takeover sailing through the House. As we got back into the cart, I turned to Ben. "My brother, what are you doing?"

He smiled, "Just having a little fun, my brother. Don't worry."

"We are playing golf with the most powerful man in Congress and the next governor of the islands. You know what they are saying to each other right now? That you are a golf cheat! Ben, this is too much. We have to do something."

"My brother, right now they are allies against me. They are frustrated that they cannot beat me. They're pulling together. They're bonding. Sure, it's at my expense, but that's OK. This is not my first time playing political golf."

Political golf? That was a first for me, but what could I do, other than pray for Ben to shank the ball over the cliff into the ocean?

Starting on the next hole, Ben put on the most masterful demonstration at controlled golf I had ever seen. Very slowly, very subtly, he let Tom and Teno back into the match. You could tell they were excited and celebrating as they took Ben apart. Ben would shoot me a smile or wink when they weren't looking, but instead of carding birdies, he was just missing and making bogeys or worse. Sometimes, he would tell me that he was going to hit the ball just to the left or to the right, so it looked like he was in trouble. On the greens, he missed putts with such skill that it would never have occurred to Tom or Teno that he was throwing the match.

When we finished, Tom and Teno had eeked out a victory and were feeling great. Ben was right to make them work together, forging what we hoped would be a productive friendship. Unfortunately, not all the conversation in their golf cart served our cause.

When we were alone, Tom told me we were going have to trouble with this new governor. He was weak and afraid of the people in Washington leading the effort to destroy the island's economy. He wanted to compromise and hope for the best. DeLay spent the better part of the round trying to convince Teno to be more like Froilan. It didn't seem to work. Tom said he wouldn't give up the fight, but that he was worried this governor would undercut us. He was more right than he realized.

A change in leadership is never a good thing when that leadership is your client. We didn't realize how bad it was for us with CNMI, our largest client, until Pat Pizzella and I sat in the audience for Teno's inauguration. Congressman Phil English, a former national co-chairman of the College Republicans, was sent by the Republican majority in the Congress as their representative to the ceremony. He was placed in the back row of dignitaries seated near the rostrum. Congressman George Miller and Interior

Department Office of Insular Affairs head Alan Stayman, both implacable foes of the CNMI, were in the front row. Worse, both were accorded high honor and recognition during the ceremony, and English was snubbed. English had personally gone to bat to save the CNMI against the perfidy of Miller and Stayman, and this was his reward.

The ceremony wasn't the only sign that a new Pharaoh had arisen in Saipan. Teno's incoming staff was quickly spreading word that a new era of cooperation between the CNMI and Miller and Stayman was at hand, and that Froilan's old pugilistic approach was now consigned to the ashbin. Teno thought the problem with Froilan's dealings with the federal government was that he was too blunt, too unwilling to be nice. Teno intended to charm his enemies and become their friends. He would even consider phasing in a higher minimum wage, even if it meant a reduction in economic opportunity on the islands. But soon Teno would discover that even his best efforts at appeasement weren't enough.

The next day, Pat and I were playing golf when we were urgently summoned to a meeting with the new governor. He had been meeting with Miller and Stayman most of that morning. By the time he got to us, he looked like he was having a heart attack.

"Those bastards will not get away with this," he shouted. "I will fight them!"

Deluded by Miller and Stayman's polite demeanor at his inauguration the day before, Teno had assumed they would give him a chance to develop other businesses on the island before the federal government would shutter the garment industry. That morning, Miller and Stayman smacked him in the face. There would be no delay—a full takeover was coming as soon as possible.

As he recounted his first morning as governor, Teno was spitting mad. I thought he was going to keel over. We had assumed that Teno would fire us as soon as he took over. Instead, we were back in the saddle.

Unfortunately for us, however, we were never actually hired. Teno re-commissioned us as defenders of the Marianas, but he seemed to think that we would just keep working for free. For months, we continued to battle the takeover efforts with no pay. Teno kept promising to formally engage our services, but every time I pushed, he had another excuse.

The truth was the CNMI had real financial problems. One day, I noticed that the television set in Teno's office was unplugged. Perhaps not understanding that televisions were no longer made of vacuum tubes, he told me that he was trying to save electricity. The lights were off as well. They were broke. When Froilan was governor, he was indefatigable in his efforts to get new business opportunities started to generate tax revenues and fees. Teno's solution was to sit in the dark.

My firm was leaning on me. We had spent over half a million dollars in billable time keeping the CNMI free from the new assaults by Stayman and Miller, but there was no one paying us. I was used to bringing in large fees, not to running up large bills at the firm, but I also knew that if we relented, even for a week, the CNMI would fall prey to the OIA and congressional enemies like Miller. After all the work we had done to keep them free of a federal takeover, how could we just let it happen over some fees? For me, it was always about more than just the money. It was about the philosophical issues involved, the competition and keeping the Washington elites from destroying my friends. But the firm was a business, and I worked for them.

Finally, after months without income, Willie Tan, the main garment producer in the CNMI, stepped in and organized the private sector to pay our fees, or at least a portion of them.

Willie was born in Guam. He had operations throughout the Pacific, but he had a soft spot for the CNMI, and did his best to support industry there. His garment factories were showcases of efficiency and cleanliness. Sure, Willie was a hard charging businessman, but he was also one of the most decent and generous members of the CNMI community. Unfortunately, Willie's kindness was not always repaid in kind. The more he did, the more the locals seemed resentful of him. Generally, he would ignore these petty feelings, but at times, the negativity took a toll on him. Eventually, he started spending more time at his other Asian facilities, particularly those in the Philippines. I considered meeting with Willie a vital part of our representation, since he played such a major role in the CNMI economy, and soon we started to meet in Manila since Willie was not visiting Saipan very frequently.

So, I would travel to Philippines to see Willie each time I was in the CNMI. On the last Thursday of my trips to the Marianas, I would fly to Manila, arriving late at night. I would then see Willie the next day.

After that, I would spend the Sabbath at the hotel and then depart for the mainland on Saturday night. After several trips to Manila, Gil Kapen— a college pal, and former chief of staff for Congressman Dan Burton (R-IN)—offered to arrange another meeting for me while I was in the Philippines—with the former first lady, Imelda Marcos.

On the Friday morning of my next trip to Manila, I was ushered into Mrs. Marcos's penthouse condominium in the Tony Makati section of town. I noticed the reception room contained scores of pictures of the former first lady and her now-deceased husband, former President Ferdinand Marcos, with world leaders. Each of the U.S. presidents from Truman through the first Bush was represented, as were the popes, kings, and prime ministers from across the globe. Photos with Leonid Breshnev from the Soviet Union, and Mao Tse Tung of China were mixed with pictures with Mother Theresa and the Dalai Lama. On the walls of this impressive room were original paintings by some of the greatest artists in history: Michelangelo, Picasso, Renoir, Monet and many others.

Mrs. Marcos entered the room with an elegant and regal bearing. She professed great interest in our discussion, as one of her passions was American politics—and the visitors from the States were less frequent than in years past. I was interested in meeting her because she was part of history. I expected very little substantive discussion from a woman known primarily for her shoe collection, but was I ever wrong. Our meeting quickly turned from pleasantries to serious geopolitical discourse. Mrs. Marcos told me about her diplomatic missions on behalf of her husband. A renowned beauty in those days, she would charm the old men who ran the world into granting her nation's strategic goals. Even approaching seventy years old when I met her, she retained much of her attractiveness. Mrs. Marcos shared with me her prolonged and deep conversations with Mao, where she came to understand the Chinese hegemonic approach to foreign policy. Mao described all of Asia as China, from the Urals east to the ocean, and from Siberia south through Indochina. All of those lands would one day return to Chinese control, he told Mrs. Marcos. She lamented that Western leaders continued to ignore this reality.

In addition to her strategic insights, Mrs. Marcos went to great pains to try to counter the commonly accepted notion that her husband had plundered their nation's wealth. At our second meeting, she showed me what she asserted was the source of the fabulous Marcos fortune. Each of more than a dozen binders contained copies of dozens of Swiss gold certificates of deposit from the late 1940s. Like most of the world, I had heard of the outlandish Marcos kleptocracy in Manila and the pillaging of that nation's wealth. But Mrs. Marcos claimed the wealth of the family wasn't derived from such misappropriation, but rather from gold—stolen Japanese gold, to be more precise.

During World War II, the Imperial Japanese forces, under the direction of General Tomoyuki Yamashita, infamously looted each of the territories under their occupation of all gold holdings and ferried this treasure to the Philippines. They planned to move their administrative capital to the more centrally located Philippines after they had won the war. The island of Japan would remain as their holy land, but all logistical control would issue from their new Philippine headquarters. To prepare for this transition, they furtively stored all captured gold in caves, tunnels, and underground complexes throughout the Philippines. This much I knew before meeting Mrs. Marcos. What I had never heard until our meeting was that many of the caves and tunnels were located on Marcos family land. According to Mrs. Marcos, when Ferdinand Marcos returned from fighting the Japanese during the war, he found the gold on his property, reclaimed it, and deposited it in Swiss banks. The certificates I saw added up to an astonishing quantity of gold, some sixteen thousand metric tons! My head was spinning. It's possible that these certificates were fabrications, but why was she showing them to me? What was her game? Furthermore, Mrs. Marcos then showed me copies of wire transfer statements from the time her husband was president in the 1970s and 1980s attesting to hundreds of millions of dollars being wired into the Philippines from those Swiss banks. She claimed that, when the government needed funds, Marcos provided them from his private accounts in Switzerland, quite the opposite of stealing from the public trough, as he was accused of doing. I could not independently assess this information, and all of this was interesting, but it was hardly relevant to my life. That changed in January 1998.

As became my custom when traveling to Manila, I would send a fax to Mrs. Marcos letting her know I was coming, so we could arrange lunch on the Friday of my visit. I admit I was as fascinated by her as she was in our discussions about American politics. Plus, I reasoned with myself, even if Marcos was not the saint she portrayed, she bore little blame for his actions. I tried not to judge her by the standards of her detractors—a tolerance I would later regret others did not extend to me. I looked forward to visiting with Mrs. Marcos as much as I looked forward to seeing Willie, which was quite a lot. In fact, after lunching with the former first lady, I would see Willie in the afternoon, spend the Sabbath and return to the United States. For me, an ideal trip.

On Thursday, January 29, 1998, I arrived in Manila late at night. After settling into the Intercontinental Hotel car sent to bring me to the hotel, I opened the local newspapers to discover a most distressing headline: "Imelda To Go To Prison!" Mrs. Marcos' appeal to the Philippine Supreme Court had been rejected and she was to be imprisoned on corruption charges. Since she had never mentioned this to me during our previous visits, I was confused and wanted to make sure my friend was OK. The next morning, I called her residence.

"Jack, you must come over to see me immediately," she said in her usual steady voice. I rushed to her building as quickly as I could and was brought to her penthouse.

As I entered, she was sitting with half a dozen men in suits—her lawyers. Mrs. Marcos rose as soon as I entered the room and asked to see me privately. Once we were alone, I asked what was happening. In control as always, she smiled.

"Well, it seems I am going to prison. A few days ago, I was given this." She handed me a copy of the Supreme Court decision reversing her conviction. It bore two of the three necessary signatures.

"I was told that the Court was going to reverse this outrageous conviction. Instead, they issued an affirmation of it the next day... There's more." I waited as she paused, undoubtedly for full dramatic effect.

Mrs. Marcos reminded me that the current president, Fidel V. Ramos, was just concluding his term in office. The race to succeed him consumed most of the attention in that nation. The leading contender was his chosen successor, then-Speaker of the House Jose de Venecia, Jr. His main opponent was a former actor, Joseph Estrada. Also contending in the race was Mrs. Marcos, who upon her return from exile was elected to the Philippine Congress. Relations between Mrs. Marcos and Ramos were tense, in part thanks to an squabble over a contested bank account bearing $800 million.

"Yesterday morning I received a phone call from President Ramos's chief of staff. He told me the president was very sorry to hear about my conviction and would extend a pardon to me in exchange for my commitment never to seek political office in the Philippines again—especially the presidency—and my relinquishing to their political party all right and title to the disputed bank account."

I was relieved for her.

"So, you won't have to go to prison?"

"Jack, I said no."

"But, Mrs. Marcos, why? Do you want to go to prison?"

"I am not going to accept a pardon, because I did not commit a crime. The Supreme Court here is packed with political cronies. Obviously they were given an instruction from the palace to withdraw the reversal at the last minute. I don't want a pardon. I want them to hear my case en banc and to reinstate the reversal."

"Does it really matter? Is it worth risking time in prison?"

She cut me off.

"Jack, when my husband was president, the rich and middle classes had medical care, but the poor people were left to die in the streets if they were sick. I implored him to find the money to build up the Philippine General Hospital so all poor people could get any medical attention they needed, but the president told me there weren't sufficient funds. I was distraught. So, with the help of some like-minded citizens, I created a way to finance the hospital. We were in the process of building an elevated train in Manila. I took the land under the tracks and leased it to businesses. Those funds were diverted to build the hospital and the poor of our capital no longer had to die in the streets. Am I supposed to be pardoned for that?"

Finally I started to understand why, in every political analysis of the Philippines presidential race, the poor voters favored Mrs. Marcos.

"Jack, I am not going to accept his pardon. I want justice. What should I do?"

I did a double take. She was asking my advice? "Jack, my people don't know how to play in this world. You do. Please tell me what you recommend."

"I recommend you take the pardon."

She frowned.

"But, if you won't . . . how bold are you willing to be?" I was trying to buy time to think of something.

"I'm willing to go to prison. Isn't that rather bold?"

I laughed, "Yes, quite." Then it hit me: "How about this? Have one of your top supporters go to President Ramos's planned successor, Speaker de Venecia and tell him that two paths lie before him. The first has you going to prison. When you walk through the doors of the prison, tens of millions of poor people in the Philippines will explode in a fury which will burn the nation to the ground, marching on the palace and making the country ungovernable. Once in prison, you will continue to run for president as vigorously as you can, but only in the districts where your presence on the ballot will dilute the vote for de Venecia. Furthermore, you will not only not cede them control of the contested bank account, you will match those funds from another account—dispatching half that amount ($400 million) to the Estrada campaign to ensure their victory. The other half will be allocated by your people to hire the world's best lobbyists and public relations companies to destroy the reputation of the government of the Philippines in every capital in the world. By the time you are done with them, they will have lost allies and seen sanctions applied for a host of reasons which have nothing to do with Imelda Marcos. That's the first path."

Mrs. Marcos leaned forward with great anticipation as I paused between scenarios. "The second path has the Supreme Court issuing the opinion they were supposed to issue, reversing this conviction for graft. You will commit not to run for president—this time—but you will keep your options open for the future. They will agree that the disputed account is, in fact, yours, but you will lend their political party half of that account for their use. The loan must be secured and repaid on an agreed timetable. That's my recommendation."

Mrs. Marcos rose to thank me.

"Jack, it is brilliant. This is exactly the plan I needed. I wouldn't change a thing. Would you please do this for me?"

My smile quickly disappeared. Did she want me to be involved in this?

"Jack, my people can't pull this off. You can. Can you please meet with the Speaker on my behalf?"

"Mrs. Marcos, I'm a stranger here with no connections other than you. I am here only for a day and then am leaving tomorrow night for the States. The Sabbath commences at sunset, as you know, and I cannot ride in a car, use the phone, or do anything like that."

"But you can meet with someone, right? You can have a conversation, right?"

"Yes, but..."

With that, she excused herself from the room. My head was spinning. What trouble had I unleashed?

"The Speaker will see you at his home at 12:00."

I looked at my watch. It was already 11:00 a.m. "Well, I'll have to call my client to postponed my lunch meeting, but..."

"No, 12:00 midnight."

I was a bit stunned. Who meets at midnight, other than vampires and drug dealers?

"Mrs. Marcos, as much as I want to help, that's during our Sabbath. I can't ride in a car after the Sabbath commences. I wish I could help, but I cannot break these rules unless a life is on the line."

"Jack, my life is on the line. If you cannot ride there, you can walk there."

The Speaker's home was two miles away from my hotel along the dark Manila streets. Against my better judgment, I agreed to be escorted by her "people" for a midnight meeting. At 11:00 p.m., there was a knock at my hotel door. It was the president of San Miguel Breweries, one of the Philippine's most established companies, a rather youthful corporate executive who was close to Mrs. Marcos.

"Mr. Abramoff, I'm here to escort you to the Speaker's home."

I looked at this well coiffed Filipino and wondered which of us would be killed first as we sauntered down the dark alleys of Manila.

"My people are downstairs," he said to my great relief. "Please come down when you are ready."

As I entered the lobby, I saw the brewer with several commandos, clad in black, bearing what looked like AK-47 rifles. We exited the hotel as a group and marched down the streets of Makati, eliciting hard stares from the passersby. After thirty minutes, we turned onto a residential tree-lined street. The homes were enormous, and most were dark, given the late hour. One house was a bustle of activity, and that's where we were headed.

Jose de Venecia was a short man, with a broad forehead. He was a loyal member of the new political elite which had run the Philippines since the demise of the Marcos regime. It was his turn to be president, and he was working assiduously to make it happen. Little did he realize what strange threats were looming.

When we entered the busy house, a dozen people were milling about. We were greeted by one of Mrs. Marcos's friends from the Philippine Senate, who would be introducing me to the speaker. The speaker's chief of staff asked me to wait in the lounge with several generals from their armed forces. After forty-five minutes of small talk, I was told that the speaker was not even home yet, but still out campaigning. I complained to the chief of staff, but my words fell on deaf ears. Finally, the speaker arrived and our meeting commenced at 1:00 a.m. The Senator introduced me, "Mr. Speaker, I present you Jack Abramoff, the partner of Bill Gates."

I was stunned by this introduction and shot a look at the hapless Senator. De Venecia, who seemed a lifeless carcass before that introduction, sprang to life, "I am honored that Bill Gates is interested in our nation and in my campaign," he beamed.

Recovering as quickly as I could, I began, "Mr. Speaker, I am actually partners with Bill Gates' father at the law firm Preston Gates." I was not really a partner, only a partner-equivalent since I wasn't an attorney, but a clarification didn't seem vital at the moment. "I'm not here to discuss Mr. Gates, however, but rather Imelda Marcos."

His face fell and then puckered with obvious confusion.

"Mrs. Marcos? Are you her attorney?"

"No, I am her friend. And I want to be your friend as well. I come to you with a most vital message, which has the potential to destroy your presidential bid, or save it."

He continued to look confused, "But why does Bill Gates care about Mrs. Marcos?"

"Mr. Speaker, Bill Gates is not the issue. Mrs. Marcos is."

He bid me continue. The hour was late, so I put aside the kind bedside manner of a lobbyist and laid on the doomsday option. His eyes widened. He started to speak, but I continued. I now offered him the second path, the one that would lead him to the presidential palace. He slumped into his chair. I waited for his considered response.

"But why would Bill Gates care about this election?"

I wanted to smack him. "Mr. Speaker, you have the choice before you. I strongly urge you not to underestimate Mrs. Marcos. She means what she says. I am likely to be the lobbyist she engages in the United States to run you guys into the ground. You don't want this fight; trust me. You need to get this deal made. You need to get to the president immediately and get this settled."

He closed his eyes and sat in deep thought for what seemed to be a lifetime. I glanced at the senator. Clearly, no one had briefed him on what I was going to say. He looked like he needed a blood transfusion. Finally, the speaker opened his eyes, "OK. OK. I will speak with the president. Please write this up for me now, and I will see him tomorrow."

I told him I could not write, since it was our Sabbath. He looked at me as if I were a Martian. I assured him that Mrs. Marcos' office would put this on paper in the morning. After staring at me for a moment, we shook hands. "My staff will drive you to your hotel."

I replied that I had to walk there, since we don't ride on our Sabbath. By now, Martians must have seemed more normal to this speaker of the Philippine Congress who had to endure a post-midnight political death threat from some strange American. I bid the speaker good night and returned to the hotel. I collapsed into bed around 3:30 a.m. only to be jarred from my slumber by banging on my door at 6:30 a.m.

"Mr. Abramoff, Mrs. Marcos is waiting for you."

I dragged myself into the bathroom, splashed water on my face, donned my suit, and followed her aide to her residence. As I entered her penthouse, Mrs. Marcos, who was most anxious to hear how the meeting went, greeted me. When I told her the outcome, she was overjoyed. I repeated the speaker's request for a written summary, and she took it from there. I returned to my room to sleep away the rest of the Sabbath. Months later, the Supreme Court reversed the conviction, and Mrs. Marcos remained free. Mission accomplished.

I wished things went so smoothly in my other Pacific Island activities, but the election of Teno changed our CNMI representation dramatically. Perhaps the most important change in our operation was the cessation of congressional trips to the Marianas.

When Froilan ran the government, he spent a fortune to bring Congress to the islands. Teno was worried about how much electricity the television would drain, so bringing Congressmen to Saipan wasn't even on his radar screen. The private sector could barely pay us the reduced fee we negotiated, but even if they had been able to afford the trips, they would have been required to report those expenses, bringing about the kind of bad press most members and staff tried to avoid. One of the grand congressional loopholes we had used to our advantage for years was the provision that when a "government" pays for travel—or, in fact, confers any gift or gratuity—representatives and staff are not required to report those expenses. With Teno's government sitting out the fight in Washington, and the private sector funding our efforts, the trips were not an option.

The inability to bring powerful government officials to the island was just one of several major problems the private sector representation created. In a foreshadowing of my catastrophic collapse less than a decade away, I sent an email to our private sector CNMI clients outlining the strategy we needed to pursue to keep the Marianas free of the takeover. As usual, the strategy paper pulled no punches. I went after Stayman with hammer and tongs, even outlining how we would control his office through congressional legislation and spending restrictions, otherwise known as earmarks.

Most Americans don't realize how many tricks of the trade are built into the federal political system. If a Congressman wished to hamstring a federal agency, he used to be able to write specific language into legislation, which would control how money was spent or not spent. The earmark system had been used for decades not only as a way for lobbyists and special interests to get what they wanted from the government, but also as a way for Congress to check uncontrolled chicanery on the part of the executive branch.

Responding to the public outcry over lobbying abuses and special interest power, Congress eliminated earmarks. But like most "reforms" enacted by politicos, the baby went out with the bathwater—now more than ever, Congress has a much harder time legitimately controlling inappropriate executive branch choices, and the reform did not significantly cut back on systemic corruption. Furthermore, eliminating earmarks did almost nothing to reduce out of control federal spending, but it was an important step in the direction of controlling the special interests.

In the case of the CNMI, we were planning to use the earmarks to stop the Office of Insular Affairs from doing anything which would have harmed the Marianas. Had we followed my memo, we would have debilitated them worse than they could ever have imagined. But the memo was leaked to the press. Led by the Seattle Times, the media unleashed a barrage on the CNMI, the firm, and me, accusing us of "defending a far away garment industry that critics have likened to slavery." The press delighted in having a rare opportunity to peer inside the lobbying world, and dissected our strategies and methods at length. This public examination did more than limit our options to defend the CNMI. It rocked my relationship with Preston Gates.

I was called into Manny Rouvelas' office one afternoon to discuss the representation of the Marianas. The firm was nervous during the entire course of this engagement, and all the more so since a retiring Lloyd Meeds had been slowly withdrawing from firm activities. The articles in the press had sent the firm into a tailspin.

I walked into Manny's modest office. He was normally pale, but that day he looked like a ghost. His sallow appearance was unsettling, but his demeanor was funereal. After a few minutes of rhetorical barbs, Manny delivered the prophetic line which would ring in my ears for more than a decade: "Jack, at the rate you're going, you're either going to be dead, disgraced, or in jail in five years."

I had previously endured a series of snide remarks about my clients from the firm. Though my clients ultimately came to represent more than half of the billings issued from that office, I was often called to task for not having more Fortune 500 clients, and instead representing Pacific islanders, Africans, and Native Americans. This racist attitude offended me, but I consoled myself that it didn't represent the leadership of the firm. Had Lloyd heard those comments, he would have punched the offender.

Manny's oracle cut into me like a dagger, but I never dreamed it would one day come true. I thought I was just doing my job. A client had slipped and let the memo fall into the wrong hands. That memo had been reviewed by at least three attorneys at our firm, one of whom had helped draft it. But none of that seemed to matter. The first seeds of my break from the firm had been planted, and there was no way to pull them out.

Our efforts for the Marianas required constant vigilance. One member of our team was assigned the often-tedious task of monitoring the daily broadcast of congressional debate on CSPAN. At 8:00 p.m. on the night of July 13, 1999, that poor researcher finally saw some action. I was about to leave the office to meet Pam for dinner to celebrate our anniversary when my phone rang.

"Turn on CSPAN!" he announced. "George Miller is offering an amendment on the CNMI."

I flipped on the television in my office and there he was. Miller was in the midst of a speech vilifying the Marianas and about to offer an amendment against our client on an appropriations bill. We needed a representative to get to the floor to oppose him quickly, but it was already late in the evening.

"Call our contacts on the Hill," I shouted to our quickly reassembling lobbying team. My staff sprang into action, working the phones to track down an allied representative. No member could be found. I called Dana Rohrabacher's cell. He answered, shouting above what seemed to be a crowd, and told me he was at a congressional fundraiser—his congressional fundraiser.

I explained the situation. "Miller is on the floor of the House, offering an amendment to hurt the CNMI. We are trying to get someone there to oppose it. The Republican chairman of the Department of Justice Appropriations Subcommittee, Hal Rogers, doesn't know the issues, and might agree to accept it as a friendly amendment."

"I'm on my way," Dana said, hanging up and leaving his own fundraising event to help us. I can only imagine what his donors must have thought, but this was Dana. He was committed to our cause and knew that if he didn't get to the House quickly that cause would go down to defeat. A few minutes later, Dana burst onto the floor, just as Miller was finishing his diatribe against the CNMI. We watched it all on CSPAN.

He began, "Will the gentleman yield?" And then he launched into a spirited defense of the CNMI. He didn't even know the gist of Miller's amendment. He just knew he opposed it. If Miller had just stayed quiet, and let Dana finish, he still might have succeeded since Dana had flown into action before I could explain what was being discussed, and he couldn't speak to the issue at hand. But Miller was as vehement in his hatred of the CNMI as we were ardent in our support, and he couldn't abide by Dana's ferocious assault. Miller, trying to throw him off course, let Dana know the precise nature of the amendment. That was all Dana, a brilliant tactician, superb orator, and master speechwriter needed. Within minutes, Rohrabacher tore Miller's amendment to pieces.

While the subcommittee chairman was still wondering how this late night session had taken such an unexpected turn, more CNMI defenders rushed to the House chamber. Ralph Hall, then a conservative Democratic congressman from Texas, bounded to the microphone. Hall quickly offered a "friendly" amendment—another congressional trick—to Miller's amendment, gutting it, and the CNMI was saved.

Miller's stealth assault on the floor of the House was not the only threat to the Marianas. In fact, the battle continued at a fevered pitch. The opponents in the House and Senate proceeded to schedule a series of congressional hearings, hoping to set the stage for a new legislative attack. Although to the outside world congressional hearings appear to be Congress doing the business of the people, most of the time, nothing could be further from the truth.

When someone is called before a congressional hearing, unless that person is cooperating with the committee, trouble will ensue, especially when the hearing is designed to attack. Lobbyists with great influence on certain representatives can actually cause the advent of a congressional hearing, and by doing so, utterly destroy whomever their client wishes to be destroyed. The cost of preparing for a hearing could easily exceed one million dollars. As I would come to discover personally in the not too distant future, hearings incur massive legal fees, as one's attorneys must review every document which could shed unfavorable light on the witness. Many parties—including all of my clients—would prepare for hearings by spending days with their lawyers fielding mock questions. These costs add up. Worse than the costs, when a party is summoned to appear before a congressional committee, their entire life stops. They lose sleep. They worry incessantly about what they say. If they perjure themselves—and they will certainly be presented with many opportunities to do so in the course of their hearing—they could wind up in prison. With little chance of presenting their case in a balanced forum, the target of the hearing almost invariably leaves with a destroyed reputation.

When the Senate Natural Resources Committee, the committee with jurisdiction over the CNMI, announced they would hold CNMI hearings prior to the summer recess, I knew trouble would ensue. We tried to get the hearing delayed until the fall, to buy more time to build our support against the latest efforts to destroy the Marianas.

As winter turned to spring, our team hit the Hill. We were relentless in pushing off the hearing. We didn't need Congress recessing in the summer with horrific images of the CNMI engraved in their minds. Murkowski's new legislative threat was a bill that would raise the minimum wage in the Marianas. We knew that Senator Don Nickles of Oklahoma—a fierce opponent of the minimum wage—would be an ally. Since he was also the Majority Whip of the Senate, second only to the Republican Majority Leader, we now had a powerful ally against the Senate takeover effort. Nickles' office besieged Murkowski.

Eventually, the Senator from Alaska couldn't withstand the leadership pressure and agreed to postpone his Senate hearing to the fall. By the time fall would arrive, we had every expectation we could kill the hearing, the bill, and any other attempt to harm our client.

For years, we had assumed that the Office of Insular Affairs at the Interior Department was a cohesive anti-CNMI monolith, dedicated to destroying our client and our firm.

One day, I received an anonymous call which led me to think otherwise.

"Mr. Abramoff, I work at the OIA and I have something you need to know. Our office is committing multiple violations of the Hatch Act and has numerous other civil service laws with blatant political attacks on Republican supporters of the CNMI. It's all in the computers here."

Click.

Knowing that no prank caller would have this kind of information on the CNMI and OIA, I immediately contacted Tony Rudy, the deputy Chief of Staff for Tom DeLay. Rudy was not only one of the most brilliant staffers on the Hill, but was a frequent traveler to the CNMI, and a complete supporter. He had started his career with Congressman Dana Rohrabacher, and then moved to DeLay's office while Buckham was Chief of Staff. He was by far our strongest ally in that office. Tony was also my best friend among the staff on the Hill. We played golf several times a week, and greatly enjoyed each other's company.

Tony clarified that the phone tip was not enough to pursue an investigation. There had to be independent confirmation of illegal activity at the OIA. Once we had that, the committee of jurisdiction—in this case the Resources Committee, chaired by CNMI ally Don Young from Alaska—could subpoena the computers and see what was really happening. To get such a confirmation, we would have to be creative.

The spring and early summer was budget time on the Hill. Most federal government agencies felt shortchanged by the Republican Congress and would do anything to appeal for more funding, but few if any had the contacts to meet directly with the representatives and staff in charge of appropriating funds. We decided the best approach to uncovering the illegalities at OIA was to offer one of the career staff a chance to present their case for increased funding and, during the discussion, try to get him to spill the beans on the illegal activities.

The staff member arrived at the appointed hour to push for more OIA funding. He was not meeting with an appropriator, though. Unbeknownst to him, he was meeting with an investigator from the Resources Committee. After hearing the case for additional funding, the investigator casually commented that getting more OIA funds would be easier if it weren't for all the political shenanigans emanating from their office. Laughing, he said he felt badly for the OIA budget staffer having to deal with such nonsense, especially since he was clearly a more model federal employee. The OIA staffer queried whether it was widely known what was going on at his office, and the investigator affirmed that everyone knew about it and thought it was silly and hilarious. That opened the floodgates. By the time the staffer was done regaling his new friend the investigator with stories about how Stayman and OIA Communications Director David North were attacking Republican representatives, the investigator had enough to issue a Committee subpoena for all computers at the OIA.

I sat back and watched this unfold, hoping that a little offense now might derail the severe attacks coming that fall. What I didn't realize was that this unleashed tempest would completely change the dynamic of the CNMI fight for almost a decade.

According to reports eventually issued by the Resources Committee, when the subpoenas were being delivered, the staff at OIA started to erase their hard drives. Being behind the times in software development, that staff didn't realize that Young's team could recapture everything they deleted, even recovering the precise time the files were destroyed. Young's committee was quickly able to reimage the erased hard drives and uncover an invidious campaign to impugn the reputations of all who might defend the CNMI—including DeLay, Armey, Rohrabacher, and several other Congressmen. They also uncovered efforts to destroy Willie Tan, Preston Gates and me.

The nasty articles resulting from my leaked strategy memos all seemed to have originated in the OIA. Tan was issued a letter from Chairman Young setting forth the basis by which he was entitled to sue the OIA and its employees. He never did. I received the same letter, but let it pass. It was enough for me that the main source of CNMI attacks was thrown into turmoil.

There were hearings in the Congress that fall, but they were about the OIA and its scandal. Member after member railed against this unprecedented abuse of power, and the nefarious ways in which this branch of government, charged with helping the Americans in the Marianas, instead used taxpayer funds to destroy them. The Committee issued a criminal referral to the Department of Justice noting clear examples of OIA employees' illegal activities. The referral went into the Clinton Administration black hole, never to emerge. Years later, while meeting with the Department of Justice and investigators from the Interior Department, I asked whatever happened to that referral. My question was met with a deafening and uncomfortable silence.

The OIA, the hostile unions and even George Miller were finally on the run. Their skullduggery was revealed. Of course, these revelations were ignored almost completely by the *Washington Post*, a key enabler in the disinformation campaign to destroy the Marianas. They were covered extensively by the then widely-read Washington Times. The enemy was on its back, but continued to launch missiles anyway. They kept us busy, but we kept winning. Their day would come, however. They just had to await my demise.

We continued to work for the private sector companies in the CNMI, though the fees they paid didn't come close to matching the amount of time we spent winning their battles. Each week, the negative cost of this effort rose and added to the strain at the firm. I tried to keep my team on course, reminding them that if the opposition won even once, it would destroy years of work. Still, time was money, and our time was not being adequately compensated.

As things continued their downward spiral, Ben Fitial offered to come to our rescue. Frustrated with developments in the CNMI, Fitial thought groveling to Stayman was a mistake. He loved Teno, but he wasn't pleased that we had not been reengaged in the fight to protect the islands. Plus, it upset him that Teno was doing almost nothing to start new business opportunities in the CNMI.

His plan was a bold one, to say the least. He would return to politics, run for the legislature, and reclaim the speakership of the House. Once he was speaker, he would have real influence, and we would be re-hired. We did all we could to support him, and in 1999, Ben won his seat in the legislative elections. But the Republicans decided to give the Speakership to Heinz Hofschneider, a local politician more like Teno and Babauta than Ben or Froilan. Ben responded by bolting the party and forming a new one, the Covenant Party.

With support lined up among Republican and Democrat members of the legislature, Ben was just a few votes short of winning the election for speaker in January 2000. In Washington, we had done all we could do to promote him, including raising money and getting members of Congress to cut taped messages in support of his candidacy. But that wasn't enough.

The election came down to the votes of the delegates from the less populated islands of Tinian and Rota. Tinian was where, during World War II, the U.S. forces launched thousands of bombers to attack Japan, including the Enola Gay that dropped the atomic bomb. The island had been neglected since the war and needed some help to upgrade its airport. Rota is the southernmost island in the CNMI chain and had needed improvements to its port for years. Ben promised the legislators from Tinian and Rota that, if he were elected speaker, he would make sure they received funds to fix these problems. By "he," of course, he meant Preston Gates. Ed Buckham knew that Tom DeLay was getting tired of battling for the

CNMI while the governor sat frozen in fear. Having Ben as Speaker would counterbalance Teno. With that in mind, Ed dispatched several staffers from his office, including Mike Scanlon, his communications director and my future partner (and co-defendant), to look into the infrastructure needs on the islands and make sure Ben got the votes he needed.

The first time I met Mike, I liked him. He was gregarious, smart and willing to think outside the box. Most staffers on Capitol Hill are cautious, or at least feign caution. Not Mike Scanlon. He was goal oriented and wouldn't take "no" for an answer. Mike was used to dealing with lobbyists who resembled Hill staff—cautious and timid. He loved that I was the opposite. Of course, in retrospect, we were both disserved by our immature bravado, but in those days caution was not on the list of desired virtues. We would ultimately pay a high price for our swagger.

Mike was no stranger to island politics. In late October 1998, at our request, he had insinuated himself into the Guam governor's race, causing a major furor in attacking the incumbent Democratic governor, and, after only one radio interview, pumping up the Republican challenger's poll numbers enough to make the race a dead heat. The mission to Tinian and Rota was fairly simple. Visit the islands, see the projects, and commit to consider funding. Scanlon brought along Neil Volz, the chief of staff for Congressman Bob Ney of Ohio, and Brett Loper, an appropriations staffer from DeLay's office. To make sure things went according to plan, Ed Buckham also travelled to Saipan, but laid low.

In short order, the legislators were convinced that we could help them, and Ben became Speaker. Immediately, our team secured the funding to conduct studies about the Tinian and Rota infrastructure projects. As soon as Ben was installed as Speaker of the Legislature in January 2000, he got Teno to retain our firm.

For the next few years, the OIA was reeling from the scandal, so they were out of the fight. George Miller redoubled his efforts in the House, but thanks to our vigilance, our allies blocked his every move. The Senate challenged us relentlessly. Murkowski and his staff continued to press for a takeover of immigration, but we parried every thrust.

In January 2001, the Republicans retook the White House, and we felt close to a final victory. Unfortunately, it didn't take the Bush administration long to create trouble for the Marianas. A draft Department of Justice letter pushed for federalization of immigration. We swung into action, calling on many members of the Administration who had enjoyed our heyday trips to the CNMI. The draft letter was withdrawn, and all seemed well.

Then Ben announced his candidacy for governor, only to be opposed by Juan Babauta. Incredibly, the people of the Marianas opted to elevate Babauta to the governorship, and when his term began in January of 2002, our representation ended.

I had to watch what followed from the sidelines.

Initially the Republicans still ran the Congress, and we had enough allies in the Administration to prevent a return to the wars of the Clinton years. The CNMI would survive Babauta's ineffectual term and live to see Ben Fitial elected as Governor in 2005. By 2006, the Democrats had taken control of the Congress, and the CNMI's days were numbered. The Democrats passed their long-desired takeover legislation as part of a federal minimum wage increase in 2007. For almost a decade, we stood between the peoples of the Northern Marianas and the hostile bureaucrats and Congressmen bent on their destruction. Now, the enemy had won. The garment industry folded quickly, and the CNMI economy tanked.

# 9

# IN BAD COMPANY

When I first joined Preston Gates, I insisted my work with the firm require no more than half my time. Back then, I was under the delusion that I might continue making films and wanted to be sure I had the time to do so. Of course, once I got involved with representing CNMI and the tribes, there wasn't much time for anything outside of my life as a lobbyist, and I bid adieu to the movie business.

My life was rich and fulfilling. I had meaningful, challenging, invigorating work, a wife I adored, and five wonderful children—Levi, Alex, Daniel, Livia, and Sarah. As they grew, we enrolled them in the various Orthodox Jewish schools in our hometown of Silver Spring, Maryland. As our eldest son started elementary school, however, the local Jewish community decided it was time to create a new school for grades K through 6, and somehow I wound up leading the effort—notwithstanding my lack of skills, knowledge, or experience. Fortunately, the headmaster of the new school, Rabbi Yitzchak Charner, had more than enough skill, knowledge, and experience, and the Torah School of Greater Washington survived and thrived. Over the next several years, I began my passionate involvement with my children's schools, serving as president, raising money, and generally supporting the professional educators in their missions.

As Levi entered high school, I was elevated to president of the local Orthodox Jewish Yeshiva High School, but felt that there was something missing and stubbornly started yet another school—Eshkol Academy. This school would offer superior Jewish learning combined with the finest secular preparatory education, and a first-rate sports program. Since ice hockey had replaced football as our family's preferred sport, Eshkol would field the world's only Orthodox Jewish high school ice hockey team. As usual, in my mind, the sky was the limit. And, as usual, reaching the goal was more difficult, expensive, and time consuming than I could possibly have imagined.

As much as I loved my involvement with my children's schools, I still had a day job. I continued to build my team at Preston Gates, trying to add the most aggressive and brightest people I could find on Capitol Hill. No one was more aggressive than Mike Scanlon. He had already proved his worth with the Guam governor's race and Fitial speaker campaign, and his contacts on the Hill were quite extensive. He tended to go overboard at times, but I loved that about him. As soon as he completed his service in DeLay's office, I hired him. I needed someone with his press contacts, and with his moxie.

As soon as he arrived at Preston Gates, Mike started to irritate the firm. While I loved his over-the-top manner, the leadership of the firm worried he was out of control. They tried to bring him into various representations, but his solutions to their dilemmas made them squirm. I wanted to propose similar solutions at times, but had the discipline to keep them to myself. Mike didn't seem to care. While I desired my team to get along with the rest of the firm, with Mike I didn't press the matter. His aggression was just what we needed for the battles to save the tribes, and our other clients were benefiting from his no-holds-barred approach. So what if they were unlikely to invite him to the firm Christmas party? I got Mike's sense of humor, even if others didn't. Once, when I pointed out that he made a typographical error in an email—typing "can" instead of "can't", he replied: "Correct my one legged friend [I had just suffered through knee surgery]—a typo indeed. I believe that typos set me apart from the rest of the pople (sic) in my line of work. The typos say 'Hey—Im so good I can make typos anytime I want' Im too cool for school." Classic Mike Scanlon. To me, it was funny. To others, it was proof that he was some evil being. I'm not sure either of us was right.

One rainy day in November 1996, I turned the car radio to a classical station on my way to the office. As the last strains of Bruckner's powerful 8th Symphony faded, my head was swimming with ideas about how to combat the latest attempt to tax the tribes, the Istook Amendment. Suddenly, a commercial brought me out of my haze. A familiar voice filled the airwaves, "I'm Adam Kidan, president of Dial-A-Mattress. 1-800-MAT-TRESS. Leave the last 'S' off for savings."

Adam Kidan? Could it be the same Adam Kidan who worked for me in the 1980s? I had lost touch with him for almost twenty years, and now here he was on the radio. I grabbed my cell phone and called 1-800-MAT-TRESS. Reuniting with old pals from my college Republican days was a lot of fun for me, but I didn't get many chances to do so.

Adam wasn't the most popular guy during our College Republican years, and in fact there were a few folks who really disliked him, but I found him to be a charming companion. Once we reconnected, Pam and I invited him to the house for dinner. Almost all our dinner meals at home which included guests revolved around the Sabbath or Jewish holidays. We invited Adam to join us during the holiday of Sukkos. Known also by its English name, the Feast of Tabernacles, Sukkos is a commemoration of the exodus from Egypt and the sojourning in the desert by the Children of Israel. Our celebration of this holiday finds us eating our meals in a thatched booth, located outdoors. Adam was not our only guest that evening, as we also had invited Professor Richard Gordon, with whom I had remained in close contact and for whom I became a regular lecturer in the Entertainment Law Seminar I had once attended at Georgetown Law Center. Adam was delighted to reunite with Pam and me, and took particular interest in our children, whose ages then ranged from two to eight years. In our college Republican days, Adam was awkward and seemed not to have his act together. The new Adam was witty, polished and even dressed with style. Adam regaled us with stories of his success in the mattress business, and mentioned that he was about to sell his interest for a major, "eight figure" score. I was delighted for him. He was, it seemed, immensely successful.

Eventually, Adam pitched me about getting involved together in deals, and I was thrilled. I figured that Adam's track record for success in business was solid and that we would do well together. So when Adam proposed

I join him in his venture to build a ferry service between Washington, Maryland, and Virginia, I jumped at the opportunity. But a few weeks later, an even bigger opportunity came along.

Because I came to lobbying from the business world, and not from either the Hill or another law firm, the partners and associates at Preston Gates thought I was far more astute about business than I actually was. They would constantly pitch me business ideas, most of which were hare-brained and easily dismissed. But when Art Dimopolous, a hard charging associate at the firm, told me he had a client who owned a cruise casino company in Florida—Sancruz Casinos—and that the client needed to sell his operations, it felt like a winner. I immediately thought of Adam and our quest to find a huge business to do together.

Kidan was ecstatic about the deal from the start. I trusted his capacity to analyze the finances better than mine, since he had already been running a major company. Art put Adam in touch with the client, Gus Boulis, and the two worked closely to get the deal done. Adam and I agreed that we would be equal partners, and split the costs of acquisition, which he estimated to be around $400,000. I eagerly provided Adam with my check for $200,000, and we were off and running. Adam predicted we could get the deal negoti-ated and that he would be able to secure the financing for the project, all in a matter of weeks. We were poised to make a killing, we thought, confident we could expand the company and build an industry giant.

Kidan handled all negotiations with Boulis. At first, things went well, but it was taking more time to close the deal than we had expected. Finally, Kidan revealed that Boulis was being stubborn and demanding a serious continuing ownership stake in the company, even though he was being paid full price for his shares. Kidan asked if there was anything we could do to scare him off this demand, so we could close the deal.

My solution was to bring in my most aggressive thinker: Mike Scanlon. Mike and I put our heads together and decided that Mike would ask Congressman Bob Ney to submit some harsh language about Boulis into the Congressional Record. We would leak this information to Dimo-polous, who would be sure to mention it to his client.

For all intents and purposes, no one reads the Congressional Record. It's an oppressively boring chronicle of pretentious congressional speeches. Thousands of pages are added to it every day. More people read the phone book. Still, it's an old lobbyist trick to tuck something into the Record, to impress a client who doesn't know any better. Usually, the insertion is in praise of some mundane action, or in recognition of an important event, like Anteater's Day, or Aunt Tilly's seventy-third birthday. For our purposes, it was ideal. We could pressure Boulis by making him think Congress was on his case. He would yield on his unreasonable demand, and the deal could close. It would only be a matter of weeks before we had control of the company and were on our way to the Forbes 400 list. Although I had decided that most of my shares would go to fund the educational institutions I was supporting, the leftovers alone were going to be substantial.

Soon, the weeks needed to close the deal stretched to months, and the $200,000 Adam requested from me to get the deal closed soon soared to almost $1 million.

With each request for funds from Kidan, I was told that he was matching the contribution and that we were heading closer and closer to conclusion. It didn't take long to deplete my bank account, and soon, in classic "good money chases bad," I was stupidly sending Adam the money I needed to survive. Pressure mounted on me and as we headed into the summer of 2000, I was under extreme financial duress.

My frantic daily calls and emails were met with calm fortitude on the part of Kidan. He was confident all would be well. I had put my neck into a financial noose, and the strain was wearing on me. I pressed Kidan to get the deal done at almost all costs, just to get me whole. I lost focus. In the midst of my normal quotient of hundreds of daily emails, I received missives from Kidan with various stratagems to get the deal done. Buried in one was a time bomb that would one day come back to explode.

The Congressional Record ploy worked, and Boulis was ready to sell. Kidan had found financing from Wells Fargo's Foothill Capital. They required the buyers—Kidan and me—to put up $23 million in equity, along with the approximately $60 million they were going to be contributing, and the millions which Boulis would finance. At the outset, I assumed Kidan would cover this requirement, since I certainly had no resources of this nature. In fact, I had no money of any kind, since it was all tied up in the acquisition costs, or so I was led to believe.

Adam had told me that he made an "eight figure" sum on the sale of

Dial-A-Mattress stake, so if need be, he could cover the $23 million. But first he wanted to try to raise these funds from a third party investor. I saw nothing wrong with this, and even tried to help him find someone, though no interest materialized. Finally, Kidan mentioned in an email that he might be able to get Boulis to take back a note for this requirement. I queried whether this would be a problem with the bank, but otherwise let it drop.

Months passed, and Kidan continued to pursue the deal. I was breaking under the financial strain of having provided my partner with nearly a million dollars and was fixated on getting this deal closed. As we entered September 2000, I was in serious financial jeopardy. Not only would my mortgage payments start to be difficult, but I might not even be being able even to pay for my son Levi's modest Bar Mitzvah celebration.

Kidan tried to keep me calm, predicting an imminent closing of the deal. By then, though, I just wanted my money back. I had lost all interest in what I thought would be a deal that would never close. Finally, ten months after it had all started, Kidan told me that the closing would take place over the course of four or five days the next week in New York City. Knowing I couldn't break away from Washington during the fall legislative session for that long, he offered me the chance to sign the signature pages of the evolving agreements in blank, so the deal wouldn't be delayed. In my frenzy to get my funds back and meet my monthly mortgage and household expenses, I agreed.

He faxed the various pages to me at my home, and I signed and returned them. Included among those many signature pages was one page in particular that troubled me—an affirmation that the equity funds were paid to Gus Boulis. There were three signature lines on that page: Boulis, Kidan, and me. I asked Adam about this one, and he indicated that my signature was required since I was to be a principal owner of the company. He had used the same rationale when he asked me to join him in personally guaranteeing the loans from Foothill and Boulis. Since both Kidan and Boulis had signed, I figured it was not a problem for me to do so as well.

With that signature, I committed bank fraud. Kidan had never paid Boulis the equity money. That document, and several others, were fabrications created by Kidan.

In fact, Kidan and Boulis had made a side agreement for payment later, backed by personal notes from Kidan. Oddly, the attorneys representing Foothill notarized them. Boulis agreed in order to receive the funding from Foothill. I read later that he had obligations to pay outstanding loans and that, as much as the delay in closing was hurting me, it was killing him.

Finally, the deal closed. Relieved, I assumed I would soon get my money back, and everything would go back to normal. But after the late September closing, Kidan called to say that the bank hadn't approved the return of my pre-closing expenses. I was furious. This was the only reason I was still in this deal, and I needed those funds. As usual, Kidan had a solution: he would cash flow the money to me by paying my expenses. Suddenly, checks from Suncruz were covering everything from my son's bar mitzvah dinner to my overextended credit card bill. I knew at the time that none of this was close to proper, but I figured I would make it up before anything blew up. I never got that chance.

Boulis had signed the closing papers in a hurry, so he could rush home to Greece to bury his just-deceased father. Within a few days of the final closing, and with Boulis in Europe, Kidan launched an assault on him in the press. I found out about this from Mike, whom Adam had recruited to do public relations for the company. Mike thought Adam was crazy to be attacking Boulis, but was not in a position to stop him. Neither was I. When I called to ask him why he would antagonize the man who not only sold us the company, but held a huge second mortgage on it, Adam was short with me, "Jack," he said, "Boulis is bad news, and our only chance to survive in the Florida market is to separate from him publicly."

Naturally, Boulis didn't take this well. Upon his return, he locked horns with Kidan. The verbal brawling reached a fever pitch and started to impact morale in the company. One day, sitting in my Washington office, I received a phone call from Gus Boulis.

"Adam Kidan is destroying the company I have built, and you need to come here to mediate between us or there will be a disaster."

I had no interest in becoming involved in the company. My only role in Suncruz was to help with the expansion into new markets and to ensure that the company didn't suffer political setbacks in the United States. I was suited for those jobs. I didn't know how to operate a casino cruise line any more than I knew how to operate a tugboat.

Still, I flew to Florida that Sunday evening and Kidan picked me up at the airport. His relationship with Gus had taken a more ominous turn, and he expressed a fear for his life. I listened with great concern, and told him he should inform the authorities and beef up security. I was truly worried about my friend.

As we arrived at the office in Fort Lauderdale, Gus and his staff were waiting. I met for several hours with them, and heard a litany of complaints against Kidan's management of the company. One grievance stood out among the rest. In the midst of an emotional harangue against Kidan, Gus roared that Kidan hadn't paid him the $23 million equity due to him. I had not remembered, at that time, the email from that last summer briefly mentioning the idea for Gus to take back notes, nor was I privy to most of the machinations of the closing in New York. I immediately replied to Gus that I had seen the document which Kidan and he had signed affirming this payment. What was he talking about?

Gus didn't respond to my challenge, but his aid Joan Wagner did.

"There was no such document."

I stared incredulously. Could I have actually misremembered this? As soon as that meeting broke, I bounded into Kidan's office.

"Adam, Gus says we didn't pay the $23 million…"

Before I could finish my sentence, Kidan launched into a tirade. "He owes us. We don't owe him. Look at this list of repairs we have had to make to the boats. It totals far more than the $23 million he claims we owe."

I was nonplussed. I figured the only thing I could possibly accomplish during this visit was to help craft a way to move forward amicably. All parties agreed to let a management committee run the company, where I would be the tie-breaking vote. Now I was doing exactly what I didn't want to do—running the company. But no more than a week later, things went from bad to worse. Adam called me late one night to tell me Gus had physically attacked him, by leaping over a table and trying to plunge a pencil into his neck. I was horrified and, in the morning, called Joan Wagner, who confirmed the attack.

I told Joan I couldn't be involved with people who resort to violence and withdrew from the management committee. As far as I was concerned, Adam could run the company. I wanted no part of this. My job was to create expansion opportunities for the company and that's what I was doing. Using my connections overseas, Suncruz was perched to open new markets in Malaysia, Hong Kong, Europe, India, and the CNMI. It was during one of our trips overseas to secure these opportunities, in February 2001, that we received a shocking phone call. Gus Boulis had been gunned down in Miami. Suddenly scenes from The Godfather and every other mob movie were swimming in my head.

Upon my return to the United States, Kidan and Boulis' estate, now being directed by Joan Wagner, were already clashing. In addition to everything else, Kidan hadn't been keeping payments current on the financing Boulis had provided for the purchase. The estate threatened foreclose. Suncruz was sinking.

So far, I had successfully kept my participation in Suncruz separate from my life in Washington, but Gus' murder changed that. Though I was nowhere near the public figure I would become with the collapse of my lobbying career, I was the most public figure involved in this mess, and to the Washington press corps, I was already a powerhouse, frequently mentioned in the *Washington Post, New York Times*, and *Wall Street Journal* as one of the nation's leading lobbyists. Now headlines about the murder would invariably include my name, and all of a sudden the venture that had so much promise was dragging down my entire career. I had to get out.

Just when it seemed things couldn't possibly get worse, I received an ominous invitation to meet with Tom DeLay in the Capitol. Tom didn't usually summon me to his office, and none of his staff knew what he wanted to discuss. I was crestfallen when, within the first few moments of our meeting, he brought up Suncruz.

"Jack, what in the world are you doing with this casino company? Do you have any idea what kind of people are involved in that business? I know we don't agree on the morality of gambling, but this is too much. If you don't get out of this, I cannot have any association with you."

I apologized to Tom for any embarrassment this episode might have caused him. He was right, and I had reached the same conclusion as soon as I heard about Boulis' murder. Nothing was worth this.

I instructed my attorneys to sell my interest in Suncruz to the Boulis estate for one dollar, tipping control of the company to them. I wanted off the personal guarantees for the financing and to get out of this business once and for all.

When I called Kidan to tell him my decision, he was calm, as usual. Immediately, he threw the company into bankruptcy to prevent the estate from taking over. The struggle lasted for months, and the company suffered. Eventually, Kidan relented after being promised a cash payout, and the company fell into the hands of a trustee, who ran the company into the ground. Eventually, the trustee sold Suncruz—a once thriving company we bought for $150 million—to an insider for $30 million . This action created a debt to Foothill and their new partner Citadel Capital and caused me no end of difficulties.

When the company was put into bankruptcy by Kidan, a legal process started which forced Kidan to be deposed under oath. I was shocked to read his admission that all along he was defrauding me. As I struggled mightily to make my contribution to the acquisition costs, he was contributing nothing. His constant affirmations that he was putting in his share, and that I needed to do the same, led me to financial strain which almost broke me. But his treachery did not end with not contributing his fair share. He was reported to be living off the money I was contributing, instead of using it for the purpose of acquiring the company. In early October 2001, with the knowledge that he might have been misappropriating our funds, I exchanged a series of emails with Kidan, asking for the books and ledgers for the company. At first he pretended not to know what my request meant and then promised to get them. They never arrived. There was more.

At my urging, Adam had hired my good friend Ben Waldman to be president of the company—but then froze Ben out of virtually every transaction. My concerns to Adam were always met with solid reasons for his approach. Ben would call me to voice concerns about Adam's leadership, but then I would hear from Adam on an another matter and he would move the conversation to the issue Ben and I had discussed, adding in a convincing rebuttal of Ben's earlier comments. My confidence in Ben flagged, as Adam's presentation was flawless. Only later did I find out that Adam had placed an eavesdropping device in Ben's office and a tap on his phone. He was listening to all Ben's communications, especially with me, and calling me as soon as he could to rebut whatever issues Ben raised. After a severe rain storm, the roof at the Suncruz office leaked, and workmen came to Ben's office to inspect the ceiling. As they repaired the damage, the listening device fell to the floor. Ben queried the Suncruz staff member in charge of electronics and he admitted that Adam had ordered the bug on his phones and office.

With the bankruptcy, Adam cut his best deal and fled. I was left to repay the personal guarantees we had made to the bank. I settled by ceding to them my retirement accounts, the money we would need to live in our senior years, but at least I was out of Suncruz. Or so I thought.

I never liked to take on elements of the conservative coalition, even when we disagreed, but it happened from time to time. One of my top clients for years was a company called Primedia, the owners of a television network called Channel One, which wired middle schools and high schools with televisions in every classroom in exchange for the school committing to air their daily twelve-minute news broadcast. I loved the public-private partnership they were fostering, and the broadcasts were patriotic and often promoted conservative core values. But the company was under assault from a coalition of the left and right. The left was led by Ralph Nader, the right by Phyllis Schlafly. Like most who knew her, I thought Phyllis was brilliant, but I felt she was wrong here.

My challenge was to smash the efforts to destroy Channel One, without harming Schlafly. Nader was a different story. For years as chairman of the College Republicans, I had directed efforts against his on-campus organization called Public Interest Research Groups (PIRGs). They had set up a mandatory fee structure through friendly student government leaders whereby they were allowed to drain money from each student on campus, without regard to that student's preference. We fought them for years. Eventually, the fee was declared unconstitutional.

For Channel One, we built a congressional coalition to protect the company and their mission, and I threw as many barbs Nader's way as possible. I was repaid in kind when one of his frustrated activists against Channel One dubbed me "Casino Jack." The attacks always seemed to get personal in politics, but I didn't much care at that point. In fact, my team joked that we should find some jurisdiction we could rename CasinoJackistan, and then sign them up as a client. Little did I realize that one day this epithet would be resurrected by detractors in the press and serve as the title for both a feature documentary film and a motion picture drama about my life.

They may have called me Casino Jack, but I certainly wasn't the only person tied to gambling in Washington. Whether it was poker, slots, horses, bridge, friendly golf bets, or fantasy football, there was a ton of gambling going on in D.C., especially on Capitol Hill. Given how many Americans engage in some form of gambling, one would think the casino industry ruled Congress, but this has never been the case. There is a deep-seated congressional guilt when it comes to gambling, and this leads to intense fighting over these issues.

One of the most explosive battles on the subject in recent years started when Congressman Bob Goodlatte of Virginia introduced a bill that would have outlawed Internet gambling. The bill was making rapid progress through the Republican controlled Congress, backed by religious conservatives. So when I was approached for help by elottery.com, a company which set up Internet lotteries for states and municipalities, I knew I would be up against a personal challenge as much as a professional one. In order to win, I would have to go into the ring against my friends on the right.

Though there were already scores of top lobbyists representing the various on-line gambling websites, they had failed. The bill was moving. It was time to try something different. My reputation saving tribal gaming enterprises preceded me, and the other lobbyists bristled at our rough and tumble style, but we weren't out to win a popularity contest. We were out to stop a bill.

The other lobbyists felt they could defeat the Internet gaming ban by pleading with Congress to respect Internet freedom of speech. They argued that Congress should regulate and tax Internet gambling, not ban it. Clearly, they didn't understand that the social conservatives who were driving this issue had no more interest in regulating and taxing Internet gambling than they did in regulating and taxing prostitution.

After analyzing the vote count in the House, I knew we needed a special maneuver to stop this bill. I found the opening in the language of the legislation itself, which provided for the protection of pari-mutuel betting, including the use of the wires, for horse and dog racing. This was the requirement of the senators from horse country, particularly Kentucky, who promised to filibuster the bill if that key industry suffered. I now had my hook.

How could a bill to ban gaming on the Internet carve out a significant part of the gambling industry as an exception? The beauty of this provision was that it actually did expand Internet gambling. It wasn't just some artifice we had concocted in our office.

Our team set out to warn anti-gambling Congressmen of this loophole. Immediately, we conjured up images of young children sitting on their computers in their homes, placing bets on the races. What had until then been the murky, gray area of Internet pari-mutuel betting now became perfectly legal, inviting far more Internet gambling than the current status quo.

I knew that if I convinced the House Republicans to eliminate this exception, the bill would be unable to survive the horse state filibusters in the Senate. If the racing exemption remained, then Congress would be voting for a bill which would increase —not eliminate—Internet gambling. The proponents of the bill would be left to argue that half a loaf of bread was better than none at all. This may be true in real life, but not necessarily in legislating. A compromise on this bill, we argued, would mean millions of children gambling for the first time in their lives.

Our opponents fell into our trap. They posited that the bill in no way legalized gambling and that we were being mendacious. I responded with a prop, a political poster reminiscent of my College Republican and *Red Scorpion* days. Posters were not used in the lobbying world back then, but I thought they could convey our message better than anything we could say. With only an hour to get something produced, we came up with a simple poster alluding to the lies which pervade the system of government we so love:

**THREE WASHINGTON WHOPPERS:**
"THE ERA OF BIG GOVERNMENT IS OVER"
"I NEVER HAD SEXUAL RELATIONS WITH THAT WOMAN"
"THE INTERNET GAMBLING PROHIBITION ACT WILL
    BAN GAMBLING ON THE INTERNET"

To emphasize the point, the poster then revealed the precise language in the bill exempting horse and dog racing from the ban.

Our team distributed the visually arresting white-on-black posters throughout the Hill. They became an instant collectible. Scores of congressional office walls bore our poster, and simultaneously our lobbyists hit office after office to secure support to defeat the bill. We also reached out to those social conservative groups who were not part of the inner circle pushing this legislation, chief among them the Traditional Values Coalition, headed by the Reverend Lou Sheldon.

Sheldon and his organization immediately understood that the bill was flawed, and they pushed the House leadership and others to include horse and dog tracks in the ban. But leadership was hesitant to take on the representative representing horse country districts, including Anne Northrup, a loyal member of the Republican caucus in the House in a marginally Republican Kentucky congressional seat. She was constantly a target of the Democrats, and the House Leadership was reticent to do anything which might cause her to lose her seat. The way we were reframing this issue was starting to cause congressional Republicans a great deal of angst.

Goodlatte noticed the shift in support, but played right into our hands. The rules of the House of Representatives permit the leadership to immediately bring to the floor a non-controversial bill under what are known as the suspension rules. In essence, the normal House rules are suspended while a bill is brought for an immediate vote. Usually, suspension bills are put through the House of Representatives unchallenged, but when there is a challenge, any representative who has opted to use the suspension route must now obtain a two-thirds majority to pass his legislation.

By our vote count, we were twenty-eight votes behind when Goodlatte made the key mistake of bringing his bill to the floor on suspension. Keeping an accurate vote count is one of the hardest but most important aspects of a congressional legislative fight. Ours was spot on. Goodlatte's vote count was off by a mile. He thought he had more than two-thirds support in the House. That might have been true before we entered the fray, but now the gap was closing. As soon as he brought the measure to the floor, our allies objected, automatically forcing his bill to a floor vote. He probably still had a majority of support, but he didn't have a two-thirds majority. We defeated him and the Internet gambling ban was, it seemed, thrust into the abyss.

But Goodlatte didn't give up. He resuscitated the bill and used his power to reposition for another shot. Now he was demanding a floor vote according to the regular rules, where he would win with his slight majority. He wasn't going to make the same mistake twice.

We needed a new approach and, since almost everyone knew by now that he had a majority, our options were dwindling. The only way we could preserve our client's position was to push the House leadership to quash the bill. Of course, getting them to do so was no easy task. This legislation had a majority of Republican members supporting it, and was not inconsistent with Republican philosophy. Moreover, the constantly overlooked social conservative movement made this their cause célèbre, and the leadership wanted to throw them a legislative bone if possible.

It was time for me to bring in my old friend Ralph Reed. In the 1980s, when Ralph worked for me at the College Republicans, he was a hard charging, fairly typical young libertine politico. Living on my sofa and eating pasta every night for dinner, Ralph was as broke as the rest of us. But he always found the resources to go drinking with the carousing congressional staff on the Hill. Night after night, Ralph would stumble out of Bullfeather's restaurant on Capitol Hill, drunk. One night, something changed. Ralph found religion. As he sat drinking with his friends, he caught sight of a middle-aged congressman, also drunk, trying to seduce a young female congressional aide. It dawned on Ralph that he was seeing his future, and it repulsed him. He immediately eschewed his decidedly non-puritanical lifestyle and left College Republicans to become a Christian political activist. He even formed a faith-based student organization, Students for America. At a dinner event a year later, he got his big break. Sitting next to televangelist Pat Robertson, Ralph was offered the chance to head the fledgling Christian Coalition. From 1987 through 1997, Ralph built it into one of the largest Christian political organizations in history before departing to become a "government affairs consultant," otherwise known as a lobbyist who spins his job title.

Ralph's specialty was organizing Christians, so naturally he was at the top of my list as the Internet gaming bill fight intensified. He was always harping on me to get him business. Now he had his chance. I wanted him to run the grassroots side of our effort to kill the Internet gaming bill.

After some obligatory pronouncements about hating gambling, Reed took the job. He didn't want his role publicized, but for the next phase of our attack, he was key. In order to convince the Republican leadership to stop Goodlatte's effort to resurrect the Internet gaming bill, we needed to scare the Republicans into thinking that just bringing it to a vote could cost them seats in the key 2000 congressional elections. Their majority in the House had been whittled down to eleven seats, and there was a real fear that they could lose the House just as they were coming to the end of Bill Clinton's presidency. We were playing with fire, but that never stopped us before.

After consulting with Ralph and the more aggressive members of our team, we opted for a strategy I would regret for years. We targeted ten Republican Congressmen with phone calls and mailings to religious Christian voters in their districts. It was never clear to me whether Rev. Sheldon understood what was about to happen, but he agreed to have Ralph's people contact Christians in key districts to fight the bill on behalf of the Traditional Values Coalition.

As only he could, Ralph crafted the script: "Hello, I am calling for the Traditional Values Coalition. I am calling because your Congressman has unfortunately voted for a bill that includes amendments that would legalize horse and dog racing on the Internet and bring gambling into our homes and community…"

The calls opened up a veritable floodgate. Members were furious at poor Reverend Sheldon. His organization was banned from coalition meetings, and his fundraising suffered. I tried to make it up to them with contributions from my clients, but the damage was done and took years to undo. Ralph skated away unscathed, but rumors circulated on the Hill—aided by our rival lobbyists—that we were behind this assault. It was a shameful and reckless tactic, but it worked. Once the phone calls and mailings hit, our operatives in the House leadership pushed to kill the bill. After a few days, I was told that the bill would die a quiet death.

It was difficult to assess the damage we had done by dropping this nuclear bomb on our own troops. Ralph posited that the calls and letters were only sent to 1 percent of the voters, and that it was a couple of months before the election in any event. He felt that if any of the Republicans on the target list were defeated, they couldn't legitimately blame their loss on this issue. I disagreed. I had allowed this to get out of hand, and I vowed I would never let it happen again.

# 10

# THE FAVOR FACTORY

With the pressures of Suncruz, the raging war against the CNMI, the battles to stop assaults on the tribes, and the fight over Internet gaming, I had my hands full at the turn of the century. Add the financial strain suffocating me personally, and you get more pressure than anybody should have to endure. Now I was going to add one more wildcard to the mix: I was switching lobbying firms.

For years recruiters had targeted me, hoping to steal me away from Preston Gates to a rival firm. I was a known entity in the media, and had been lauded for the success I enjoyed and the money I made for my clients across the board. All of this was flattering for me, but I remained loyal to Preston Gates, even as tensions mounted. Though I was not happy with some of the bad vibes at the firm, they did provide me a platform to build a lobbying practice, and I still liked most of the leadership there.

For a long time I found it odd that the Washington executive recruiting business was able to target well functioning firms for the sole purpose of stealing their most talented professionals, just to move them to another firm and pocket a fee. Then I realized: this is Washington. In a town where legions of politicians spend a lifetime draining the public treasury or enacting special privileges, why would anyone have a problem with employee poaching?

At Preston Gates, it didn't bother me to be a conservative surrounded by liberals, but my clients seemed to rub the firm the wrong way, as did my fight-to-the-death ethos. Time and again, I was encouraged to seek out corporate clients and forgo my representation of "those people." In the polite and careful parlance of a Washington law firm, that meant those pesky Pacific Islanders and Native Americans. I was sure that many Preston partners squirmed at their wine and brie parties when their peers confronted them with tales of Team Abramoff. As each year passed, I became closer and closer to my clients, and these thinly veiled barbs rankled me.

In 2000, I began to seriously consider breaking away from Preston Gates and taking my team with me. I was sure I could make it work on my own. But when I had my assistant, Susan Ralston, run the numbers, it was clear to me that I couldn't afford to start my own firm. All of my money was still tied up in Suncruz. So when headhunter Avery Ellis called me that summer to see if I was interested in joining his client, Greenberg Traurig, I told him to set up a meeting.

At first, it didn't seem to be a good fit. I was far from impressed with their key "player" in Washington, Ron Platt, who seemed to be a typical lobbyist. I hated typical lobbyists. They had nothing going. Their idea of a successful day was meeting someone at a cocktail reception. Our idea of a successful day was obliterating our clients' enemies.

Then I met Fred Baggett, their national director of government affairs. Fred said one thing that played right to my heart: "At our firm, we believe it's better to seek forgiveness than ask for permission." To me, that meant, "Act now and we'll figure out the consequences later." Finally, I had found a firm that thought just like me! While at the time that sounded ideal, hindsight would show me how much I needed someone like Manny Rouvelas telling me I was going to be dead, disgraced, or in prison if I didn't watch myself. I didn't need someone telling me to just do what I wanted, and that we'd sort it out later.

I tried to keep my discussions with Greenberg quiet as I privately asked the top members of my team—mostly Republicans, but some Democrats as well—to join me were I to make a move. Almost all of them said yes. A few declined because they wanted to join what they hoped would be the new Bush administration. Most were discreet about this, but one of them—a liberal Democrat named Daniel Ritter—apparently decided his future was more secure playing the role of spy and reporting everything he could back to the Preston leadership. This leak caused great tension and pressure. Compounding that leak was the reckless Platt, who ran around town bragging that our team was about to join Greenberg.

One morning, I received a call from a client asking me when I was moving to the new firm. Thanks to Platt, word was all over town. My enraged calls to the national leadership of Greenberg quieted him for a while, but it was too late. Ritter and Platt—two almost comically minor characters—precipitated a show down at Preston for me as 2000 drew to a close.

With the nation mesmerized by the recount of the 2000 presidential race, I was racing to get my deal done with Greenberg so we could join as of the first of the New Year. Manny had picked up rumors of my possible departure, but it was still premature. He asked me to email the firm to deny I was leaving, but I couldn't do that. I hadn't made a final decision. I sent an email which left my options open.

At the same time, after months of carping, the tension between Mike Scanlon and the Preston Gates leadership came to a head. Mike had done a masterful job for our clients, with his effective combination of pluck and punch, but he carried an almost open disdain for the non-political members of the law firm. Almost hourly, I'd hear his displeasure with lawyers and what he viewed as timid bureaucrats. When I wasn't hearing complaints from Mike about the firm, I was hearing grievances about Mike from the firm. It seemed obvious to me that they were on a collision course, but since I was leaving and taking Mike with me, I figured things could hold. I was wrong.

Once the firm realized I was departing, they summarily fired Scanlon. I counseled Jonathan Blank that it was a mistake. We were all likely to be leaving in a few weeks. Why create an enemy with media contacts? My advice was ignored, and Scanlon was fired the first week of December. He was furious.

Almost immediately, he got his chance to strike back, using my announced departure as his platform. They had treated him with open disdain for so long that he couldn't wait to return the favor. He hit them with so much negative media that I had to beg him to stop. His actions reconfirmed two things for me: First, Mike Scanlon knew how to work the press. Second, he knew how to bury the hatchet—in his opponent's head. In the years to come, he would put these skills to work over and over again.

Once the deal was out in the open, all of my clients agreed to follow me to Greenberg Traurig. It was my team who had served them, not Preston Gates, and it was me to whom they were loyal. As to my staff, ten people made the jump with me: Michael Scanlon, Susan Ralston, Amy Berger, Alan Slomowitz, Todd Boulanger, Shawn Vasell, Kevin Ring, Pat Wilson, Sara Rizzo, Julie Plocki, and Michelle Diedrick. Tony Rudy, DeLay's Deputy Chief of Staff, also came on board immediately.

Once at Greenberg, we started to attract some other strong lobbyists, including Mike Williams, a top legislative director from the National Rifle Association, Duane Gibson, the chief counsel of the House Resources Committee, Eddie Ayoob, the legislative director for Senator Harry Reid, and a number of other top former Hill staffers.

Our physical move from Preston Gates to Greenberg Traurig felt like a giant step up for us. Preston was housed in a stodgy, poorly constructed building. The floors were slightly on a tilt, so depending on which side of the building you were on, your door either swung open or closed. This was particularly ironic considering it was the headquarters of the American Institute of Architects.

Greenberg's headquarters were in a stately marble building at one corner of Lafayette Park, across from the White House. The building gleamed, and projected an image of power and elegance. As we moved into our new digs, my team was quite excited about our new beginning. We were given half a floor to settle, and quickly made ourselves at home. Almost immediately, we started to remake their lobbying shop in our mold.

But from early on in the transition, there were signs of trouble ahead. Although I had clashed with my former colleagues at Preston Gates on so many levels, I had always appreciated the intellectual caliber and modest demeanor of most of the partners and associates. For all its faults, Preston Gates had an aura of appropriate dignity. In terms of interpersonal dealings, Preston was straitlaced, which suited me just fine. Within a week of our arrival at the new firm, I began to see how different Greenberg Traurig would be for all of us.

The atmosphere here was casual. Too casual for my taste. At Preston

Gates, I had objected to "casual Friday" in the office. My team always wore business suits, and it seemed to me that clients who were paying upwards of $500 an hour for our services did not want to see us dressed as if we were off to the movies. Not to mention that we were lobbyists, and a lobbyist never knows when he or she will be summoned to Capitol Hill where jeans are not well received. When I convened my first meeting at Greenberg, my new colleagues commented that we looked like a cult in our suits, but my guys thought the Greenberg staff members looked like college kids on spring break.

But the bigger issues at Greenberg lay below the business casual surface. The female members of our team were made to feel uncomfortable by one senior partner at the firm. The women of our team were used to an office atmosphere informed by my strict adherence to Orthodox Jewish law, forbidding any physical conduct between unmarried males and females, and prohibiting a man and woman from being alone in a room with the door closed. So when I walked in on a very upset Susan Ralston with this senior partner standing behind her, massaging her shoulders, I knew there was trouble coming. She looked like she was going to kill him. I defused the situation by asking him to come with me to review a document, but Susan was miserable.

The harassment from this predator was bad enough, but when Susan was stuck with the job of organizing hundreds of requests for tickets to the Bush inauguration in January 2001, I could tell she was fed up. Susan was remarkable. I routinely assigned my assistants upwards of fifty tasks a day. As my practice grew, and I took on other businesses and activities, the daily tasks increased to over 100 a day, and I needed three assistants to do the work which Susan had, until then, done all by herself, never making a mistake. She was one of the great wonders of my world. When the transition to Greenberg became rocky for her, I worried, but thought she would get things under control. I found out differently on a dusty road to Tel Aviv.

A few weeks after the inauguration, I was in Israel with my Russian clients. They were seeking a permit to explore for oil in the Negev desert. On the way to the Petroleum Commission offices, Susan called from the States. She told me that Karl Rove—the newly installed counselor to the president and my friend from the College Republicans past—had called.

When I told her I would return Karl's call in a day or two, she informed me that Karl had in fact called for her. He had offered her a job as his top assistant, and she was leaving to take it before I returned from overseas. I was disappointed, but not surprised. After I overcame my irritation that this had taken place behind my back, I realized that Susan's move to Karl's office was not a blow; it was an opportunity. Sure, I'd have to find another assistant, but that was nothing compared to having Susan in the West Wing of the Bush White House.

As soon as she started in her new job, she was instantly recognized as the most valuable member of their support team. Suddenly, my potential access to Karl and information from within the Administration was improved, though most of our practice still revolved around the machinations of Congress, not the Administration. In fact, I only saw Karl a few times during this period and only requested his guidance on a very few matters. Of course, that didn't prevent the media from making more of our relationship than it was when my collapse came. Misinterpreting everything from my staff's regular visits to the White House to Karl's attendance at the NCAA Tournament in our box (he paid for his tickets), they sought to portray a relationship which never existed. Even my chance encounters with Karl were blown out of proportion. When a boneheaded political consultant saw me greet Karl on the way to a dinner at Grover's home, he reported having witnessed a secret curbside meeting between the powerful White House Counselor and me. I was fond of Karl, but there was precious little we needed from him or of his boss, President George W. Bush.

While some thought different, I was never very close to the Bush family. I admired their sense of dignity and commitment to our nation, but I was among those who regretted that Ronald Reagan hadn't chosen Jack Kemp as his running mate in 1980. Most people forget that during the 1980 campaign, thanks to Jimmy Carter's horrific administration, the common wisdom was that the presidency was too big for any one man. The establishment feared Reagan. When he wasn't being called stupid or senile by the press and the chattering classes, Reagan was derided as a warmonger. Though he sailed to the nomination, the party grandees were pushing him to put former President Gerald Ford on the ticket and run as co-Presidents. While Reagan had the sense to reject that plan, he did accede to the next demand from the country club wing of the Grand Old Party: to put George H.W. Bush on the ticket as vice president.

Notwithstanding his having maligned tax cuts—the central feature in the Reagan economic program—as "voodoo economics," Bush was a loyal and devoted vice president. My dealings with him while I was College Republicans chairman were minimal and by the time he became president, I was already in my filmmaking mode and out of politics. When he broke his promise not to raise taxes, like most conservatives, I hearkened back to the bad decision Reagan made by including him on the ticket in 1980. Then there were his harsh fulminations against Israel. Enough was enough. When he ran for re-election, I opted not to vote for him again. Being a conservative, I couldn't bring myself to vote for Clinton, so I voted for the only true conservative in the race, my dear friend Howard Phillips, nominee of the Tax Payers Party. I found it gratifying that scores of Orthodox Jews throughout the nation told me that they, too, voted for Howard. Unfortunately, he didn't win.

The next time I had to think about a Bush was right after the midterm elections of 1998. The Republicans had, again, retained their majority, though they were not able to score the overwhelming victory a party sees in the off year when they don't control the White House. I was balancing the various lobbying efforts with my usual free lance political activities, including the battle against the Guam governor, when Ralph Reed approached me to support the next Bush to make a run at the White House: Texas Governor George W. Bush. Ralph wanted me to contribute funds and to get active. I told him I didn't donate to Bushes, but he assured me this one was different. Then-Governor Bush was a born again Christian, deeply committed to Israel, and a conservative. I listened, thinking Ralph was conning me, and asked how that was possible. How could such an avatar emerge from the kin of Kennebunkport? Ralph explained that George W. Bush's life experiences had brought him to a worldview at variance with his family tradition and that I should feel quite comfortable with him. I wrote a check.

Ralph told me that Karl Rove, former chairman of the College Republicans, was running the Bush show and had done so for years. That, too, was comforting, as I liked Karl. He said that, as conservatives, the Bush presidency would be everything we ever wanted. In classic Ralph Reed overselling fashion, he then went further, saying that Bush personally told him that his presidency would make all of us very rich. I thought that an odd comment, and discounted it immediately. If Bush had said this, then he wasn't very wise. I imagined this was Ralph's hard sell. Ralph never lost an occasion to regale me with stories of the moonlight strolls he would take with Bush, ruminating on a glorious future. Several of my friends had made the trip to Austin, Texas to meet Bush, and Ralph suggested I do so too, but I could never find the time. I didn't see the point. I had given money to Bush, but my focus was on Congress. Presidents can do little on issues of importance to most lobbying clients. They deal in big issues of national concern, not minute provisions of the tax code or other such details. The only thing most clients wanted from an American president was a photograph or souvenir. I hoped Ralph was right that Bush was a good guy, but I wasn't going to take time out of my crazy schedule to find out. No matter what, he would never be as bad as Clinton, and we had figured a way to ensure our clients' survival and success through that administration.

My indifference ended after the 2000 New Hampshire primary. I was generally rooting for Bush from the sidelines, but his campaign seemed dysfunctional. When they lost New Hampshire to the surging "Straight Talk Express" of John McCain, I got a phone call. Ralph was Bush's key Southern campaign advisor, and was personally involved in directing their grass roots and voter identification programs. The race was heading into South Carolina where he feared Bush was going to lose to McCain. He pushed hard for funding so he could launch a massive effort for Bush among the churches in the Palmetto State. Ralph knew how I'd react to the prospect of a McCain nomination. I set about finding the money and hoped Ralph could work his magic. He didn't disappoint. Thanks to Ralph distributing millions of voter's guides in South Carolina's churches, the so-called Straight Talk Express hit a speed bump on its way to the White House. Rove took things from there, and finished him off.

Unfortunately, the South Carolina race didn't fade into the night. As I rushed to get Ralph whatever funds I could and he, in turn, used those and other funds to turn out Christian voters for Bush, another politico who hated McCain was busy with a dirty trick worthy of Tammany Hall. Taking a photo of Senator McCain with his adopted foster child from

Sri Lanka, and charging that McCain had fathered a black child out of wedlock, this repugnant scoundrel introduced a vile, racist tone into the election. I read about this skullduggery and, like most Americans, was appalled and disgusted. While I had no patience for McCain, his self-less and benevolent act of aiding this child deserved nothing but praise. Unfortunately for me, years later I would be told by several lobbyists close to McCain that he blamed Ralph Reed, and by extension, me, for that horrific episode, confusing Ralph's legitimate voter education campaign with that loathsome slander.

With a South Carolina victory notched in his belt, Bush navigated his way through the rest of the primaries to the general election. During the post-election vote recount in Florida, I dispatched virtually my entire lobbying shop to aid the Bush efforts. At the end of the long war, Bush emerged as the victor.

After he became president, I met Bush on numerous occasions, though never one-on-one. I had no business with the president, since my issues were dealt with at a much lower pay grade. Mostly, my interest in seeing him was to enable others to get their pictures with him.

What struck me about George W. Bush was that, unlike most presidents, he seemed to be having fun. Even when things were tense, he kept his sense of humor. He also had one of the best memories for faces, names, and details of any politician I had met. I had the occasion to bring each of my children in to meet with Bush over the course of his first term in office. My eldest son, Levi, was first. Bush asked him about his studies. Levi was in high school at the time and replied that he was doing well, but having trouble with an English assignment. When my son Alex came to see the president a few months later, I was stunned when Bush asked Alex how Levi was doing with his English class.

In 2002, I brought my youngest son to see the president at a political fundraising event. Daniel was just nine years old, but already an aspiring businessman. Indulging his entreaties for the trappings of the business world, I provided him with business cards and a Motorola PageWriter, a precursor to the Blackberry. Clad in his businessman's suit and bearing his business cards, Daniel accompanied me to see the President backstage prior to his address. After a warm greeting from Bush, Daniel solemnly extended his business card to the leader of the free world, "My card."

Bush barely could contain his laughter when thanking Daniel, but the little future captain of industry was not done: "Do you have a card?" he asked.

Bush fought back peals of laughter to inform Daniel that no, he didn't have a card. The little guy was astonished: "You should get a card! Do you have email?"

Daniel's agenda was to get the president to join a myriad of unsuspecting business colleagues of mine who were daily recipients of Daniel's email missives. They were usually hilariously innocent, and the source of much good humor.

"No, Daniel, I don't," Bush replied.

Daniel, thinking he could help this poor Luddite president offered, "You really need to get email. Lots of people have it!" Bush couldn't contain himself any longer and burst into laughter. We quickly ended our chat and left the poor man to lead the nation. Bush, that is.

A few months later, Daniel joined me again for an encounter with the President. This time it was a reception for Senator John Thune of South Dakota. Though he had nothing to do with any of our client issues, I was a donor to Thune and thought him to be one of the finest men in the Senate. I was invited to a donor reception, and the President was going to be in attendance. As we waited for the president to work the crowd, I could see poor Daniel feeling quite overwhelmed by the rush of big adult bodies. I kept him close to my side to ensure he wasn't swept away. As we stood girding ourselves against the crush of the mob, Bush approached. As he saw me, he called out my name. Immediately he saw Daniel at my side and halted in his tracks. He rifled his inside suit jacket pocket and revealed a cream colored White House note card. Quickly he scribbled a message on it and offered it to Daniel.

"Here you go Daniel... Here's my card!" Bush beamed as he closed the matter of the missing card.

Daniel didn't miss a beat: "Hey, you forgot to get email! There's no email address on this card!"

Laughing, Bush moved along and I was left shaking my head in disbelief. If I would have ever seen, let alone met a president of the United States when I was a kid, I certainly would never have had the boldness to ask for his card or berate him for not having email! But to his great credit, in the dignified and elegant manner of his parents, George W. Bush made this little boy—and his father—feel very special. Sadly, the glow of that encounter and many others faded years later when I was constrained to hear President Bush deny he had ever met me. I guess I can't blame him. I was, by then, the ultimate albatross, and he was still steering the ship of state.

Settling into Greenberg was an adjustment. The existing lobbying group at the firm had an attitude problem. The Greenberg staff was used to being inconsequential and to thinking small. We thought big. We saw every representation in grandiose philosophical terms and all our clients paid huge fees. Like most other lobbyists in Washington, the Greenberg gang were used to charging clients around $10,000 a month. Ours paid over $100,000 a month, with many paying up to $150,000.

In later years, critics would express shock at these amounts, but we were neither the first or only firm to charge fees of this magnitude. Our billings were derived from the time spent on the representations. Since most of the clients who hired us had sink or swim issues which required massive and extensive Congressional lobbying efforts, it was not unusual for us to assign a dozen or more lobbyists to these efforts. Law firms usually value the work of their employees on an hourly basis. From the initial years of representing Choctaw and the CNMI, I saw that extensive representations averaged around $150,000 per month. The CNMI representation immediately consumed large numbers of our staff and many of their hours, and never dipped below $100,000 per month when one multiplied the hourly rates of the firm by the staff hours spent on the client. Some months, the bill exceeded $300,000, especially when a Congressional hearing was slated. Choctaw started a bit slower, as we only worked on one issue, but once we took on a host of matters at their request, the bills soared as well. A flat fee is easier for the client, since they are able to plan their year's budget in advance. But a flat fee can either be a bonanza for a lobbying firm, or a disaster. If the firm miscalculates the work required, and quickly uses up the flat fee amount in hourly billings, they are left with the probability of loss. This often happens in Washington, and the consequence is that the client suffers. Lobbyists are not the most loyal outside contractors, and any disincentive is enough for many to drop the ball. This could prove deadly to a client, when an inattentive lobbyist misses a key issue or allows a bill to slip through the process.

Eventually, all of my clients opted for a flat fee, except Choctaw. Their budgeting process did not permit flat fees. To accommodate Nell Rogers's need to plan ahead, we agreed on a target fee of $150,000 per month, with the understanding that we would reduce our billings in the heavy months and increase them in the lean months. This would enable her to plan the tribe's finances, yet enable our firm to be paid for its work. This arrangement would later be attacked as billing fraud, which it certainly was not, but by then everything I did, thought or said was treated as a crime or worse. In fact, our clients knew we charged a lot, more than most of the other lobbying firms—but they also knew we delivered. Virtually all of my clients stayed with me for years, of their own volition. No one forced them to hire us, and none of the clients ever indicated they felt we were not providing more than their money's worth. Unlike most lobbying firms, which required clients to commit to a one or two year minimum contract, my deal with my clients was simple: fire us the minute you think it's not worth having us. Until my tribal government clients lost their internal elections, no one ever fired us.

When my team arrived at Greenberg, we found a sluggish operation, riven with jealousies and pettiness. Their lobbyists never saw billing numbers like ours and disbelieved them for a few months, until my clients started paying their bills. In our first year, Greenberg shot from ranking a lowly thirty-fifth among the lobbying firms to the top five and remained there the entire time I was employed.

In addition to our personnel and clients, we also brought our lobbyist tool bag to Greenberg, filled with baubles, trinkets, and other goodies for those we were lobbying, and the firm loved it. Our seemingly unlimited ability to dispense sports and concert tickets to the Hill left scores of representatives and staff thinking we were Ticketmaster. For their purposes, we were.

Most lobbying shops in Washington made efforts to secure choice tickets for Congress and staff, but few, if any, went as far as we did. We had more tickets at our disposal than most ticket brokers. And we also had a staff of former jocks who loved to go to the games with Hill staff, which made our investment worthwhile, as the jocks were our best lobbyists. The amount we spent on getting the best tickets to every event was astounding. There were years where we spent in excess of $1.5 million on event tickets alone. An entire sub-industry developed at the firm to acquire, dispense, and track the tickets. We had prime seats to every game and important event.

During football season, I had two double suites at Fed Ex Field where the Redskins played, the equivalent of seventy-two tickets per game, including a double suite in the Owners Club, which had the best view of any luxury suite in the nation, and room for twenty-seven people.

For Washington Wizards basketball, I had four tickets on the court, front row at the MCI Center. I also had a smattering of other tickets in the arena, and a large suite which I was able to obtain thanks to some clever maneuvering. For Washington Capitals hockey, our family's favorite sport, we had twelve seats in the first row, and several more in the lower tier. Our tickets just off the first base dugout and our suite on the third base bag at the Baltimore Orioles stadium were immensely popular, though the hapless Orioles rarely won a game.

Lobbyists on my team understood why we purchased these tickets, and it wasn't to indulge memories of their days on the playing field. It was to build relationships with the staff or representatives who attended these events. A sporting event or concert gave us at least two hours of face time with important people. With only a few rare exceptions, my guys had to tell me who they were bringing to any given event and what they were going to discuss there before they were granted tickets. When the game was over, I expected an email telling me about that discussion and what the follow up would be. Everything had a purpose. Even the process of acquiring our seats and suites provided us with opportunities to lobby.

I obtained the incomparable double suite at the Owners Club at Fed Ex Field after sending a memo to Dan Snyder, the owner of the Redskins, just one month after he assumed control of the team. I was one of his larger customers, but I had a number of frustrations with the amenities of the facility. Since my primary purpose was to entertain clients and the powerful people who could impact their lives, and since I was spending a fortune, I didn't hold back on my critique. One of my main suggestions was that he convert the choice location the press commanded close to the field to prime suites and catapult the media to the upper reaches of the stadium. The final item on my long list of suggestions was that he should try to change the offensive name of the team.

Although the Choctaws had long ago assured me that a team named the Redskins didn't bother them, I figured I would take a shot at trying to undo this insult. In my letter to Snyder, I asked him how we would feel if the New York team were called the Jew Boys, or worse. Moreover, I knew that all Native Americans resented the use of the feathered headdresses in the team band's uniform. I asked how he would feel if that New York Jew Boys band had a uniform of black hats and prayer shawls. I further argued that, were he to make this change now, he would immediately establish himself as a moral leader in our nation's capital, and garner the respect of those who were likely to look askance on him.

Snyder called me within a few hours of receiving the letter, and reviewed each point with me. He was kind and gracious, not the imperious brat the media had portrayed him to be. He said that he sympathized with my points about the team's name, but he had been a Redskins fan since he was a kid, and he couldn't bring himself to change it. His business acumen led many to think he was only a cold-hearted, cutthroat shark, but he was nothing but decent, honest and straightforward with me. A few seasons later, I was given first choice of the new suites in the former press section and our expenditures at Fed Ex Field grew exponentially.

Our football tickets were in the highest demand, but when I first started acquiring sports tickets for lobbying, back in 1998, I didn't have the best seats at the MCI Center (later called Verizon Center). All the executive suites on three levels were taken, but I knew I needed one to use for fund raisers and to host Congressional members and staff. I found out that Marion Barry, the Mayor of Washington, D.C., was purchasing one of the choice suites with city funds. Somehow Barry didn't request or receive a free box for city officials when Abe Pollin, the founding father of sports in the Capital area, built the new stadium. Of course, Barry had little claim on the box, since the city did precious little to make Abe's life easier. In fact, their financial insolvency caused him endless heartache. Abe and I would soon become close friends and, along with a very few other public figures—such as Dana Rohrabacher—Abe stayed loyal and supportive of me throughout the storm which would engulf my life.

As for the MCI Center suite, the Republican Congress had been warning Barry for months about his prolific spending. At the Washington Redskins game against the Denver Broncos on September 28, 1998, I hosted a fundraiser in our box for North Carolina Senator Lauch Faircloth. A solid conservative and one of our favorites, we tried to raise funds for him whenever we could. As I stood to the side, Faircloth held court in our box at halftime. Our clients in attendance, as well as my lobbyist team, peppered him with questions about the legislative calendar. He was chairman of the D.C. Appropriations committee, so one of the guests asked him whether he read that Marion Barry had bought a box at the MCI Center. Faircloth laughed and said he had, but that the Mayor better not pick out his seat just yet. He planned to nix that item from the D.C. budget that week.

The next morning, I called the MCI Center again. I asked to be put on the waiting list for that particular box. The manager laughed and said I'd be waiting a long time, since the D.C. government was never going to give up such a prime location. I asked if there were any others waiting on the list, and he said no—no one was that crazy. I asked that he send me a fax confirming my position, and he did.

Faircloth, true to form, attacked the box a few days later. By week's end, it was mine. Scores of fundraisers were held in Marion Barry's box, and I proudly told each of my Republican honorees that they were particularly distinguished in having their fundraiser in a suite with such provenance.

Later, as the world dissected my activities, many asked how it could be that so many representatives and staff could accept so many tickets from my team, and others. The answer lies in the purposeful ambiguity of the gift ban. Putting aside the inherent conflict of congressmen and their staff making rules about how many perquisites they can accept, the rules themselves were confusing. For example, senators and their staff could accept any gift from an Indian tribal government under the government exemption, but representatives and staff could not. Therefore, when we gave sporting and event tickets to the Senate, we did so freely. When they went to the House, we had to issue the recipient an invoice for them to reimburse us. Of course, we never pressed anyone to actually pay—and most didn't. We felt that all of this was legal, and were never told otherwise. That even part of it could have been legal is just one example of what's wrong with Washington.

At Greenberg Traurig, I usually ran behind in my schedule. I tended to chat too long in meetings and wedge in unscheduled discussions. My secretaries were always driven to distraction, but they knew what I was like. What caused the most eye rolling among my staff was seeing me in my office with someone not on my schedule or involved in our businesses, and then asking my assistant to cut him a check. Whether it was a mortgage payment missed for months, or a deposit needed for a car, I was there to help people in need. When our seats were not in use at games, I gave them to the guys in the mailroom and maintenance departments. I noticed that the so-called progressive attorneys who ran the firms ignored the very people who made sure their lives ran smoothly, so I went out of my way to help when I could. I always gave these employees my own cash Christmas bonuses, even though the firm disliked it, and even found myself giving them personal loans and grants when they came to me for help.

This charitable giving was good for my soul, but soon it became something of an addiction. I was providing millions of dollars to finance Jewish schools, and few people in my life could understand why. Todd Boulanger would rib me. My accountant would frequently email me, admonishing my giving practices, adjuring me to stop giving away so much of my money to charity. She had a point. Jewish law provides a guidepost, which I should have followed. The minimum amount one is required to give is ten percent. Most people know that. But what they don't know is that, according to our strictures, the maximum amount one can give is twenty percent. I was giving away virtually everything.

My response to my intrepid accountant was typical of an addict: "I'll make more money." And I did. But with that money, I ventured into another realm that might have fared better without me, the field of fine dining.

Kosher restaurants never seem to survive in Washington, D.C. Whereas New York, Los Angeles, and Baltimore have a nimiety of fine dining establishments, the nation's Capital cannot seem to supply enough customers to keep a restaurant in business. For part of my lobbying career, I took most of my business lunches at L'Etoile, a kosher restaurant off

Dupont Circle in Washington. Whenever I could convince my staff, clients, or friends to dine there, I would. Most abhorred the place. Adam Kidan called it Le Terrible. But it was kosher.

One day L'Etoile followed suit and closed like all the other kosher restaurants in DC. The next day, one of my assistants, Rodney Lane, bounded into my office with a plan. Rodney had started at the firm as the assistant to my assistant, Susan Ralston. A lanky young man in his 30's, Rodney wanted to be more than an assistant. He wanted to run something. In my world, at that time, ambition was greatly admired—even if the ambitious one lacked the skills and experience to carry out the plan. This was one of my many weaknesses—I admired moxie far too much.

"You have a dozen lobbyists wining and dining staff and Congress on a daily basis," Rodney said. "They spend upwards of a half million dollars a year at the various restaurants around town. Sometimes more. You also dine out, but now you've lost the kosher restaurant and have nowhere to go. There are dozens of similarly situated local kosher consumers, and scores more who visit. I have an idea."

I could already see where this was going, but I listened.

"You should open a restaurant. It would be a fine dining establishment, so that your lobbyists could eat there with clients and folks from the Hill. It would be a kosher restaurant so you could eat there, too, along with the kosher consumers from this area. We'd make it the nicest kosher restaurant in the world, and you would be the owner. Can't miss!"

That's where I should have told him to go back to his filing work. I was always flying 10,000 miles a minute and was getting careless. I had habitually given people too much of a chance to succeed, even when they were likely to let me down. I had always done what I wanted and usually succeeded, so I mirror imaged that onto others, assuming they too could do whatever they said they could. Of course, people lie, and people are incompetent, and you should probably never allow a clerical assistant to open a restaurant for you. But in the moment, I got excited about the idea. I had, by then, recovered from the Suncruz losses and, while not flush with money, had enough to launch such a project. I told him to proceed.

We found a choice spot on Pennsylvania Avenue, across from the Archives building, and the plan was to open a top-flight kosher restaurant called Archives. Our very name would be a marketing tool, directing people right to the restaurant.

Rodney claimed to know about restaurants, having worked as a restaurant consultant. It was insane to promote him from his clerical job to head of this million-dollar venture, but with the whirl of activity on too many fronts, my admiration for his determination and his savvy presentations, I made a hasty and soon-regretted decision to move forward. Rodney spent money like the proverbial drunken sailor preparing the restaurant space, but was clearly out of his depth. We were within weeks of opening when we decided to have a tasting dinner to see if the chef we hired could deliver. I invited several representatives and senators to our home, and the chef worked diligently preparing a sumptuous meal, while a sommelier from the finest kosher wine company in the nation brought his choice wines.

After the guests left, Kevin Ring from my staff remained behind. Kevin is a bit of a wine connoisseur, so I invited him to give me an unvarnished view of the proceedings. The meal was fine, he said, but the wine was putrid.

"Putrid?" I asked. I never drank, so I couldn't weigh in on this one.

"I don't want to use profanity, so go with putrid, Jack. You can't serve that to fine dining consumers in Washington, D.C., and certainly not lobbyists. You'll be closed in a week."

The restaurant was slated to open in a very few weeks. I had poured almost one million dollars into renovating the space, acquiring the furniture and fixtures and preparing for the opening. Now I was being told my restaurant would be closed within a week? A day? Talk about Le Terrible.

That next morning, I called Marina Nevskaya, my Russian client. She was a genius, with an unrivaled photographic memory. One of my favorite diversions was showing Marina a few pages from a book and having her repeat verbatim the contents. That she could memorize texts in six languages was even more impressive. More importantly, for my restaurant woes, she was also a wine expert and had contacts everywhere. I called Marina to discuss the kosher wine problem. She had heard that kosher wines were subpar, but had had no reason to look into the matter. She did, however, maintain close ties to wine maker Baron de Rothschild in Paris, and was immediately able to set up a meeting with him at his private kosher wine cellar to sample his finest stock and assemble a wine list for my restaurant.

A few days later, the chef, manager, and rabbi who would certify the restaurant's kosher status were winging their way to meet her in Paris. After the tasting session, I received a call from Marina.

"Jack, it's you reen."

Rarely did I have a problem with her accented English. Perhaps the phone lines were weak. "What? What's you reen?"

"The wine. It's you reen."

"You mean urine!?" I couldn't believe this. Putrid sounded good just about then.

"Yes, urine. It's horrible. And these are the best of the world's kosher wines. Just terrible. I couldn't drink it. The rabbi is in heaven since he has never had non-kosher wine, but the chef and manager agree with me. You cannot serve this stuff."

"But if this is the best, how could that be?"

Ever the curious investigator, she vowed to find out. She never did.

By then I knew we had problems. When Rodney—now the restaurant manager and no longer the file clerk—returned to Washington, we met.

"Jack, there is only one solution. When you first went to see the rabbis about certifying the restaurant, they asked you why you wanted to have a kosher restaurant. They told you to just open a small kitchen for yourself alone, and not to bother with the rest of the restaurant being kosher. In their view, it would not work."

Maybe they knew about the wine.

He continued, "I suggest we make Archives a non-kosher restaurant and then just build a separate kosher kitchen for your use. Otherwise, I fear you will lose all your money on this venture."

I was crestfallen. I had dreams of the finest kosher restaurant in the world dancing in my head for months. Kosher Kobe beef. Kosher Alaskan Mountain Goat. Kosher everything. It would have been historic, and now it was over. I called one of my out-of-town rabbinical friends and ran the problem by him. Could I have a kosher kitchen in the restaurant and use it? He said yes, though the safeguards would be onerous.

But I had a different problem. I had told several of my friends in the Jewish community my plan for Archives, and they had spread the word far and wide. Jewish publications overseas were reporting the coming kosher Valhalla. And they were calling it Archives. Worse, religious Jews were already showing up at the site to see if we were open. Worst of all, several of the community leaders had approached me to thank me for making the sacrifice of opening a restaurant in town. The lack of a nice place for young people to dine was causing them to move to other cities like New York or Baltimore. Opening Archives would not only provide the community with a nice place to celebrate occasions with their families, it would in fact help ensure a future for Washington, D.C.'s Jewish presence. Talk about pressure.

I had to do something. I called Rodney in and asked whether we could open the restaurant at the present location as a non-kosher venue, and at the same time open a kosher restaurant to fulfill the promise I had made to the community. He said it would work just fine. What a miscalculation.

Now, instead of having to bear the expense of opening one restaurant, I had to open two. I decided to use the name Archives for the kosher place, and choose a new name for the original location. Since my plan was to adorn the walls of the restaurant with original historic documents, in the hopes that they would engender conversation among diners about the history of our nation, we chose the name Signatures. We were able to conclude an agreement with a major purveyor of historic documents to serve as their D.C. showroom, taking hundreds of fascinating original historic instruments on consignment. In addition to serving Beef Wellington, we would be selling the Duke of Wellington's letter to his wife Catherine Pakenham.

Complications arose left and right. The local Jewish community had a rule that no one could own both a non-kosher and a kosher establishment. To solve this problem, I transferred ownership of Signatures to a small group of friends, with the terms of ownership protecting them from losses. I also arranged an agreement that I would oversee the restaurant, so as to ensure it would meet my main remaining goal, to serve as a venue for our lobbyists, clients, and Hill contacts. I also had to control that kosher kitchen, or I would get nothing to eat!

I called my out-of-town rabbinical counselor to run this by him. He was not delighted, but said that it met the technical requirements, as he understood them. I was forum shopping and pushing the envelope—but that was my normal modus operandi. I could have just returned to the local rabbis, and requested a ruling and method to do this, but since I was by then running a competing religious high school at Eshkol, I felt I might not fare too well. That was wrong of me, but I was moving at such a quick pace and trying to protect my investment, that I made a number of foolish mistakes.

With the opening of Signatures, I now had a base for entertaining clients and Congress. I used it to the hilt. Flaunting the by now much-trampled gift ban rules, I became a virtual cafeteria for large groups of representatives and staff. Signatures had a diverse menu, including the finest sushi near the Hill, and quickly became one of the hotspots. I secured a corner table and conducted most of my meetings at the restaurant.

Signatures also became a key venue for political fundraisers. On any given night, the place would host events for several senators, representatives, and even aspiring governors. When Arnold Schwarzenegger decided to convene several dozen Republican representatives to get a feel for his political prospects, he booked the entire main dining room at Signatures. When freshly minted Washington Wizard Michael Jordan wished to break from his usual haunts, he took a table outside on our patio. When Senator Conrad Burns—who, at the height of the scandal which would bring us both down, would later proclaim to the world his greatest wish that I was never born! —held his birthday party, it was at Signatures. When the founder of Home Depot hosted the leaders of the Christian political world to meet with then-Deputy Prime Minister Ehud Olmert, it was at Signatures. Our chef, Morou Outtara, was the finest in Washington. The décor was the talk of the town. It was glorious.

Meanwhile, construction continued on Archives, now moved several blocks down Pennsylvania Avenue toward the White House. Unfortunately, my erstwhile assistant didn't really know what he was doing, and I surely didn't have a better idea. He secured space far too large for our purposes and almost bankrupted me with the expenses. We decided to make the restaurant into a kosher deli, since that was more likely to survive without a fine wine list, and we even opened a smaller kosher fine dining facility in the cavernous rear space we had let. It took forever to get the place open. We named the deli Stacks, as in where the books in the Archives go, and opened with my son Alex's bar mitzvah party in November 2002—seven months after his actual bar mitzvah date.

Once open, the community rushed to patronize Stacks. But even with packed houses, the operating cost was prohibitive. I soon found myself subsidizing this social venue for the Jewish community. I spent several million dollars opening and operating Stacks and Archives, but since the venture was, in my mind, a charitable endeavor from start to finish, I didn't really think about it. After all, I could always just make more money.

# 11

# TRIBAL INFLUENCE

By the time we left Preston Gates, our representation of the Choctaws had become iconic in lobbying circles. Not only did we stop every tax proposed for Indian country, but we also beat back attempts by legislators to gut the Indian Child Welfare Act—the only law stopping wholesale adoption of Native American children by non-Indians. This victory was especially sweet for me because it defeated John McCain.

I had few direct dealings with McCain until I started representing the tribes. On scores of issues, McCain paired with liberals. Carbon credit. Immigration. Campaign finance. On tribes, he supported a communistic redistribution of the wealth system which infuriated my clients and scores of other tribes. He didn't seem to understand that tribes may all be called Native Americans, but they are as different to each other as the Swiss are to the English or the Russians are to the Spanish. He had been chairman of the Senate Indian Affairs Committee since the Republicans took control of the Congress in 1995, and many tribal leaders were repulsed at his paternalistic approach.

I avoided McCain whenever possible. I didn't attend his fundraisers, and I steered clear of his acolytes. But, when the Indian Child Welfare Act came into play, I had no option but to meet with him. We were trying to stop efforts to gut the act, which had served its purpose well and didn't need tampering. McCain and other critics of the status quo felt that the act gave too much power to the tribes, and that it was time to revise it. History showed, however, that once Congress started to "revise" something, the proverbial can of worms was open, and anything was possible—including denuding the act of all meaning. This threat led me to a testy meeting with the all-wise senator in his office.

McCain, a classic narcissist, viewed the meeting as his chance to tell me that they were going to change the act, so my clients better just accept it. His staff director—who was far more of an ally of the tribes than his boss—squirmed uncomfortably and shot me furtive, frustrated glances. I calmly explained that, while the changes did not impact the Choctaws, Chief Martin had instructed us to protect Indian country in general whenever possible, and in this matter in particular. We were opposed to any changes in the act. McCain's piercing gaze locked into my eyes, but I didn't blink, nor did I back down. The noble senator quickly informed me that it didn't matter what we wanted. What he wanted would prevail. I knew better, since the House was in our corner and we could even work our magic on the Senate to frustrate his designs. I could tell that my refusal to bend to his will was angering McCain, so I did my best to draw discussion to a close. The meeting ended abruptly, and I left upset but determined that he wouldn't have his way with our clients. He didn't.

McCain's connection to and relationship with the tribes was anything but straightforward. While they were one of the first groups he assaulted for campaign contributions for his ill-fated 2000 run for presidency, he hardly had the track record worthy of their support—financial or otherwise. As chairman of Indian Affairs, McCain should have been at the forefront of efforts to frustrate those attempting to tax or regulate the tribes, but he was A.W.O.L. Instead of assisting the tribes in building relationships, he criticized those tribes who hired lobbyists to provide the help he refused to give—except when a tribe hired a lobbyist affiliated with his political machine. For the most part, the mainstream media gave McCain a pass on these matters. He was, after all, their favorite Republican, at least until he secured the Republican nomination for president. I found it ironic that he would eventually serve as my hangman, given his checkered record in dealing with lobbyists and his dubious reign at Indian Affairs. In fact, even as The Village Voice excoriated two of his biggest supporters—Roger Stone and Scott Reed—for tribal rapine, McCain and his staff sermonized ad nauseum about my abuse of the tribes. When asked why these two lobbyists weren't also the focus of his committee's invective, McCain or his staff would claim they had limited time and resources.

The Indian Child Welfare Act was the tip of the iceberg. The number of bills of urgent concern to the tribes was astounding. We were constantly on alert for seemingly minor references that could have set precedent and harmed their sovereignty. Fortunately, we had some observant monitors in our office who didn't let anything slip by. Plus, we had built a network for Choctaw on Capitol Hill similar to that which we had for the CNMI—and this time it was bipartisan. That network was critical in beating back the myriad attempts to tax the tribes in Congress and would be vital when two major issues solely related to Choctaw came to a head.

One evening, over dinner, Chief Martin told us how dysfunctional the Bureau of Indian Affairs office was in their region. The tribe had applied to move parcels of land that they had purchased into trust. The federal government holds tribal land for them in a trustee system, which protects the land, and removes jurisdiction from localities which are often out to harm the tribes. The Chief said that some of their parcels were submitted to the BIA to be placed in trust in 1927—the year my father was born—and they still hadn't heard back. He shook his head as he recounted the dozens of times that the tribe had to re-submit applications since they were "lost" by the BIA.

Did he want us to seek a legislative solution to this problem, I asked. My fellow lobbyists' eyes widened. They knew, better than I, that what I was proposing was impossible. Congress didn't take land into trust. The Administration, through the BIA, did that. Since their legs weren't long enough to kick me under the table, I continued: "Chief, how about if we get all the details from you and see if we can get a legislative remedy to this problem."

The Chief was happy to hear that we would try, though I don't think even he believed it possible. I just didn't know any better, so I assumed we could do it. We hadn't failed him anywhere else, so why should we falter here?

As soon as we started to move legislation through the Congress, the Interior Department awoke from its 1927 slumber and weighed in heavily against the proposal. I focused our entire squad on this bill. Todd Boulanger went to work with the senior senator from the Choctaw home state of Mississippi, Thad Cochran, and his key staffer, Ann Copland. Cochran had been an unqualified friend of the tribe for decades, a highly intelligent and socially astute Senator who embodied all that was good in politics. He virtually ran to the well of the Senate and proposed the legislation immediately. Since he was a powerful appropriator, he was able to steer the bill through the Senate. There were no real obstacles there, notwithstanding the Administration's remonstrations to the contrary. Our job was to move the bill through the House, and then protect it in conference. That meant lobbying scores of congressmen and senators in a very short period of time to ensure no opposition.

Other than the snide comments of rival lobbyists that Choctaw got too much of what they wanted in Congress, we had no blowback. With one legislative move, we were able to shift over 8,000 acres of land which Choctaw had purchased over many decades not into trust status, but into "original reservation" status. In Indian country, that's the gold standard. A tribe has far more control over land on the reservation than land in trust, and they can use that land more flexibly for economic development. Not only that, but the legislation we passed provided for annual updates of the reservation to accommodate future purchases. The client was ecstatic. My staff needed a vacation from the Herculean effort required to get this bill through, but we delivered something worth hundreds of millions of dollars. In later years, as I was being accused of ripping my clients off and not delivering value for their fees, this achievement, like so many others, was ignored. In the words of a French nobleman: Hypocrisy is the tribute that vice pays to virtue.

The second special issue facing the Choctaw tribe had less immediate financial impact than getting the reservation land secure, but was all the more fraught with danger. When Congress codified the court decision allowing for casinos on Indian reservations, they passed the Indian Gaming Regulatory Act, or IGRA. They also set up a supervisory body called the National Indian Gaming Commission (NIGC), so tribes which could not afford to self-regulate their operations would have a federal regulatory body overseeing their businesses. Most tribes submitted themselves to the NIGC, but Choctaw and a few others had already spent millions of dollars to create legitimate self-regulating gaming commissions and blanched at the notion of having to spend more money to support a redundant federal system. Like most Washington bureaucracies, the NIGC grew and grew, and eventually, in their quest for more money, tried to sweep all tribes into their orbit. The NICG was taking a huge fee from virtually every tribal casino, but Choctaw was not having any of it. They had no need for them, and IGRA was clear that they were under no obligation to submit to this scheme.

That didn't stop the NIGC from trying to force Choctaw under their control. To stop them, Senator Cochran inserted language in the Interior Department Appropriations bill exempting from the NIGC fee regime all "self-regulated tribes, such as the Mississippi Band of Choctaw Indians." We worked to protect the language in the House, and that became the law. The NIGC chaffed at this fee-collecting limitation, but there was little they could do.

Then, a year later in the midst of a heated congressional debate on an unrelated tribal issue, Dale Kildee, liberal Democratic Congressman from Michigan and ersatz friend to the tribes, snuck to the podium to offer a "technical corrections" amendment, which are unopposed provisions usually proposed to correct a technical problem in the language of legislation. Kildee's faux "technical correction" was to remove the words "self regulating tribes, such as" from Senator Cochran's provision, leaving the exemption from the NIGC tax only to apply to Choctaw. Since he disingenuously offered this amendment in the midst of a major floor fight over another tribal issue, our attention was diverted and none of our team caught what he was doing. Once the dust settled, we realized Kildee had struck a blow against all the self-regulating tribes, except Choctaw. Kildee was no dummy. Choctaw had the most powerful political operation on Capitol Hill, thanks to our efforts, and to battle them directly meant not only a stinging defeat, but a possible political storm which could sweep him from office. He figured the other tribes didn't have our muscle, and he was correct. The problem for us, though, was now Choctaw stuck out like a sore thumb. Plus, the other self-regulating tribes included the Chitimachas, a tribe based in Louisiana that Choctaw recently had asked us to represent.

After huddling with Senator Cochran, we tried to get some of the other self-regulating tribes into the fight. This sneaky Kildee amendment was going to cost them millions, so they should have been well motivated. Cochran told us that he didn't wish to carry the water for tribes from other states, but if their home state senators would request it of him, he would insert their names along with Choctaw when he restored the language Kildee had removed.

I went to Terry Martin, the Chitimacha's government affairs liaison, and one of the most impressive client representatives we had. His quiet, humble manner barely masked a keen intellect, and he was instantly the favorite of every Congressman and staffer on the Hill he met. Terry made every effort to get Louisiana Senator John Breaux to support the provision we proposed. Breaux's office was rather explicit that if the Chitimacha wanted the senator to help, they better hire former Senator Bennett Johnston from Louisiana as their lobbyist. One hand washes the other in the U.S. Senate. Terry hesitated because they had just hired our firm to help them in Washington. I told Terry to hire Johnston, and give him whatever money Terry had set aside to pay us. We didn't need the money and were happy to keep representing Chitimacha gratis. One of the most honorable men I had the pleasure to meet during my Washington years, Terry refused to do so. He didn't like this kind of blackmail and wouldn't play ball.

Then I tried the Oneida Tribe of New York. Their representative, Keller George, was a friend of Choctaw and someone we really admired. I called Keller and told him that Cochran had agreed to get them exempted from the fee if they could get a New York Senator involved. I recommended Senator Alfonse D'Amato, who was supportive of the tribe. Keller told me that he would speak with their attorneys and someone would call.

I was finishing a round of golf a few days later when I got the call from the Oneida's lawyer, who was also their lobbyist. I explained what we were doing, and he replied that he didn't recommend we proceed since the tribe was suing in the NIGC over this matter, and the legislation would disrupt the suit.

"Precisely!" I exclaimed into the phone, much to the shock of my guest at the course that day. I put on my headphone and excused myself. "This legislation would make your lawsuit unnecessary. You would win by legislative fiat. What could be better than that?"

"Well, we think the lawsuit has merit and don't want anything to disturb that."

Was I not speaking English? Did he not understand what I was saying? I repeated myself, this time more forcefully. He reiterated his concern, and then it dawned on me: he was their lawyer. He was making a fortune out of this lawsuit and didn't want us to pull a fast one and end it. This guy was actually going to recommend to his client that they stay with his lousy lawsuit when we had a solution to end it. It would cost them millions.

Disgusted, I called Nell Rogers who managed to calm me down. She said that this was typical of tribes and tribal attorneys in general. I asked whether I should call Keller, and she said to forget it. Just leave the language where it was.

And so ended that legislative fight. Our client was still OK, but Kildee had delivered a deathblow costing the other tribes millions of dollars. Later we discovered why he was willing to throw years of supposed support of the tribes to the wind. His former chief of staff, Larry Rosenthal, was the executive director of the NIGC. Together and separately, Rosenthal and Kildee would soak money from the tribes for years to come. Incredibly, both would be at the forefront accusing me of corruption and ripping off my clients when the time came.

The state of Louisiana had three federally recognized Indian tribes with gaming interests: the Chitimacha, the Tunica-Biloxi, and the Coushatta. These tribes were granted seven year compacts to operate casinos on their reservations, all coming due in 2001. Just as I moved to Greenberg, in January of that year, Terry asked if we could help him get the Chitimacha compact renewed for another term. That meant lobbying the Republican governor, Mike Foster. Foster liked the Chitimacha tribe. So did everyone. They were involved in their local community and supported every charitable event they could. The Chitimacha casino was relatively modest, and they did their best to ensure no infrastructure stresses or social ills resulted from their presence. The problem was the Coushatta tribe. Foster hated them and was holding up renewal of any compacts because of his animosity. Terry needed to break through the logjam and thought I might be able to help.

I flew to Baton Rouge, where Terry and I negotiated with Foster and his staff. Everything was pleasant and orderly. The governor was friendly and expressed his great affection for Terry personally. As we chatted, he let loose a series of invectives against the Coushatta. They were rude, bad neighbors, arrogant. He vowed never to give them a compact renewal, unless they submitted to an onerous state tax. I listened impassively. I didn't know the Coushattas, and really could not have cared less. My client in this state was Chitimacha, and they got what they needed. Mission accomplished. I headed back to Washington confident I had seen the last of Louisiana for a while.

A few weeks later, Terry called again. "Remember the Coushatta tribe?"

I didn't. Why would I?

"They were the ones Governor Foster said would never get a gaming compact while he was breathing."

Oh, those guys. Sure, I remembered.

"Would you be willing to represent them, and try to get them a compact?"

I thought Terry was joking. He wasn't.

"Sure, why not? Nothing like a challenge."

Terry set up a phone call with Kathy Van Hoof, the tribe's outside attorney, who brought me up to speed. The tribe was viewed with hostility by their neighbors, who seemed jealous of their success. This was typical. The Indians were pushed around for centuries and then, when they finally got something going, they were resented.

Governor Foster had demanded an 18.5 percent gross tax of their gaming revenues. Since those revenues amounted to almost $400 million a year, and the tribe was already making a contribution of approximately 6 percent of their revenues to offset the stresses on infrastructure, they were obviously up for the fight. This increase was egregious, but I knew from what the governor said that day that quashing it would not be easy. His dislike of the tribe stemmed primarily from the fact that they would not truckle to his whims. Where the Chitimachas were polite and helpful, the Coushattas were brusk and not interested in problems outside their reservation.

We soon found out that Governor Foster was not the Coushatta's only problem. There was a disaster brewing across the border. The Texas tribes were about to launch a legislative effort to get gaming approved in El Paso and Houston. Since Houston was home to virtually the entire Coushatta customer base, this threat was equally scary to the tribe. First we had to make sure they could keep their casino. Then, we could focus on their competition.

We needed a plan. Mike Scanlon was, by now, spending most of his time on outside consulting, and had started working with me to assist Choctaw with political and grass roots matters in their state. The need for grass roots activities for the tribes in their states was a mission apart from the capacities of Greenberg Traurig, or most lobbying firms, so Mike decided to build a separate business focused on this need. When he joined Greenberg, he was hired as a part time consultant, so this did not conflict with his relationship there. Thinking I, too, was permitted to engage in outside activities—after all, I came to the firm during my Suncruz involvement and started numerous other businesses, such as restaurants, while there—I joined Mike in crafting the grass roots programs. He was as brilliant at grass roots organization as he was at communications, so it was only natural that Mike was my first stop after Kathy Van Hoof asked for my help.

Mike and I sat for hours with various members of the Greenberg team to see what they suggested. Most of our lobbyists thought every fight could be won in Washington, and usually they were right. The absurd power that the federal government has usurped from the states meant there was almost always a federal solution to any problem. This nettled us, since we were conservatives, but until the nation could be returned to constitutional government, we felt our job was to work with the tools at hand. The problem here, though, was that there were few federal solutions available. It was perfectly within the rights of Governor Foster to deny the Coushattas their compact. There was no way the Bush administration was going to override a governor—a Republican governor, no less—on denying an Indian tribe a gaming compact. This problem had to be solved in Louisiana.

While no one in their area seemed to like the Coushattas, plenty of folks made their living off them. We had to harness that group. Somehow, we had to organize a mass army and march on Baton Rouge to force the governor's hand. Foster might resist capitulating to the tribe, but what if it weren't the tribe asking for the compact? What if it were his best friend? What if it were all his best friends? His donors? The leading business leaders in the state? What then?

Mike and I devised a plan to create support for Coushatta within

Louisiana and to use this to beat back the governor. Then we went to meet the Coushattas. Unlike most tribes, the Coushatta only had five members on their tribal council. We were ushered into their conference room and introduced to four genial council members and one council member who could easily have fit in among our most aggressive lobbyists. His name was William Worfel and, in introducing himself to us, he declared: "I'm William Worfel and I'm a pit bull with AIDS!"

Scanlon and I smiled. Worfel was ready to fight.

I told the council about my meeting with Foster two months earlier, and none seemed surprised. In fact, the vitriol exhibited toward the governor and almost every state official down to the dogcatcher took Mike and me by surprise. At least they seemed ready for battle, which was good, because the brawl was soon to begin.

To build an army, we were going to call the head of every company in the state which did business with the tribe. We figured that there were at least three hundred companies that sold products or services to the casino, and this group was likely to include a few donors, friends, and relatives of the governor. We were hoping half of them would be willing to call or write the governor, asking him to renew the compact so they wouldn't lose business. A hundred and fifty calls from prominent Louisianans would turn the tide for us, we estimated. As it turns out, there weren't three hundred companies doing business with the tribe. There were four thousand. And we didn't get half of them to call—we got almost all of them. And they were mad. None could understand how their Republican governor was going to ruin their business. It was perfect.

We flooded Baton Rouge with calls. And these were not the typical callbank-generated "robocalls". These were from heads of companies. Many were the governor's donors. Some were his friends. Our staff called the company presidents, explained how their Coushatta contact would soon be gone, and when they agreed to call the Governor's mansion, their call was immediately transferred to the governor's office. Some of the company presidents had the governor's home phone number. Some planned to stop by his house. A few were going to speak with his wife. This was far more serious to these companies than we imagined. They were furious that their governor would even contemplate hurting their business, and they were going to let him have a piece of their mind.

In addition to the calls, we generated letters to the governor by the thousands. These, too, weren't the standard, factory-generated, cookie cutter letters. They were individual letters delineating the precise problem each vendor had with what the governor was doing to their client, the tribe.

When the dust settled, Foster was angrier than ever at the tribe, but he signed the compact. Not only that, but instead of having to pay the 18.5 percent tax he proposed, or even the 6 percent of their gross they were already providing, the tribe was ultimately permitted to pay a mere 4 percent. The Coushattas had another seven years for their casino.

Months later, Mike and I returned to the tribe's headquarters in Kinder, Louisiana for a victory lap. The council meeting turned into a celebration. Even the pit bull was happy. We explained the effort in detail and postulated that their new political prowess might have other benefits. We encouraged them to use the victory as a way to reach out to the community and make new friends.

After the meeting, Worfel pulled us aside.

"Be careful in what you say to folks here. Some of the council members aren't loyal to this tribe."

Those remarks struck us as bizarre, but we would soon come to understand his concerns. With the compact in hand, the tribe asked us to tackle the situation in Texas. The Lone Star State had three recognized American Indian tribes: the Kickapoo, the Alabama Coushatta, and the Tiguas. I represented the Kickapoo briefly while at Preston Gates. Since they were recognized by the federal government as a tribe under the Indian Reorganization Act of 1934, they were able to operate a legal Class II casino, meaning they could have video slot machines, but not the Vegas-style slots or table games such as poker, blackjack, and craps. Almost every tribe in the United States organized under the 1934 Act had the same rights, as did many additional tribes recognized by federal legislation. The only ones I knew of that didn't have the right to even a Class II casino were the two other tribes in Texas.

Recognized by a special Act of Congress in 1987, the Alabama Coushatta and the Tiguas were forced to forgo any casino opportunity which was not already legal under Texas law. Since all gambling was illegal in the Lone Star State, these tribes were prohibited from operating casinos of any kind. That didn't stop the Tiguas. Based in El Paso, on the far western end of the state, the Tiguas opened a rogue casino with full Las Vegas style gaming in 1993, when Democrat Ann Richards was governor. Though she voiced token opposition to the casino, her administration did little to halt its activities. Some speculated that, since the Tiguas were major donors to the Democratic Party, she didn't want to kill the party's golden goose. In 1994, George W. Bush defeated Richards and became the next governor of Texas. His Attorney General, John Cornyn, launched a legal assault on the Tiguas in an effort to shut their casino. The Tiguas responded by hiring lawyers to do battle in court, and lobbyists in Austin to push legislation that would legalize their casino. Almost a decade later, their efforts in Austin started to bear fruit.

The effort to bring gaming to El Paso was of little concern to us. That was over 800 miles from our client in Louisiana, and no one travels that far to gamble unless they're headed to a destination resort. Instead, our clients, the Louisiana Coushattas, were worried about the Alabama Coushattas of Texas—otherwise known as the Alabamas—their distant cousins, who were trying to open their own casino on the doorstep of the Coushatta market. Plus, as Worfel informed us, some Louisiana council members were regularly passing along sensitive political information to their actual cousins on the Alabamas tribal council.

The Alabamas' tribal land was in Livingston, Texas, just east of Houston. The tribe benefited from oil and gas leases, and were flush with money. That enabled them to hire lawyers and lobbyists to join the legislative effort by the Tiguas to legalize gambling. The legislation would have provided these tribes full Las Vegas style casinos in El Paso and Houston. The Houston casino would crush our client's facility in Kinder. Why would anyone drive three hours to Kinder if they could gamble thirty minutes away in Houston?

The Texas tribes were well ahead of us in this fight. In fact, they had already passed their legislation in the Texas state house by a close vote. That stunned us. We had assumed conservative Texas was anti-gaming, but we were wrong. Scanlon ran some quick opinion polls, and we were shocked to find a majority of Texans favored gambling. So much for stereotypes.

The tribes' lobbyists in Austin intuited the same information, and had assembled a coalition of western (Tigua) and eastern (Alabamas) legislators to pass the bill in the state house. Our vote count in the Senate was grim.

We had to shake things up with a third force.

A few years before the Texas rhubarb ignited, Scanlon and I had been fighting a similar battle in another part of the South. Located on the eastern border of Mississippi, our Choctaw client relied almost entirely on a customer base from Birmingham, Alabama, where Democrat Don Siegelman became the 51st governor in 1998. Siegelman vowed to enact legislation permitting a state lottery, which would have been the first breech in the Alabama anti-gambling wall. One of his main campaign financiers, Milton MacGregor—later indicted along with Siegelman for corruption—owned several dog tracks in the state, and wanted to enhance his operations with slot machines. Seeing the rumblings of gaming, the state's only federally recognized Indian tribe, the Alabama Poarch Creek Indians, made a run to get approval to open their own casino.

The Choctaws were in the process of opening a second, massive casino across the road from their initial facility in Mississippi. Suddenly, they were facing the possible obliteration of their market, and we were sent to stop it. Once again, a federal solution would not be sufficient. We had to stop these efforts in Alabama. Scanlon embarked for Birmingham, and I called Ralph Reed.

Time and again, Ralph had shown the world that he knew better than anyone how to motivate the faith community to get politically active. It was obvious to me that the only way to stop Siegelman, MacGregor, and the Poarch Creeks was to organize the Christians. Ralph could do this in his sleep.

While Ralph didn't want his co-religionists to know he was accepting funds from an Indian tribe with a casino, he threw himself into these efforts. With Scanlon on the ground and Ralph organizing a blitz of the state house by pastors, we were able to defeat the assaults on the Choctaw gaming markets time and again.

Ralph wasn't the only one who wished to work in silence. Nell Rogers made it clear to me that our efforts had to be carried out in stealth, since they didn't want the Poarch Creeks to know it was the Choctaws who stopped them. Chief Martin had previously met with the Poarch Creeks to dissuade them from encroaching on the Choctaw's Birmingham market, even offering to help them get a compact with the governor if they would keep their casino in the southern part of the state and forgo Birmingham.

When they refused, the Choctaws called me in. I thought the Poarch Creeks should know who was stopping them, but my loyalty was to my client, and so I kept the secret as Nell requested.

While Ralph went to work for us, Scanlon and I war-gamed our approach. We set up a political infrastructure in Alabama which would have enabled us to stop the Poarch Creek in the event our legislative lobbying failed. We drafted city regulations closing the streets surrounding the competing casino and denying the tribe access to the curb. These seemingly minor annoyances can actually shutter an enterprise.

Then Scanlon and I came up with another aggressive tactic. While Ralph organized the African American churches to oppose the introduction of gambling, we designed a different campaign for those members of the African American community who weren't opposed to gambling. Facing abject poverty and the need for better social services, this community needed money. If our efforts to stop the gaming juggernaut started to falter, we were going to direct African American leaders to make contact with MacGregor and offer their support—in exchange for five percent of all gross revenues at all his tracks. Based on our calculations, a loss of five percent of gross revenues would have sapped his profitability, making the entire endeavor fruitless. He would be torn, however, seeing a massive block of the African American community willing to support him. We chortled at the possibilities of this devilish plan. We even gave it a name: Gimme Five. As in, "Give me five percent." Eventually, Scanlon and I started referring to all those activities which we thought clever as "Gimme Five." But, we were too clever for our own good. When my life came crashing down, McCain and the media hounds attacking me misinterpreted the term to be a code for our planned fraud. Some felt it meant "gimme a five percent profit". Others were convinced it meant "gimme five million dollars." Neither made any sense since the media were accusing us of defrauding our clients for far more than five percent or five million dollars, but our attackers loved the satiric catch phrase.

Our efforts for the Choctaw in Alabama were extensive and expensive, and included radio and television advertising. We organized scores of pastors and voters to lay siege to the statehouse and the Governor's office. Between MacGregor and the Poarch Creeks, the fight continued to flare up repeatedly. When we defeated them, they would try another tack, so we would defeat them again. Over the course of almost five years waging this battle, we saved Choctaw's gaming market—which provided them with over $400 million a year in revenue. It cost the tribe approximately $20 million to wage these battles, but the returns were worth it to them, Chief Martin called us the "best slot machine" they had, and he was not exaggerating.

Eventually, our grassroots expertise for the Choctaw was required in their home state of Mississippi. State Senator Jack Gordon was chairman of the powerful Appropriations Committee. Having served in the Mississippi legislature almost continuously since 1972, Gordon was hardly ever challenged for re-election. One day, Senator Gordon announced he was going to introduce legislation to undo the perpetual tax-free compact Chief Martin had signed with the state for Choctaw gaming rights. Gordon wanted to tax the tribe.

Immediately, we launched our grassroots offensive. There were few people on earth who could have matched Scanlon in this arena, and he didn't disappoint. Within eight days, Mike had blanketed Gordon's district with radio, television, and print advertising, but he had an even bigger weapon—one we would employ with great effect in many future battles. Just as we had with the Coushattas and Foster, in addition to the short-term allies we found in faith communities and tribe members themselves, we targeted the vendors of the casino. In the case of Choctaw, we found that there were thousands of them. Getting these vendors organized in a political force became our passion, and like our efforts in other tribal fights, the vendors responded beyond expectation. Mike had the Choctaw vendors, some of who were donors to Gordon, rain calls into the senator's office. At the same time, Scanlon located a potential election opponent and started pushing his name with phone banks. He even conducted a poll, which showed the challenger within striking distance of Gordon. All in eight days. Furthermore, we made sure Gordon knew everything we were doing.

On day nine, Gordon took to the air himself. On a local talk radio program he apologized for the "misunderstanding." Later that day, the Chief called and told me that Gordon wanted to come to the reservation to apologize in person. I was glad that Gordon got the message, but wanted him to do something more than apologize and urged the Chief to request action as well as words. Gordon offered to sponsor legislation to widen the main road leading to the reservation. Mike's self-congratulatory praise was well deserved: "Sometimes," he said, "I even amaze myself!"

These Choctaw grassroots efforts gave us the experience we needed to wage a similar war in Texas for the Coushattas in 2001.

The Texas tribes had succeeded in pushing the gambling legislation through the state house prior to our engagement. Now the battle was focused on the state Senate, and Lieutenant Governor Bill Ratliff, a gaming opponent, was the president pro tempore. He didn't intervene in legislation often, but he controlled the senate's schedule. The Texas tribes and their allied Democrats pushed the bill through the Senate Criminal Justice Committee and were ready to bring it to a vote on the floor. I called Ralph Reed. Immediately, the tribe hired him, though, again, Ralph wanted to do so indirectly and quietly. He did not want word out about his involvement with tribal gaming. We were more than willing to oblige and crafted a structure which would protect his privacy, but not violate Texas law. Once we were able to engage him, Ralph called Ratliff to get him to delay the vote. He then alerted the Christian community that the legislature was about to pass a gambling bill, and they were outraged. We coordinated their activities, and pummeled the legislators responsible for this bill with phone calls, letters, and angry visits. Without the funding provided by the Coushattas, we wouldn't have been able to mobilize these troops to defeat the legislation, and the bill would have easily passed.

The Texas legislature meets in regular session once every two years, and then only for 140 days. Texans know how to keep their politicos out of the state house, limiting them from doing too much to meddle in their lives. Since it was already late April, we just had to hold on for another month, and the session would end. We added television, radio, and print advertising to our campaign, and activated thousands more to fight the bill. Ralph made contact with the African American pastors in Texas, as he had done earlier in Alabama, and they incited their members to stop the coming gambling scourge. But even with everything we were doing, we weren't certain we had moved enough votes to prevail. It was rumored that the tribes' lobbyists had been spreading cash around, but we couldn't get this confirmed.

After an intense few weeks, Ratliff's hold on the legislation prevailed, and the Senate adjourned its session without taking up the bill. We had won. It was a harrowing battle, requiring round the clock vigilance, with the frenetic pace of an election campaign. We targeted legislators and directed our supporters to bombard them. Each day required our political armies to shift battlefields and attack, but Scanlon and Ralph were masterful. When the clock ran out, we joined the chief of the Coushattas, Lovelin Poncho, and Worfel in celebration. This time, we were cautious to avoid the rest of the council. Worfel later told us that some of our updates were taken from their office and passed to the Alabamas, and on to their lobbyists. We had won a most hard fought battle, but it wasn't over yet.

Almost as soon as we wiped our brows of the Texas challenge, the Coushattas faced several fights back in Louisiana, and we were at it again.

Governor Foster didn't go gently into the night. He knew the Coushattas had bested him politically, and he was going to try to get the last laugh. Anyone who knows about casinos knows that market share is one of the key determinants of success. If another casino is drawing your gamblers, you will have less revenue. If they draw enough, you are out of business. That was Foster's plan.

The first volley was his effort to place a riverboat casino on Lake Charles, to the west of Kinder. Lake Charles is thirty-eight miles closer to Houston, and directly off US Route 10, the main interstate road to Kinder. Foster's proposal was no mistake. He was going to kill Coushatta with this new facility and make it look like he was just trying to improve the economy of the state. For the third time in less than six months, our team, Scanlon, and I were suiting up for battle. This time, the anti-casino effort would be brought into Louisiana. We launched a statewide media and grassroots campaign to stop the expansion on the lake. Since none of this could take place in the name of the tribe—because otherwise the effort would be seen as one competitor fighting another, he had to set up an outside organization to lead the fight. Immediately, we launched a non-profit group called Citizens Against Gambling Expansion, or CAGE. This group was the face on the anti-gambling expansion efforts we ran in Louisiana. Through it, we launched direct mail, television and radio assaults on our opponents and organized our anti-gambling supporters in the faith community. It was common practice to use non-profit organizations to front for lobbying efforts, and it still happens today. This practice was legally questionable, but that never occurred to us. We figured that the groups were engaged in non-profit activities and that, therefore, our activities were permitted. Even the attorneys at our firm didn't see the issues when these matters were discussed. But, it was wrong of us to use the system in this way, and I would pay dearly for it in the future. In the meantime, CAGE served its purpose and we were able to beat Foster again.

He took the blow, but got right back up again for more. Next up, horses.

Delta Downs Racetrack Casino in Vinton was even closer to Houston than Lake Charles. They already had a few slot machines, but Foster proposed expanding that exponentially. He wanted a full casino. Scanlon and I prepared a plan to stop this, but the tribe dithered and only gave approval at the last minute, which meant we would only be able to slow Foster down, but not stop him completely.

The next assault was far more serious, and came from yet another tribe. Though there were three tribes engaged in gaming in Louisiana, there were four tribes recognized in total. The fourth was called the Jena Band of Choctaw Indians. We already had experience in dealing with the Jena when they attempted to acquire land for a casino in Tishomingo County in neighboring Mississippi. Acting on behalf of the Choctaw, we stopped that effort by lobbying the Bush Interior Department. It would have required federal approval for this tribe to move across the border into another state, and we blocked them.

The Jena's base was in Northeastern Louisiana, near the border of Mississippi. Had they attempted to secure a casino in that location, it's unlikely any of the other Louisiana tribes would have opposed them, but instead they tried to locate two and a half hours away, between Kinder and Houston. What a coincidence.

Foster backed the initial effort to move the tribe to southeastern Louisiana and they soon found a location: right near Vinton, the home of Delta Downs. Adding insult to injury, the site they grabbed was actually ancient Coushatta land! In response to the thousands of hostile calls and letters we initiated, Foster indicated that he was considering backing off. Instead, he secretly signed a compact with the tribe and shipped it off to the Secretary of the Interior in Washington for ratification, the final step in granting a tribe a casino compact. Now the fight was in our own backyard of the nation's capital.

I had developed good relations with the Interior Department through the Deputy Secretary of Interior, Steve Griles. A southern gentleman with a charm and intellect rivaling most of Washington's luminaries, Griles was a delight to be around and, more importantly, the number two person in the department. He was no fan of gambling, and no friend to tribes attempting an improper expansion. With the Jena situation, though, we were up against a powerful Washington lobbyist, future Mississippi Governor Haley Barbour. Haley was close to Interior Secretary Gail Norton, and we feared Griles wouldn't be able to overcome that alliance.

But Foster and the Jena made a key mistake. They added a state tax provision to the compact, and federal law prohibited a state tax on Indian tribes. We had been through this fight many times before, when we fought the Istook Amendment, which would have enabled states to tax tribes located in their borders. When we reviewed the Jena compact, we knew we had a way to stop it. It was only a matter of activating the legions of tribal supporters we had organized on Capitol Hill and directing their fire against this provision. A few weeks later, a letter was dispatched from the Assistant Secretary of Indian Affairs to the Jena chief: there would be no casino.

Each of these threats to Coushatta would have eviscerated their annual gaming receipts, estimated to be well over $300 million. They spent millions with us protecting their markets, but, like any prudent business owners, they felt it was worth spending millions to protect hundreds of millions a year.

We worked long and hard for the tribes we represented and in return, the law firm and Scanlon's company were making a lot of money. Millions. Our efforts were saving the tribes hundreds of millions, if not billions. Each effort would require grass roots mobilization, as well as radio and sometimes television advertising. For each Coushatta campaign, like each program we provided to any of the other clients, we would assess the threat they presented to us and return with a proposal to eliminate that threat. Mike would usually label the project with a mission name, such as "Operation Tishomingo" or "Operation Orange." The proposal would usually be quite extensive, including every possible method of ensuring victory. Since hundreds of millions of dollars were at stake, we tried not to leave any stone unturned. Usually, the tribe would review the cost of the plan and make a counter offer. If, for example, Scanlon and I proposed an effort costing $4 million, they would counter with $2 million. We would adjust the proposal and re-counter, as would they. Eventually, we would come to an agreement, which their attorneys and Mike would document. Almost invariably, the tribe would then ratify the agreement at the tribal council level. Then we would launch the campaign and see it through to victory. After that, Mike would insist on written confirmation that the tribe was satisfied with our efforts.

The Coushatta tribal council was more than satisfied with our efforts, or at least those members of the council who did not have a conflicting relationship with their competition were. But the many battles they had to fight were draining them of funds. Later, I was told that the Coushatta tribe was paying us from their education fund. That seemed unlikely to me since they claimed to be reaping hundreds of millions per year in casino revenues, but I never saw proof either way.

Scanlon and I had beaten back all threats to the Coushattas, and were continuing to wage wars on behalf of the Choctaw and tribes in three other states. I could tell he was getting fatigued, but we had to keep going. For Mike, it was no longer enough that we were making a fortune. He was sick and tired of the late night calls from worried clients and the frenetic pace of it all. He wanted to stop. I told him we couldn't stop for two reasons. First, our clients needed us to protect them. No one could match our track record, and we couldn't risk a defeat. One loss, and they would be out of business. Second, I couldn't afford for us to stop.

Mike and I split the profits of the grassroots efforts. Sometimes there were no profits since the fees were eaten up by the immense cost of the lobbying. Most of the time, though, there was a healthy profit margin, especially when we figured out a way to stop the threat to the client more quickly or inexpensively than usual.

By the time our operations reached their zenith, I was funding schools, restaurants, charity efforts, and a host of other activities. My addiction to charity and schools was draining me and, though I was making millions of dollars, I was actually living hand to mouth. I never even paid off the mortgage on our home since I figured there would always be more money to come. In a way, I was acting exactly like the irresponsible spendthrifts doling out taxpayer dollars to a myriad of federal programs. They spend with abandon, always confident that the American taxpayer will cough up more money. Now, of course, that reckless behavior has come back to haunt our system, as we deal with massive deficits and debt. Unfortunately, I was a miniature version of that system.

Worse than my proliferate charitable spending, in the heat of battle, and the triumph of success, I neglected to tell my clients how much I was profiting from these grassroots efforts. I reasoned that the tribes and clients were happy with their victories, that our efforts were priced in accordance with their value and that they were paying what they agreed to pay to stop threats they identified to us, after proper fee negotiations. Plus, I wasn't even keeping the money I made anyway. I was giving away upwards of 80 percent of my income for good causes and to help people. What could possibly be wrong with any of this? Sure, I didn't tell all my clients that I was sharing in the profits from Mike's operation, but did I really need to do so? Wasn't it obvious? Did they think I was doing all this extra work—work that had nothing to do with the D.C. lobbying—for free? Surely some of them knew. Others must have figured it out. Did I really need to be explicit here? Yes, I did.

While my clients almost certainly didn't decide to hire us based on what Mike did with the profits from his work, and while splitting the fees wasn't illegal, they had a right to know. I didn't tell them that Greenberg paid me approximately 30 percent of the revenue I brought into the firm, and I reasoned that, similarly, I didn't need to tell them that Scanlon and I were splitting his fees. But I should have. And I paid a heavy price for it when everything came apart.

Jack Abramoff, age six.

The 1965 Miss America Pageant dinner with Arnold and Winnie Palmer and children, and Frank and Jane Abramoff and children.

LEFT: In July 1969, Jack Abramoff was the youngest student at the Arnold Palmer Golf Academy in Vail, Colorado. Pictured here with Palmer and Frank Abramoff.

RIGHT: In March 1972, Jack Abramoff holds the Torah scroll in preparation for his Bar Mitzvah.

Don Rickles, host of the Sugar Ray Robinson Youth Foundation Telethon, directs his good-hearted insults at young Jack Abramoff.

LEFT: Abramoff breaks the power squat weight lifting record at Beverly Hills High School with a lift of 455, June 1976.

RIGHT: Official high school football picture, September 1976.

LEFT and RIGHT: President Ronald Reagan greets Jack Abramoff in the Oval Office, December 1981.

Poster against nuclear freeze, April 1982.

TOP: Grover Norquist, Paul Erickson, Ted Higgins, Larry Copperman, Ian Ballon, Andy Smart, and Steve Bowling join Jack Abramoff in celebrating his election as national College Republican chairman, Chicago June 1981.

BOTTOM: Grover Norquist and Jack Abramoff exit the West Wing of the White House, December 1981.

TOP: Jack Abramoff listens as President Ronald Reagan confers with conservative leaders about the nuclear freeze movement, March 1982 .

BOTTOM: President Ronald Reagan speaks at his seventy-second birthday party in the East Wing of the White House, February 1983.

TOP: Jack Abramoff introduces then-Vice President George H. W. Bush at the 90th anniversary College Republican National Committee Conference, June 1982.

BOTTOM: New York City Mayor, Ed Koch, interviewed by Jack Abramoff for Fallout Radio Program, June 1984.

Artist Phil Groves painted what was to be the ultimate College Republican political humor poster, *The Empire Strikes Out*, as a parody of the Star Wars hit film *The Empire Strikes Back,* only to see the quick demise of Soviet dictator Brezhnev and several of his successors end the effort, November 1982.

# Stop The PIRGlars
# From Stealing Your Student Fees

# RESTORE STUDENT RIGHTS NOW

Published by the USA Foundation, 214 Massachusetts Ave. NE, Washington, D.C. 20002

A Public Interest Research Group poster, August 1983.

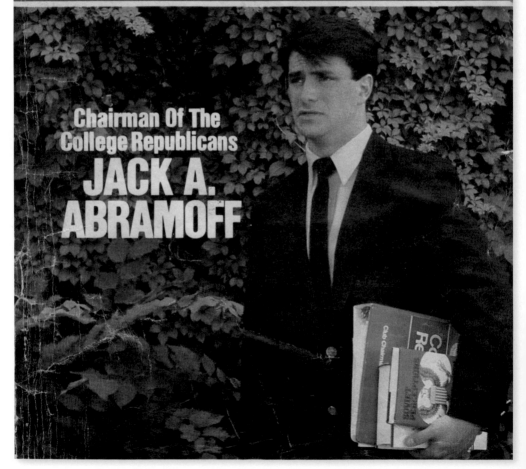

STUDENT SPECIAL
See Pages 43-44.

# The Review Of The
# NEWS

ONE DOLLAR                    September 8, 1982 • Volume 18, Number 36

## How The West Created The Soviet Chemical Warfare Machine

## CONGRESSMAN PHILIP CRANE BLASTS NEW TAXATION OF TIPS

### Chairman Of The College Republicans
# JACK A. ABRAMOFF

*The Review of the News* magazine, September 1982.

TOP: The iconic "Fritzbusters" campaign button became a collectible in 1984.

BOTTOM: Jack Abramoff addresses Republican National Convention, Dallas 1984.

Poster about El Salvador, March 1983.

FIRST ST. S.E., WASHINGTON, D.C. 20003

TOP: Two Jacks: Jack Abramoff and Jack Kemp were friends and allies. Kemp was the biggest congressional booster of Abramoff's College Republican efforts, and Abramoff organized the Kemp for President rally at the 1984 Republican National Convention.

BOTTOM: Republican National Committee Chairman promises financial support for all College Republican training schools, as Jack Abramoff and Paul Erickson look on, June 1981.

National College Republican Chairman Jack Abramoff, December 1983.

As executive director of the president's grassroots lobby, Jack Abramoff briefs President Ronald Reagan and lobby chairman Lewis Lehrman, March 1985.

Citizens for America poster in support of the MX Missile Vote, June 1985.

TOP: Americans for Tax Reform Chairman Grover Norquist and Jack Abramoff meet with Speaker Newt Gingrich, October 1995.

BOTTOM: Russian Prime Minister Viktor Chernomyrdin meets Speaker Newt Gingrich, as Jack Abramoff and Jay Kaplan look on, February 1997.

Jack Abramoff makes the case for the CNMI with Speaker Newt Gingrich, October 1995.

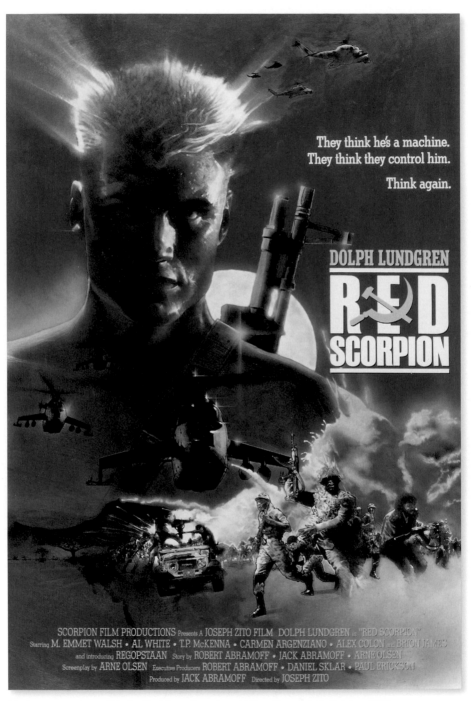

Movie poster responsible for *Red Scorpion* sales at Milan film market, October 1986.

TOP: On the set of *Red Scorpion* with actor Dolph Lundgren, December 1987.

BOTTOM: Jack Abramoff and Dolph Lundgren discuss filming challenges on the set of *Red Scorpion* in Namibia, December 1987.

TOP: Neil Volz, Ralph Reed, Paul Vinovich, Bob Ney, David Safavian, Michael Williams, Alex Abramoff, and Jack Abramoff outside the plane which took them to Scotland, August 2002.

BOTTOM: Jack Abramoff hits approach shot to the green on the 18th hole at the championship course at Carnoustie Golf Links in Scotland, August 2003.

ack Abramoff, Ralph Reed, David Safavian, and Congressman Bob Ney complete a round of golf at Carnoustie
Golf Links in Scotland, August 2002.

TOP: Jack Abramoff and Chief Philip Martin greet Majority Leader Trent Lott, May 1998.

BOTTOM: House Majority Leader Tom DeLay makes his point to Choctaw Chief Phillip Martin and Jack Abramoff, September 1998.

TOP: Jack Abramoff joins Majority Whip Tom DeLay at a charitable golf event to benefit foster children, April 1998.

BOTTOM: Jack Abramoff at Stacks Deli, December 2003 (photo by Richard Bloom).

TOP: Jack and Pam Abramoff with Vice President Richard Cheney and Speaker Dennis Hastert, October 2003.

BOTTOM: President George W. Bush and Speaker of the House Dennis Hastert gather Abramoff children for a photograph, February 2002.

TOP: Jack Abramoff and son Daniel meet President George W. Bush, September 2002.

BOTTOM: Jack Abramoff and son Daniel welcome Arnold Schwarzenegger to Signatures Restaurant, January 2003.

Jack Abramoff is sworn in before United States Senate Indian Affairs Committee, September 2004.

obe Lowell confers with Jack Abramoff at Indian Affairs Committee Hearing, September 2004.

TOP: Sarah Abramoff meets with Kevin Spacey, who plays Jack Abramoff in *Casino Jack*.

BOTTOM: Jack and Pam Abramoff at Cumberland Federal Prison, June 2008.

# 12

# FIRE UP THE JET, BABY!

With victories over Foster on the compact, the Texas tribes, the Lake Charles river boat, and, in a more limited fashion, the Delta Downs Track, we were riding high. In addition to these efforts, our team in Washington was helping create the same solid relations for the Coushattas on Capitol Hill that we built for Choctaw. But there were still clouds on the Louisiana horizon.

Word leaked back that Foster was going to make another attempt to get Jena approved in Washington. That would mean another conflagration. At the same time, Ralph Reed called with intelligence that the Tiguas and Alabamas were preparing to launch another assault in the Texas legislature when their next session commenced. While I normally would celebrate additional grassroots efforts, and the attendant fees, this time I was concerned. The Coushatta were spending so much money, and yet it seemed there was no end to the threats they faced. Like some bad whack-a-mole game, the opponents just kept coming back for more. Mike and I were heavily engaged in battles for other tribal clients, and my practice continued to expand. I was worried that constant war would kill the Coushatta golden goose.

One night I sat and thought anew through all of their issues. And then it hit me. We might be able put an end to the fight in Texas permanently, stopping that drain of Coushatta funds, and even pick up another client on the way. It was a perfect solution. Or so I thought.

How could we make this happen? By enabling Tigua to obtain a casino. Not a full Vegas casino, but a Class II casino with video poker machines and bingo. Since they had no gaming competition anywhere near El Paso that might just satisfy them. The Texas Attorney General was days from concluding a several year battle to close their illegal casino. Wouldn't it be amazing if we could march right in and get them re-opened with another one? We could achieve this by slipping an amendment through Congress to the 1987 Act which recognized the tribe, eliminating the gambling ban against them. Removing the explicit prohibition against gambling would put the Tiguas on the same footing as every other tribe in the nation. They would be permitted a Class II casino without any further governmental approvals. Once the Tiguas were satisfied with a legal casino, the entire coalition of western Texas legislators would peel off the bill in Texas. Those politicians had no fealty to the Alabamas. Once that part of the coalition was gone, we would have no problem beating the bill in the Texas statehouse, and the Coushattas would be safe. Plus, if we played our cards right, once we got Tigua open again, they'd be our client.

I ran the plan by Mike who had a one-word response: "Perfect." It was the ultimate bank shot. Our client's Texas problem would be solved for good, and we would gain a new high paying client. What could be better than this? Now we just had to pull it off.

I made contact with the Tiguas through Nell Rogers' ex-husband, who was a prominent Indian law attorney, and landed on the phone with Marc Schwartz, the tribe's outside political consultant. At first he was cautious since I was the bad guy who stopped their bill in Austin. Fortunately, the fact that I had been their relentless opponent gave me a strange credibility in presenting this new plan. When I finished, he said he would discuss with the tribe and get back to me. It didn't take more than a day for him to return. I told him that Scanlon and I would come meet them at our expense, and he agreed. I was ecstatic. In my exuberance, I sent an email to Scanlon that, like so many others, would be used to slander me: "Fire up the jet baby! We're going to El Paso!"

Scanlon and I met Schwartz at the airport in El Paso. On the drive to the tribal offices, he explained we would be meeting with the entire tribal council, but not the chief, Albert Alvidrez. He was a committed

Democrat and didn't want to have anything to do with an effort by Republicans to re-open their casino. Considering the tribe's troubles stemmed in part from their partisan embrace and funding of the Democrats, I found this disturbing.

Scanlon presented our plan to the tribal council, which we called Operation Open Doors. This was unlike any other effort in which we had engaged. We had to sneak a provision onto a moving piece of federal legislation in the Republican Congress which would legalize a casino in a state where the Republican Party opposed it. The effort had to be kept secret from the Republicans as well as the Tigua's previous partners in the state legislative initiative, the Alabamas. If the Alabamas found out what the Tiguas were doing, they would try to stop it because they would be left alone and helpless. Any effort against the legislation could topple it. One alert to Senator Phil Graham—a major opponent of the tribe—and he would put a hold on the bill, effectively killing it.

Once the bill was passed, we had to brace ourselves for the backlash. The Republican opponents of the tribe would be furious that the casino in El Paso was back in operation and would undoubtedly try to reverse our success with legislation of their own. To prevent this, Scanlon was to build a database of the vendors and motivate them to act. Additionally, through Tigua contributions to the Republican Party, we would construct a cadre of supporters. Since we would be on defense in the backlash, we had a better chance. It's always easier to stop a bill than to put one through. All of this depended on keeping the Alabamas and everyone else in the dark, and finding a moving train--congressional legislation which was currently progressing—to jump on.

Last, but far from least, we had to keep our own presence quiet. By now I was a known media entity. Every time I landed a new client, the *Washington Post* would feature the news in the front section of the paper. These articles were in no way hostile, but they were certainly public. Any mention of the Tiguas would alert the Texas Republicans and, particularly, the Alabamas that something was afoot. So I told the tribe that Greenberg would depart from our normal practice of insisting on being engaged, and work for the tribe without compensation and without registering under the Lobbying Disclosure Act.

I thought I was using a loophole in the law to conceal our presence in this representation. Of course, this was wrong. While my motivation was, in part, to protect the client and maintain silence about the effort, I was making a mockery of a law designed to shed light on a corrupt and secretive business. But I wasn't thinking about that then. I was thinking about slipping legislation past the most powerful Republican state delegation in the Congress and keeping the Houston-based Alabamas from opening a casino.

When I returned from El Paso, I called Jon van Horne to my office. Jon was one of our most valuable team members, a legislative and process genius. When I first arrived at Greenberg, I was told that Jon, who was approaching retirement age, was on his way out—a tired, useless holdover that I should feel free to dismiss as soon as possible. But as soon as I met him, I recognized a master craftsman whose talents were either unknown or under appreciated. No, Jon Van Horne was not going to be fired by me. He was going to be promoted. I had emailed ahead to Jon about the new project and asked him to get up to speed for my return.

Back in D.C., Jon entered my office and sat down. "Jon, I need legislative language we can slip into a bill. I want something so cryptic, so enigmatic, so opalescent, that it would take a computer to discern what we were trying to do. And I need it fast, like yesterday."

Jon flashed his trademark grin and handed me a piece of paper. "Funny, that's when I wrote it." On it was written the poetry I craved: "Public Law 100-89 is amended by striking section 207 (101 Stat. 668, 672)."

It was a thing of beauty. No one would know that these abstruse words would magically open the doors to the Tigua casino, and forever doom the Alabamas' chances to steal the Coushatta's Houston market. Now we just had to find a moving train to throw this on.

The expansion of our tribal gaming representations did not end with Coushatta and Tigua. As my practice grew, I sought new Indian tribal clients throughout the nation and was able to secure representations in Michigan, New Mexico, Arizona, Oklahoma, and California. I was particularly happy to commence a relationship with the Agua Caliente tribe in Palm Springs, California, since my parents had recently moved from Beverly Hills to Mission Hills, which borders Palm Springs. Each time I met with the tribe, I was able to see my parents—except once.

The Agua Caliente had a myriad of Washington issues which our lobbying team, under Duane Gibson's leadership, was able to solve. They also had a compact with the state of California that limited the number of slots they could operate, and Scanlon and I were brought on to run a grassroots effort to help them get that limit raised. Most of our other tribal government clients had over 4,000 slots (which, in casino economics, calculates to over $200 million dollar in annual revenue), but the Agua Caliente were limited to approximately one thousand machines. The tribe was enmeshed in a lawsuit over their campaign contributions, which made our job more challenging, but we were finally starting to make some real progress when the tribe asked us to come brief their council. The meeting took most of the morning, but finished just before lunch. We weren't planning to fly back to Washington until the next day, so I asked Mike if he wanted to play some golf. It was rare that we had a chance to play golf together. Our usual sports competition was racquetball. Since both Mike and I were hypercompetitive, those bouts seemed to be fought to the death, and almost always ended in a good-natured verbal fusillade. Well, sometimes it was not so good-natured.

My parents were, by then, living in Rancho Mirage. Their home was situated on the fairway of the 11th hole of the championship course at Mission Hills, the site of the annual Kraft Nabisco Women's Golf Major Championship. Dad kept several sets of clubs and a golf cart at the house. Since they were traveling when I was in town, Dad had arranged for us to play at the course if desired. Mike and I arrived shortly after the conclusion of our meetings and headed straight for the tee box. As usual with Mike, the verbal taunting started as soon as we pulled out our drivers. Mike and I decided on a friendly bet of one dollar a hole. After easily vanquishing him on the first few holes, Mike declared he couldn't treat a one-dollar bet seriously, ergo his inability to win. He raised the stakes to ten dollars a hole. I was fine with that, as long as I didn't lose too many holes. I calculated that I would end the bet after two losing holes, but that didn't happen. Instead, I won the next two holes and Mike was starting to get frustrated. The worst emotion for a golfer is anger, or, in Mike's case, rage. You start making mistakes in what is very much a mental game. Somewhat sadistically, I was enjoying Mike's explosions, as he thrashed his ball all around the course. I calmly shot bogeys and pars, but he was putting up some very big scores, and losing every hole. After about four more holes, Scanlon pulled his signature psychological warfare move: "Jack, I can't get serious about ten dollars a hole. Let's play for one thousand dollars a hole."

Normally, Scanlon's opponents would fold, intimidated and afraid to play his version of the game chicken. But I accepted. I figured we made a good living, and it was worth it to counter his posturing. But, I decided I would quit this insane game the minute I lost any of these gargantuan bets.

The first hole of the new betting regime didn't go well for Mike. His drive sliced into the rough and his irons were not working well. By the time he reached the green, he was already out of the hole. I was up one thousand dollars, plus the now less relevant sums of our earlier bets. The second one thousand dollar hole proved equally frustrating for Mike, and his rage started to return. After a third consecutive defeat, he was down three thousand dollars. I tried to let him out of the bet, telling him I had no intention of collecting, but that's not Mike Scanlon. He was going to win or die trying. That's one of the things I loved about the guy.

Mike demanded we raise the bet to three thousand dollars. I agreed—quietly knowing that I was always one lost hole away from quitting this insanity. Mike's intensity and frustration wreaked havoc on his swing, and he was out of that hole by the time we reached the green. I calmly continued to make pars and bogeys, taking no chances with any shot. Anguished obscenities flowed from his mouth. I could barely keep from laughing at the site, and continually looked away as he let loose strings of vulgarities. With each lost hole, Mike's taunts and bravado would return—but only for the walk to the next tee box. He raised the stakes and lowered them depending on his manic mood. As we approached the seventeenth hole, Mike was down twenty-five thousand dollars! He hadn't won a single bet, and continued to pile on the debt. I played steady golf, as he proceeded to meltdown.

The seventeenth hole at the Mission Hills championship course was a par three, playing almost 200 yards. Guarded in front and back by sand traps, the green sits perched on a hill, with a dramatic slope falling to the left. Mike set the bet at ten thousand dollars. If anyone had told me that I would ever bet ten thousand dollars on a golf hole, I would have laughed, but I took the bet, knowing, even if I lost, I was still ahead by fifteen thousand—of his money. As I struck my tee shot, I felt myself pulling the club to the left, sending my ball hooking toward the left side of the green. A bad bounce propelled the ball down the hill on the left, into the abyss. Mike cracked his first smile in hours, realizing I had finally opened the door to a comeback. His confident swing sent his ball soaring toward the green, but it didn't soar high enough, and landed in the sandtrap in front of the green. But that didn't dampen Mike's spirit. As we settled into the cart for the ride to the green, Mike was explaining how, in two holes (this one and the final hole, the eighteenth) he would undo all my gains of the day. I just listened and didn't respond. A lot can happen in two holes.

I found my ball at the bottom of the hill, surrounded by trees. I searched for a smart way to play the ball back toward the green, but few paths out of this jail were evident. Finally I spied a slight opening among the branches, though I didn't think I had the shot to propel the ball straight up with the force required to get to the green. Mentally, I had already conceded the hole, and felt no real pressure. I thrashed at the ball and saw it clear the limbs of the trees, heading into the sky. As I couldn't see anything, I had to wait to hear Mike's anguished expletive scream to know that the shot worked. I bounded up the hill to discover my ball at rest no more than three inches from the cup. An easy tap in gave me a score of three, par on this hole.

To win this hole, Mike now needed to sink his ball directly from the sand trap, a feat highly unlikely even for the most accomplished professional golfer. Mike wasn't even playing like an accomplished amateur golfer, and promptly skulled his ball out of the trap, over the green and into another sand trap! This shot was followed by a hail of invectives roaring Mike's disapproval. Now, he had to sink the ball from the second trap, just to tie the hole, and not sustain a ten thousand dollar loss. His attempt made it to the green, but not to the hole. He was now down thirty-five thousand dollars. I offered, again, to call it quits, and forget about it. No dice.

The eighteenth hole at this course is one of the most celebrated finishing holes in professional golf. A par five, which played on that day at 613 yards, the hole invariably plays into a stiff headwind, and ends with a most difficult shot to a green surrounded by water. Mike announced the bet as fifteen thousand dollars. I accepted. If I lost, I would take home twenty thousand dollars. If I won, it would be fifty thousand.

We both hit nice drives, roughly into the same area. As we rode to the fairway, I spotted a ball in the rough and took out my fairway wood to advance it into position. After stroking the ball, Mike claimed I had hit his ball by mistake. We rode to the ball, and he was right. I told him I would have to re-hit, once I found my ball, and would be penalized two strokes. He replaced his ball and proceeded to shank it forty yards to the right. He was upset, but that was only his second stroke. After finding my ball, I applied what was now my fourth stroke to it, advancing it into the wind, but not as far as I had hoped. Mike's next hit landed him 150 yards from the green. I was laying about 205 yards staring into a stiff breeze. Knowing my only chance to catch Mike was to land this next shot onto the green, I pulled out my five wood and pounded the ball into the sky. Somehow, it landed on the green and held position. Mike approached his shot with a seven iron and clocked it. As it soared toward the green and took a huge bounce, the ball hopped past the putting surface. Mike flashed a toothy smile, "Well, only a chip and a putt to victory."

I reminded Mike that the green did not just have water in the front, which was visible to us, but also behind—it was an island green. Mike's smile disappeared as he realized his ball was in the water. With the stroke he would be penalized for that miscue, and the shank earlier in the hole, Mike had given back the two-stroke advantage I had given him by mistakenly hitting his ball. Now, I was sitting on the green and Mike had to pitch up from the drop area and hope for the best. My first putt came within a foot of the hole, and I easily made the second. Mike now had to sink the ball from off the green to win, or miss and one-putt to tie. He did neither. I learned some new curse words on the ride back to our hotel that day. Mike wasn't happy, and I was $50,000 richer.

As I repacked my suitcase that night, I noticed a United States Golf Association rule book tucked into one of the pockets, left over from some other golf trip no doubt. I decided to leaf through the book, and came to the rules about hitting another's ball by mistake. The rules provided for a two stroke penalty, but only in stroke play—where the score is based on the total number of strokes a player takes over eighteen holes. We were engaged in match play, where each hole is a separate contest. In that circumstance, I should not have been penalized two strokes; I should have forfeited the hole. The next morning, as we piled our bags into the taxi, I told Mike the good news: he only lost $20,000, not $50,000. I might as well have told him he won the lottery. He was ecstatic and immediately demanded a rematch.

Our chance for a rematch wouldn't come for another few weeks until we returned to Palm Springs for more meetings. This time, the golf match was no casual last minute event. Mike was fixated on getting to the course, almost rushing the client through our meetings. I could tell he was out for blood. I decided to stick with my previous approach: as soon as I lost money, I would stop. Whereas my parents were away during our previous visit to Palm Springs, this time they were home, and Dad was delighted to have two guests to join him for a round of golf. I told Mike that under no circumstances was he to reveal to my father the size of our bets. We would denominate our wagers in cents, not thousands of dollars. My father was not opposed to a friendly side golf bet, but these numbers were absurd to anyone on the planet other than Mike Scanlon and Jack Abramoff —oh, and maybe Michael Jordan. If my father heard us betting ten cents, he would think we were frugal. If he heard ten thousand dollars, he would have thought we were psychotic—which we were!

Starting twenty thousand dollars down, Mike bet five thousand—that is, five cents—on the first hole. Bringing the same bad game with him, Mike lost the first hole by two strokes. The next hole, Mike lowered the bet to two thousand, causing Dad to joke that, at this rate, one of us might be able to buy an ice cream cone if all goes well. Little did he know. Mike quickly settled into the same loss pattern of our previous bout, and I was playing bogey golf, with the occasional par. Mike kept doubling the bets and losing. By the time we completed the first nine holes, he was down an astounding sixty-eight thousand dollars—or sixty-eight cents in Dad money. On the tenth tee box, Scanlon finally humbled himself and asked me to give him strokes, to even his chances. It only took him twenty-seven holes of losses to realize that he needed and deserved an advantage to equalize the match. I gladly gave him a stroke per hole. If we were to tie on a hole, for example, the stroke would give him the victory. If I beat him by a single stroke, his advantage would equalize our score. With his new stroke advantage, Mike came alive and won several holes in a row. On the thirteenth tee box, Mike, having won the last two holes, was feeling confident and declared, "OK, on this hole, the bet is ten thousand dollars."

I froze. Dad turned to me: "What did he say?" I stammered, but Dad continued, "Are you guys betting ten thousand dollars on this hole? Were you really betting cents on those others? That's not like you, to think in pennies. Are you betting thousands?!"

I couldn't lie to my father. "Yes, but let me explain…" Dad's face seemed to drain of all blood. I pulled Dad aside as Mike teed up his ball to start the hole. I quickly explained what was going on, and that I was playing with Mike's money, not mine, and that as soon as it was my money, the game would be over. For the rest of the day, Dad acted like someone placed a motion activated explosive bomb in his hands. Every putt became a potential life-ending event. Now I was not only playing Mike, but also playing to keep my Dad calm. Mike and I traded holes and I started to pile up more winnings. When we tapped our putts into the cup on the island green at the final hole, Mike had lost sixty-five thousand dollars. As we rode to the clubhouse, Dad quipped, "He'll never pay that bet." He would soon find that statement to be wrong. Back at Dad's house, Mike promptly wrote a check for the full amount and handed it to me. I could tell from his face that Dad thought the check had more bounce in it than Mike's previous shot through the eighteenth green, but he was wrong there as well. The check cleared and I notified my accountant that I had a new source of income—golf.

Like most of my activities with Mike, the golf match in the desert was thrilling, with high stakes and big sums on the line. But it was also an allegory for how things can quickly spiral out of control in the high-stakes world in which Mike and I lived. While at the time it felt only slightly crazy to be betting so much money on a golf game—even though it was all his money—upon reflection I now see how symbolic it was of our lives, which were far more than slightly crazy.

Americans love reform. Each election is about reform, change, throwing the bums out. And yet, nothing ever changes. We see new faces, but we face the same problems. Why? Because it's the system which needs to be changed, not the current cast of characters running the system. But systems are hard to change. Each year, the congressional high priests offer a sacrifice to the idols of change. They pass reform bills, or change the rules in Congress. Ostensibly, these alterations are done to fix the system, yet nothing seems fixed. Is corruption in Washington really ended by insisting congressmen eat their food with their fingers standing up, rather than seated with forks and spoons? Yet, this is the kind of reform which Congress proposes, passes, and then congratulates itself about.

For years, it has been difficult to pass legislation in the charged partisan congressional atmosphere. So a lobbyist trying to enact his client's wishes needs to get his amendment onto a bill likely to pass both the House and the Senate, to then be signed by the president. No bill is more likely to pass than a reform bill. While there may be hiccups on the way, most reform bills will make it all the way to the president's desk, so smart lobbyists always keep an eye out for reform bills.

It's ironic, if not horrific, that this is the case. The very bills designed to limit corruption and improve our system of government sometimes serve as vehicles for special interests. Like fugitives surreptitiously searching for an escape car in the dead of night, too many lobbyists prospect for reform bills in the hope of attaching their amendments. To my great shame, I was part of that group, too.

Congressman Bob Ney, whose former chief of staff, Neil Volz, joined our lobbying team at Greenberg at the end of 2001, was a regular at Signatures. Ney had inserted the Suncruz flummery into the congressional record. Twice. Now, he would assume an even greater place in our pantheon. He was chairman of the House Administration Committee. With his control over all things material in the Congress, from office assignments to ordering supplies, Ney was known as the "Mayor of Capitol Hill." But the mayor was never as important to us as when we found out he was moving a reform bill. The "Help America Vote Act," or HAVA, was originating in his committee.

HAVA was to be the legislation which corrected the hanging chad issue from the 2000 Florida ballot. While liberals and conservatives will never agree as to the fairness of that election's results, most do agree that the election system is antiquated and flawed. HAVA was to correct all of that. And for our purpose of slipping Jon van Horne's unfathomable amendment quietly past the Congress, it was perfect.

Most Americans would be appalled at the number of bills working their way through the Capitol which are never read by anyone, other than the staff director in charge of that particular bill. Once the chairman of the committee and his staff were on board and the Tigua language was included in the legislative draft, the odds of anyone catching and stopping it were long. Since Jon had crafted the most opaque language possible, the odds of our legislative fix surviving the drafting process were good.

On March 20, 2002, I met Ney at Signatures. Between trays of sushi, I explained the situation in full, focusing on the arbitrary denial of low level gaming to the Tiguas when almost all other tribes in the nation were permitted. I was clear as to the political upheaval this might create, but, in revealing our post-passage plans, assuaged his concerns. Ney agreed to move forward. His bill was slated for passage within a couple of months. He asked that we contact Senator Christopher Dodd, the Democrat from Connecticut who was chairman of the companion committee in that body. I was elated and immediately emailed Scanlon. Mike had the contacts to get to Dodd and was confident we could line him up. In mid April, he came back to me with Dodd's assent and a request for a $50,000 contribution to the Democrats in Dodd's name. Mike said he would cover the contribution from the budget the Tiguas had provided him, and the pieces were falling in place. Of course, neither of us considered for a moment that this "contribution" was, in fact, merely a bribe. To us, it was just how politics worked.

The regularity with which my staff would return from congressional offices with requests for funds, on the heels of our asking for help should have disturbed me, but it didn't. It was illegal and wrong, but it didn't register as abnormal in any way. I was so used to hearing senator so-and-so wants $25,000 for his charity, or representative X wants $50,000 for the Congressional Campaign Committee, that I would actually double check with my staff when they didn't request lucre for the legislators. The whole process became so perfunctory it actually seemed natural.

In short order, Mike forwarded the donation Dodd required. I saw Ney and told him Dodd was on board, and asked that he confirm with the senator. Neil Volz coordinated with Ney's staff to get them in touch with Dodd's people. Ney reverted to me in a week, saying he had spoken with Dodd and that they would deal with the matter at the end of the conference on the bill. Since they were both chairmen, I had little doubt things were moving according to plan. Then trouble struck.

A non-controversial reform bill, HAVA should have sailed through.

Both the House and Senate had passed versions of the bill by wide margins. Yet, the bill was stuck in a conference to iron out differences between the House and Senate versions, and it continued to be delayed. Ney would report the progress to me almost daily as he gulped down sushi and wine at Signatures, on the house, of course. As we neared summer, I started to worry. A partisan fissure had emerged between the House and Senate. The bill started to look like it was in trouble. The tribe was stressed, as were we. Ney's staff asked if we could launch a grassroots effort to push the senators on the bill. We immediately started phone banks, but still no one budged. The dispute was too esoteric to register with the callers. I instructed my staff to start looking for other moving trains.

As the summer session commenced, the logjam remained. No other moving summer bills would suit our effort, but we were already creating a list of options for the fall. It was a short list. The Republican House and Democratic Senate were not joining to pass anything. We needed to move HAVA and keep Ney focused to make sure we were in the final bill.

I made sure Ney ate at Signatures as often as possible, even getting Volz to dine with him daily at times. It was not a heavy lift, since Volz loved Ney, and we all enjoyed each other's company. I just didn't want Ney too far from my sight. This was too important to the Tiguas and to us. I took him golfing. In fact, I took him, Ralph Reed, and a number of staff members to Scotland where we played the Old Course at St. Andrew's, the home of golf. I lavished all I could on our champion in the hope that we could get our provision passed.

Our rounds of golf in Scotland included some discussions of the Tigua situation, and Ney was solid. But while we were in Scotland, Ney apparently attended to other business as well. Years later, I was told he had met with an Iranian expatriate interested in gaining permission from the U.S. federal government to sell airplanes to Iran. Ney accepted $50,000 in casino chips from this businessman, which, along with his dealings with me, served ultimately to land him in prison.

These idyllic golf pilgrimages to Scotland had become an annual event for me and were generally devoid of tension and strife. Other than playing golf with Ralph Reed, that is. Ralph is a good golfer, but he is not the best sportsman. I found his antics humorous, but the others in the group did their best to avoid him. When he made a good shot, he was a one man

Golf Channel acclaiming his prowess. When it was a bad shot, watch out. I was already used to his temper from our rounds at various American golf clubs, but in Scotland, things almost got out of hand.

One of the courses we played was in Carnoustie, a hard scrabble town on the east coast of Scotland, and it was one of the most difficult courses in the British Open championship rotation. It is at Carnoustie that French golfer Jean Van De Velde had his famous meltdown in 1999. Leading the Open by three strokes as he started the last hole, he shot a seven and lost in one of the most famous collapses in golf.

I had played Carnoustie before with Adam Kidan in 1999. We were paired with a couple from the United States. Our misogynist caddy, Paul, had nothing but disdain for them because the young man had the temerity to bring a woman to Paul's holy golf course. At each hole, Paul would cast aspersions, and Kidan and I could barely contain our laughter. The couple took it in good cheer, ignoring Paul who seemed quite inebriated at the time. On the last hole, the three men teed off, and Paul started walking down the fairway, right in front of the young lady as she prepared to tee off. As he was only fifteen feet in front of her, I thought there was no way he wouldn't be killed by her drive. I shouted for him to watch out. He replied in his thick Scottish brogue, "Why, she can't hit it this far!" We all fell over laughing, including the nice young lady. Even Paul cracked a smile, and there was peace in golfdom.

There was little such peace the day I played Carnoustie with Ralph. Caddies were assigned to each golfer, and Ralph's immediately got a taste of what to expect. On the first hole, Ralph skulled his approach shot to the green, and promptly let out a yelp and threw his club. On the second hole, his caddy was in his peripheral vision, inviting mordant censure from Mr. Reed.

The day was far calmer than the tempestuous weather that usually added to the challenge of my previous Carnoustie outings. In the past, with wind gusting to fifty miles an hour, I was lucky to keep sight of the ball, let alone place it anywhere in bounds. On this day, the sky was clear, and the sun was shining. My game came together, and I was playing my best golf. As we came to the tee box of the sixth hole, the famous "Hogan's Alley" named for the innovative shot-making of past champion Ben Hogan, I was only one over par. I dreamed of a career round of golf, and teed my ball. As I commenced my downswing, Ralph's caddy shouted a question his way, "What club do you want to use here?"

If I were Tiger Woods, I could have stopped my swing and started again, but I'm no Tiger Woods. My ball shanked to the right, and I was in deep trouble. And I was steamed. My dream of a career round turned into nightmares with one bad swing. Ney patted me on the shoulder as we started walking down the fairway. I strolled over to Ralph and asked, "Would you mention discreetly to your caddy that he might want to wait to speak until after I swing?" Ralph nodded, and we continued play. My game was gone, and the dream of a great golf score died. I carded a ten on that hole, instead of the par five.

On the next hole, I asked Ralph if he had a chance to speak with his caddy. He looked at me and plainly said, "Yes. I told him if he does it again, I'll wrap my five iron around his neck." He wasn't kidding.

Things were getting so bad between Ralph and his caddy that the other caddies approached us to ask if there was something wrong with that "bloke." One of the caddies, a rough and tumble Scotsman named James, spoke for them all when he said, "If I get that bastard into a pub, he won't get out." I chuckled. There were probably a few political folks in the States who felt the same way.

On the last hole, Ralph's caddy sidled up to me and popped the question, "You a lawyer, eh?"

"Sort of. Why?"

"I want to know if there is a law in the States about murder."

"Of course there is. Just like here. Why?"

"Because I want to know whether to expect the noose or a trophy when I kill this little numpty."

And so ended another round of golf with Ralph Reed.

When we returned from bonny and sunny Scotland, Ney had a deep tan. The tribal council visited Washington, and Ney greeted them in his conference room. Though they had sponsored the Scotland trip, I encouraged them not to focus on that tan too much for fear that it would make Ney uncomfortable. Bob brought them up to speed on the bill. Finally, there was to be a conference with the Senate, and things would move forward. The council left, satisfied. I was thrilled to have Ney. I can't think of too many other members who would have stayed on such a relatively small issue as long as he did.

As the fall session started, so did the conference. We followed the conference with great interest, passing each detail to the tribe. Our matter was to be dealt with by the chairmen privately, just as the conference ended. Like an expectant father, I called Ney's chief of staff, Will Heaton, constantly. On October 2, the conferees were locked in a room all day to iron out the final passages of the bill. Then the call came.

It was Ney. "Dodd is not on board. I thought you told me he was. He won't allow the provision. What's going on?"

I was caught off guard, and immediately called Scanlon.

"Mike, what the hell is going on here?"

As it turned out, in the intervening months, Dodd got cold feet. The tribal councils in his home state of Connecticut were creating immense traffic problems and the population was up in arms. He didn't want to do anything to help Indians right now. It was too tough on him politically. There was no chance of turning this around now. I almost collapsed in depression. We had never failed one of our clients before. Whenever things got tough, I just put on the pressure, and our guys came through. If one attempt didn't work, we tried over and again to succeed. Now, on one of the biggest efforts of my career, I had to rely on others, and they failed. I failed. How could I possibly face my clients?

Ney agreed to call the clients and promise that he would find another vehicle to move this bill. They were grateful, but we were all despondent. For the next eighteen months, I would continue to try to find a way to help the Tiguas. Mike insisted that we had fulfilled our contractual obligations to the tribe, and nothing more need be done, but I couldn't let it rest. I tried everything. I drove my staff to distraction looking for another bill, but to no avail. I was consumed with getting this done for the Tiguas. They weren't only great clients; they were my friends.

Throughout the next year, I approached dozens of staff seeking the right bill. None were interested. I tried to craft novel approaches to the problem, including proposing the Tiguas cede some of their land to the Kickapoos, who already had a legal facility in Eagle Pass, near San Antonio. Then, the Kickapoos could open the El Paso casino and take a small fee, leaving the bulk of the revenue for the Tiguas. I even looked into moving the Tiguas across the border to New Mexico, where the state would be more amenable to gambling.

I was so obsessed with getting a win for the tribe that even after my career was over, and I was being investigated by the U.S. Senate, I met with staff from the Hill at Signatures to seek a way for them to pass the bill. As my life was being torn apart, I remained committed to the Tigua cause.

I tried and tried, until the day came when the Tiguas publicly attacked me. The Senate Indian Affairs committee had worked them over, convincing them that I was a racist and that I had ripped them off. Once that happened, I finally let go. There was no sense in helping people who were now bent on destroying my life.

In the midst of the Tigua project, our success in getting clients out of last minute disasters brought us a new client. Tyco Corporation is one of the biggest defense and security companies in the world and was once headed by Dennis Kozlowski, who was convicted of fraud and sent to a New York State prison. Tyco had scores of lobbyists, but they had all failed to stop a congressional finance bill which would have retroactively taxed the company over $4 billion. The House and Senate each had bills with this provision, and they were moving. The sponsors were the most powerful people on the finance committees, and included Senator Harry Reid, the then-minority leader in the Senate, as well as Chuck Grassley, the Republican Chairman of the Senate Finance Committee from Iowa. Every other lobbyist had failed. Tyco wanted to know if we could somehow stop this.

By the time of this discussion, we were charging each of our clients approximately $150,000 per month. Considering the stakes of the tax threat, Tyco didn't balk at the amount and hired us immediately.

Obviously, the matter revolved around a tax increase, but this would be even harder to stop than the tax attacks on the tribes. Because of the Koslowski publicity, Tyco was seen as a bastion of corruption, and Members loved to attack corruption. It's one of the great hypocrisies of the system. Members swim in a swamp of corruption, and thrive in it, but they are able—with a straight face no less—to accuse others at will and sanctimoniously punish what they see as malfeasance. This kind of hypocrisy led Governor Eliot Spitzer of New York to take on the scourge of prostitution while partaking in the vice himself.

I was confident we had a winning hand with the tax issue, but the problem was that the Democrats on the attack did not care—they loved to raise taxes, especially against big corporations. And the Republican involved, Grassley, wasn't much better. Sure, he would pay homage to the tax movement and say the right things when asked, but Grassley was a moderate, not a conservative. He saw no problem with raising taxes, at least on a company as reviled and corrupt as Tyco.

But corruption was truly a side issue here. The commissars of our nation's capital were after more revenue for their uncontrolled federal spending, and, more to the point, they were after inverted companies— corporations which reincorporate themselves overseas to avoid the high U.S. corporate tax rates. To the Congress, those escaping the U.S. tax system in this way were traitors. I guess it never dawned on the sheriffs of Capitol Hill that, were they to lower corporate taxes so the United States didn't have the highest rate in the civilized world, more of these companies would forgo the option of reincorporation overseas.

Ironically, Tyco wasn't even an inverted company, at least in the purest form. They were acquired by and merged into ADT, a security company based overseas. For purposes of this assault, that's what made them inverted. But the real issue was more banal. Tyco had successfully purchased scores of companies over the previous few years. They built their corporation into a megalith, comprised of over three hundred acquisitions. Some of those companies were won in hard fought battles. The losers in those fights decided to get their pound of flesh, and launched the assault on Tyco under the veil of fighting tax scofflaws. Most Americans are blissfully unaware of how often public officials will crush the corporate competitor of their donors. It's one of the best pay-backs legislators can provide.

Beating back this inverted tax required a lot of effort, and we needed more than astute lobbying on the Hill. There were too many Tyco opponents with too many powerful lobbyists doing their bidding. Plus, the main Congressional players were already publicly against us. We needed an edge, and our edge was our signature grassroots work.

Tyco had more vendors than all our tribal clients combined. When I requested the company compile a list of every company in the country that sold any product or service to any of their multitude of corporate subsidiaries, they thought I was crazy. Then I told them of our success with this approach on behalf of the tribes. No one had proposed such an approach to them before, but, once I was finished, I promised them they would be rid of this tax. They had little choice but to trust me. The Angel of Death was knocking at their door. Had they lost this and taken that tax charge, their stock would have collapsed and the company would have been destroyed. Their enemies knew exactly what they were doing.

My problem was that Mike Scanlon, the mastermind of grassroots campaigns, was barely interested in continuing his work with the tribes, let alone taking on a new battle. Even though he was making millions, he was exhausted and he was finished with having to take calls at every hour of the day and night from the clients. He disdained their representatives, such as Marc Schwartz, and wanted out. Had Mike actually bowed out of our work together, it would have been a disaster for our tribes. One only has to lose one fight over a single rival casino, and the tribe's entire market is decimated. I could not implore him to stay involved so I could continue to feed my charitable addiction, and his contempt for the clients was growing daily. I had to think of something.

Faced with a steady stream of complaints and trying to keep Mike in the game, for the sake of winning these fights, I took a tack with him which worked, but which later came back to haunt me. I started to act as though I, too, was upset with the clients, and that, in fact, I was even more upset than he was. I started to use inappropriate language to show my angst was as great, if not greater than his. I was using reverse psychology on my friend, hoping that, instead of continuing his threats to leave the clients, he would spend his spare energy to buck me up, and keep us both in the fight. It worked, but the juvenile, jocular and, at times insulting and repulsive language I employed in my emails to Mike would later be thrown in my face by the press. I will regret that unfortunate strategy for the rest of my life. It was colossally stupid, but, with the tribes at risk, and no way to imagine these pronouncements would one day be aired publicly, I felt I had to try it. Losing Mike was not an option for the tribal efforts.

With Tyco, I chose not to involve Mike, and instead built a separate organization to establish Tyco's political machine. In my weakness of character, and my desire to get the client to do quickly what I thought would be necessary to save them, I didn't reveal that I was the one who set up this company and subsequently profit from it. In my mind, it was a win-win situation. They would get the result they needed, and virtually all of the profits would be going to charity. But it was wrong, and I would pay dearly for it in the future.

I brought in a few of the best field organizers I knew, and we set about the task of organizing the vendors of Tyco. The heads of thousands of companies received calls from our phone operation, and most of them put calls directly into their senators' offices. When the president of a major employer in a state calls his or her senator, that call gets through. Our guys ran cross tabs between the owners of the companies and the Federal Election Commission lists, and now I had a list of hundreds who were not only major employers, but also major donors. I knew there was no way a Washington lobbyist opposing us could compete with that. After a few weeks of calls, I had generated enough pressure to stop the bills.

Even Senator Grassley, the original sponsor of the bill, backed down after we employed a two-pronged, "good cop, bad cop" approach to him. Our grassroots operation poured it on from the field, with scores of Iowa corporations calling him, interrogating him as to why he was killing Tyco, their golden goose. And our Greenberg team played the 'inside the beltway" game of cajoling and pampering him. We became one of Grassley's biggest fundraisers and hosted event after event for him. We flew him to the Greenberg offices in Florida, Boston and Chicago for fund raisers. We plied his staff with every trinket we had. When we were done, they loved us. Our only request? Stop this attack on Tyco.

When the dust settled, Tyco survived the assault, and Grassley became one of our most dependable Senate assets. His assistance was key a few months later when both he and the other senator from Iowa, Tom Harkin—also a major recipient of our beneficence and campaign contributions, combined to help our Iowa tribal client—the Sac & Fox nation—beat back a rogue hostile takeover. Grassley and Harkin donors dined at Signatures and relaxed at our sports boxes with great frequency. While neither senator would draw federal corruption charges during the coming scandal, like many of their colleagues, they had no problem extending their hand and taking the silver.

Unbeknownst to most, when the lobbying scandal surrounding my demise was in full swing, with McCain and his staff preparing to drag me before the Indian Affairs Committee, I received a letter from a second

Senate Committee preparing to skewer me. It was from the Senate Finance Committee, chaired by our old friend Senator Grassley. It was immediately clear to me that his campaign finance staff was not communicating with his Committee staff. It didn't take them long to connect, and I heard nothing more from the good senator. I guess he didn't wish to take a chance that I might not take the Fifth in front of him.

Our Tyco victories did not stop with the tax bill. On November 17, 2003, I received a call from the chief of staff of the General Services Administration, my good friend David Safavian. David was one of those who joined us in Scotland during the Ney golf trip. He had seen an internal memo at GSA putting Tyco on the debarment list for the federal government. Apparently this, too, had been ginned up by Tyco's competition in the defense industry. David asked whether Kozlowski was somehow still involved in the company. I told him no and asked why. He told me about the memo, but said he thought it might not be accurate. I did not wait. I immediately contacted the company and told them of this looming threat. They had been suspecting a new assault, and my call confirmed it.

Tyco's lawyers wanted to take a tack that I thought would backfire on them. I called David to run my thoughts by him. He was reticent to react, but it was clear that the lawyers' approach would have caused grave difficulties. David didn't want to say more. I understood his discomfort and asked if he would facilitate a meeting to get this resolved. This assault on Tyco was a misunderstanding, but if it became public, my client would be finished. The reaction in the market to the debarment of a corporation heavily focused on defense contracts would have been devastating. David agreed, and the meeting was set. After some light pressure I added from Capitol Hill, the deal was done. Tyco was off the debarment list, and the stock was not affected.

The client was delighted. They wanted to know how to compensate me. They were paying me a ton of money already, I replied. But this was extra, they insisted. I told them not to worry about it. It was part of my job. I was sure they would one day show their gratitude. I was wrong.

Like the rest of my clients, when my career started to crumble, Tyco initially stood by my side. Then, after being told that I had abused them, they abandoned me. I should have expected it. How would their stock have survived headlines like, "Tyco Defends the Most Evil Lobbyist in History"?

# 13

# NIGHTMARE ON K STREET

In the fall of 2003, opponents of Chief Poncho and Council Member William Worfel started to stir discontent within the Coushatta tribe. A series of articles appeared in a small local newspaper, critical of decisions the tribal council had made and of the amount of money they had spent on our efforts to preserve their market share. The articles spread like wildfire across the nation to our other tribal clients. Nell Rogers saw copies circulating among the Choctaw. Our clients, the Saginaw Chippewas of Michigan, were inundated as well. My tribal clients, the Agua Caliente, in California called to ask about the articles, which were mailed anonymously to their membership.

Additionally, the tribes also reported receiving a wave of articles about my Suncruz experience and suggestive letters questioning whether I had a role in the murder of Gus Boulis. Someone was expending a lot of energy on this.

At the time, I didn't think much about these attacks. I was proud of our record with the tribes, and I knew that tribal government politics was vicious, much like any other scrappy political environment. I had seen the personal invective and fists thrown with equal enthusiasm.

Unfortunately, the deluge of negative materials seemed to have a dramatic impact on the Saginaw Chippewa tribal election. We had achieved monumental milestones for this tribe, including stopping numerous efforts to dilute their gaming market. We shepherded them through the appropriations process in Washington, securing funding for their water and sewer plant, the tribal police force, a domestic violence treatment center, school construction, roads, and a senior center. We put them on the map as a political force, both in Washington and their home state. None of this sat well with the political opposition to our clients, and the campaign to dislodge them from power was a bloodbath of slander against both the tribal council and us.

In November, the Saginaw Chippewa voted out the incumbent leaders and installed a new council. Scanlon and I were concerned since we were in the midst of a number of market-saving activities on their behalf. We deluded ourselves into thinking that, because we had done so much for them, the new group would continue with us.

In December, the new council invited Mike, Todd, and me to make a presentation of our progress. We flew to their headquarters in Mount Pleasant, Michigan and brought thick binders detailing the effective work we had done for them over the past two years. Scanlon brought a power point presentation showing the market threats we had thwarted. We were even able to quantify the value of our representation, showing we had brought a return to the tribe in excess of 10,000 percent.

As we sat in the waiting room, anxious to commence our briefing of the new council, a tribal staff member approached. "Mr. Scanlon, they will see you first for fifteen minutes, and then they will see you, Mr. Abramoff."

Why were they separating us? I had a role in each presentation and representation, and had material to report on both the grassroots efforts and the Washington campaigns. Fifteen minutes? We flew for half a day to spend fifteen minutes with them? That made no sense.

Mike shrugged and took his materials to the conference room. He was back in fifteen minutes exactly, carrying all his materials. He looked miserable, but there was no time to talk. On his heels was the staffer. "Mr. Abramoff and Mr. Boulanger, please follow me."

Todd and I cautiously entered the room. The council was seated in a horseshoe arrangement and we were bidden to take seats at the table before them. Not more than twenty seconds into my presentation, I was cut off and told I would be subjected to some questions. I halted and awaited the query. One of the council members asked if I paid a gratuity to Maynard Kahgegab, the recently defeated chief of a tribe for whom we worked. I said I didn't. They asked whether I shared our fees with either Kahgegab or Chris Petras, the now former head of government affairs for the tribe. I said we did not. They then thanked me and were prepared to dismiss us.

I spoke up. I had come half way across the country with information for them about pending grants and benefits. Didn't they want to hear about these funds? I mentioned that we were still in the process of obtaining the grants we secured and that they needed to know where things stood. They asked me to leave the materials on the table on my way out the door. And with that, our two-year representation of the Saginaw Chippewas came to an end.

Todd and I walked back dejectedly to the waiting room to fetch Scanlon. As I entered, we exchanged exhausted glances. The tribe had paid us handsomely and we'd done effective work in exchange, work for which any tribe in the nation would have been happy to pay. But thanks to the recent elections, the tribe was now controlled by a council bent on vilifying their predecessors and all they achieved. Since we produced their greatest achievements, we were at the top of the villain list.

After returning from Michigan, I received a phone call from Greenberg Traurig Chairman Cesar Alvarez, the Miami-based national managing partner of Greenberg.

"Jack, I heard we were fired by our client in Michigan. What's going on?"

I explained as best I could that our clients had lost their election, and now the new council didn't wish to retain our services. It seemed pretty simple to me.

Cesar pressed.

"But I heard we did a terrible job representing them and that was why we were terminated."

I tried again to explain that the matter was political. Just as a new political administration anywhere would fire the old consultants, we were being fired. Usually my conversations with Cesar were friendly, uplifting, and encouraging. But this time, as I hung up the phone, I could tell something was very wrong.

The loss of the Saginaw Chippewas was not the only crisis of this period. Governor Foster and the Jena tribe were making another run at our Coushatta clients, trying to secure a casino location on yet another piece of historic Coushatta land. With our emblematic fury, we attacked the effort and, thanks to significant help from the House leadership and some key senators, including then-Minority Leader Harry Reid of Nevada, we were able to choke off what turned out to be Foster's final stab at the tribe.

Reid was very much a secret weapon in our lobbying efforts. In 2002, we hired Eddie Ayoob, Reid's legislative director and top political operative. Eddie was a master lobbyist and connected to virtually every office on the Hill, but his real power derived from his history with Reid. The clients showered Reid and his staff with contributions, tickets to events, and every other gratuity imaginable, and they responded in kind. During the first Jena battle, Reid fired off a firm letter to the Interior Department to protect our clients. When the next fight erupted, his staff coordinated with ours to stop the Jena tribe from gaining their casino. Reid was not the only politician to come to our aid in this battle. Nor was he alone in denying his involvement in our lobbying activities when things blew up a few months later.

In September 2003, I tried to pull up to the front of Signatures restaurant, but was blocked by scores of large trucks and a bustle of activity clogging Pennsylvania Avenue. Immediately, I realized it was a motion picture production company shooting a film. I was furious that they were blocking access to our restaurant, as we were never consulted and their presence would kill business. Normally, film permits are only granted after the business establishments likely to be impacted by the filming have given consent.

The film was *National Treasure*, a Disney production starring Nicholas Cage. I found the production manager to query how they were able to block the street. He smirked, saying the District of Columbia Film Commission permitted filming if businesses in the vicinity were OK with it, and he checked with several of the businesses a few blocks away. None seemed to mind, so it was our tough luck. He said they'd be there for three days! We had fundraisers booked every night for senators at Signatures, all of which would be ruined by having the street blocked. I told him it would be well advised for him to have his producer call me as soon as possible. Giving him my card, I ducked into Signatures to see what I could do about this.

My calls to the D.C. Film Commission were met by their answering machines, with no return calls. I called Griles. "Steve, there is a film crew outside blocking Pennsylvania Avenue and the Naval Memorial (which stood just outside our door),effectively closing Signatures to public access. They plan to be there for three days. They claim to have a permit, but I can't imagine they have one from the Department of Interior. Can you help us remove them?"

Griles got the head of the National Park Service on the phone with us and directed him to go immediately to the site to see what he could do. Twenty minutes later, Griles and the Park Services head were on the phone. They told the film company that they had to move off the Naval Memorial, since that was federal property and they had no permit, however there was no way to stop them from blocking the streets, since they were under city control. I thanked them, as the production manager entered the restaurant.

"Who do you think you are?!" he shouted as he approached my table. I sat impassively waiting for him to finish. "We are making a multi-million dollar film and I have never seen such ingratitude. Most restaurants would pay us to be outside filming, as it attracts visitors."

When he finished, I started. "First of all, don't you ever come barging into this restaurant shouting like a lunatic again. Second, who I am is not the issue. The issue is that you are hurting our business and we're not going to just sit here and let you do it. You guys need to reschedule your shoot and come back on Friday when business is light. If not, I will get you shut down. End of discussion."

He turned on a dime and blurted out "we'll see," as he headed for the door. I called Todd Boulanger at Greenberg. "Todd, get to the staff director of the D.C. Appropriations Committee in the House and have him call the mayor's office so we can get this crew away from Signatures." Todd was the organizer of that night's Senate fundraiser and was steamed that these Hollywood types were going to ruin it. Todd didn't much appreciate Hollywood guys. An hour later, he called to say that his connection was on the case and would be calling the mayor that next morning, as it was already well past business hours.

The next day, the film crew was still blocking the restaurant. I had meetings and could not spend much time on the matter, but was confident things would be resolved with Todd on the case. Late that afternoon, my cell phone rang. The caller identified himself as the producer of the film and took a decidedly different tack with me—he was friendly. He apologized for the "mix up" and wanted to make it up to me. His idea of making it up was to offer me passes so I could bring my family to the filming and meet the star. I politely declined his offer. My kids were in school and I had a restaurant to run. I asked him to reschedule the filming. He started to tell me that they couldn't do that, when I reminded him that every production has to keep interior sets in reserve in case it rains. Rain is a killer for movies, since the look of the set before and after—let alone during—rain is completely different. Consequently, prudent productions prepare interior sets, often in a warehouse when on location outside the studio, for a weather event. I told him to pretend it was raining and just come back Friday. He refused.

Todd called me a few minutes later to say that the mayor's office was stalling the request from the appropriations staffer to move the crew from in front of the restaurant. I called my friend who headed the lobbying shop for Disney. By now I was angry. When Richard Bates, vice president of government relations for Disney, called me back, I told him what was happening and he solved the problem. The crew returned on Friday and we were able to have our fund raisers. I made sure to be there when they were packing up the trucks to wave goodbye.

Meanwhile, just as we squashed the final Jena attempt, another crisis exploded on the Coushatta reservation. A rogue group opposed to Chief Poncho and William Worfel staged what quickly evolved into an armed takeover of the tribal offices. Only later would we discover that this group was coordinating with the new Saginaw Chippewa council members, assisted by some of our rivals in the lobbying industry.

With our attention completely focused on getting the Interior Department to restore order in Louisiana, as well as the normal stress of running our lobbying efforts, keeping the restaurants afloat, and making sure the schools had what they needed, I didn't have much time to contemplate what turned out to be the biggest threat on my horizon: the *Washington Post*. Rumors of a forthcoming article assaulting my lobbying practice had circulated months before, but nothing had materialized. Then, in early February 2004, Post reporter Susan Schmidt emerged and called me for an interview.

Schmidt had a stern expression on her seasoned face as I entered the conference room near my office for our meeting. I brought Allen Foster, one of the firm's top litigators, as well as Kevin Ring, Todd Boulanger, and Jon van Horne from my team. She brought a tape recorder. So did I. I didn't trust her. She was, after all, a reporter from the *Washington Post*.

Immediately, she started firing questions at me about our representations. I answered some, but not all. She wanted to know about Scanlon. I told her to speak to Scanlon, but that I wasn't going to speak about third party vendors. She asked if I owned part of Scanlon's company. I didn't, and told her so. She had been told that I was profiting from Scanlon's company, but she never asked me that question directly. It was true, but since she didn't ask, I didn't answer. I saw no reason to help her do her job of assassinating me. Later she would misrepresent her question, claiming she asked me whether I shared in Scanlon's profit, but I had the interview on tape.

Her posture in the room was utter hostility. She was writing a scathing hit piece and had come to believe what others had told her. She inferred that our clients paid us a fortune and got nothing in return. I started to review what we did for our clients and why they did in fact get a return, but she seemed completely disinterested in that discussion. She was there to make her accusations and to try and elicit a quote she could ultimately use against me.

The interview lasted about an hour, and then she left. She said she might have some follow up questions. I did my best to be friendly and polite, though she was hardly either. She left and we convened a post-interview meeting. Allen was upset by her aggressive and hostile posturing, and we decided to write to her publication. But it was all rearranging chairs on the deck of the Titanic. Her piece was already written before she entered the room. She had only interviewed me as a formality, to make it seem fair.

On Saturday night, February 21, 2004, the *Washington Post* Sunday edition came online. Pam and I were dining with friends at Signatures when I received a copy of the piece on my Blackberry. I read it quickly. It didn't seem so bad. I read it again. Had I missed something? No, it was not the horrific assault I had expected. It was critical, but not devastating.

When we returned from dinner, I sent it to a dozen or so folks, including my clients and the leadership of Greenberg. Nell Rogers replied immediately: "This could have been a lot worse," she wrote. She felt that Mike was the target of the article, and that Schmidt didn't have a clear story to tell. It seemed to her that the assault was launched by other lobbying firms who were disgruntled about how much money we were making and how little success they were having keeping up with us.

The next morning, Richard Rosenberg, second in command to Cesar at Greenberg, wrote that although the press wasn't good, it wasn't as damning as its author intended it to be, probably because she couldn't find the hard facts to support her theories. He said it was a good thing I had taken the interview, as it seemed to have resulted in a more balanced piece than we expected. I agreed completely. Most of the people I'd talked to about this were perplexed as to what the story was really about, and why it was front page worthy. I was confident that the storm would pass, and thanked Richard for his friendship and support.

Two days later, Congressman Frank Wolf, a Republican opponent of gaming, called for a federal investigation into the accusations made in the *Post* article. Senator John McCain followed with a call for congressional hearings. At first, I assumed McCain was jumping on me as payback for the Bush 2000 race, but later I heard that lobbyists close to him were possibly responsible for the Saginaw Chippewa firing of our firm and the armed takeover at Coushatta. When these lobbyists wound up representing our former clients, it was bad enough, but when McCain sent a letter to the new chief of the Saginaw Chippewas lauding the participation in my investigation of their lead lobbyist, Scott Reed, I thought I was in a bad episode of Twilight Zone. This was the same Scott Reed who was exposed in the Village Voice articles and purposely ignored by McCain and his committee.

He was also the same Scott Reed who boldly predicted to former Deputy Assistant Secretary of Indian Affairs Wayne Smith that he would one day become the "king of Indian gaming", primarily by destroying my career. When Smith came to my office in April 2002 to tell me about Reed's efforts to dislodge him from the Interior Department, he told me about Reed's plans, which were described to him directly by Reed. My initial reaction was outrage that anyone—especially someone not a Native American—could espouse a goal to become "king of Indian gaming." Foolishly, I dismissed this detractor, naively suggesting he focus himself on the 540 tribes I did not represent. Unfortunately, he didn't.

Meanwhile, the *Washington Post* continued to hit me on the front page. The firm held a conference call for the staff in our Washington and Northern Virginia offices, and I did my best to put a positive spin on what was happening. Greenberg hired an outside investigator to look into the accusations, but this was leaked to the *Post*. Todd Boulanger called for the firm to get aggressive with the *Post*, to stop their assault. No one in the firm responded. Worse, the firm continued to give no comment to the *Post*, a sign they weren't as supportive of me as I'd hoped and thought I deserved.

Shortly after, I was called to a meeting at Greenberg's headquarters in Miami where I was asked about the accusations in the article. The meeting was formal and the questions difficult. They were going to call my clients, which was fine by me. I called Nell Rogers to give her a heads up, still confident I could get through this. After her talk with the firm, our follow up call seemed very positive.

Fred Baggett, head of lobbying at the firm, was coming to D.C. that Monday, and I was hopeful the firm would finally mount a defense so we could turn this around. I waited all day Monday for an answer.

Late in the afternoon on Tuesday, March 2, 2004, Cesar, Fred, and Richard came into my office. I usually had music playing in the background. At that moment, the mournful Scottish tunes of the Braveheart soundtrack gently filled the air. Not a good omen. Hoping they were there to signal the start of a firm-wide defense strategy, I waited with great anticipation. Cesar spoke first, followed by Richard.

They weren't going to defend me. They were firing me. They believed I had done indefensible things and that I would face serious consequences for my actions. They asked me to leave by the end of the day.

I sat there, dumbfounded, as they left my office. They didn't wait for my response. This wasn't a conversation; it was an execution. I felt like a house had landed on my head. Consequences for my actions? I was in shock, and the full ramifications of what they were saying were unclear to me, but I had heard enough to know that I needed an attorney. I crept to my phone and called my friend Ollie North. Brendon Sullivan, Ollie's lawyer during Iran-Contra, was the only criminal lawyer I could think of, and I wanted to hire him. Ollie got me on the phone with Brendan, but we soon found out that there was a conflict of interest. Greenberg Traurig had hired him several weeks earlier.

The fog of shock was dissipating by the second, and soon it was clear to me: I was a dead man walking.

There was no time to lose. I called in Shana Tesler, my top aide, who recommended I hire Abbe Lowell. I remembered working with Abbe on behalf of another client. I liked him, and I liked the fact that he was a Democrat who also represented Republicans. Since I was convinced that the attack McCain was pressing would soon spread, hiring Abbe might be helpful in discouraging Democrats from jumping on board.

Abbe quickly made contact with Cesar, and we negotiated a departure statement. I called my staff in and told them the news. They were as stunned as I had been a few moments before. I told them that I would work to get a new position for any of them that wanted it and that I hoped to land somewhere else soon. I truly believed I could get through this.

After instructing my assistants to ship my personal property and files to the business office we maintained for the restaurants, I sent out emails to friends, letting them know I was leaving Greenberg and how they could reach me.

I walked down the hall to where the firm's triumvirate was meeting and knocked on the door. Fred answered. They looked a little surprised I was there. I told them that, while this was a difficult time, I otherwise appreciated being at the firm and wanted to say goodbye to them, rather than just sneaking out. Baggett and Rosenberg rose to say goodbye, but Cesar kept typing at his computer. Finally, he rose and repeated that I was in for some difficult times, and he felt badly for my family. Right.

I headed back to my office to shut off my computer one last time when I noticed an email from a Capitol Hill reporter. He asked if I wished to reply to the statement he had just received from the firm. That must have been what Cesar was typing. When I read it, I was floored. Notwithstanding that Greenberg had agreed with Abbe to a mild, neutral statement about my departure, the firm lashed out at me.

The firm's decision to turn their back on me and pursue me as a villain stung, but fortunately, many friends tried to help where they could. Abe Polin called within hours of hearing the news of my demise. He hired a public relations firm in New York to "turn this around." At first, I, too, believed the crisis would run its course and that I might even be able to regain my footing. Abe's assistance was invaluable in that regard, but after several months of constant attacks, Abe and I agreed that a public relations firm could not even impact—let alone turn around—this tsunami. At first, the tribes I represented came out strongly in my defense, with both Chief Martin and Maynard Kahgegab, chief of the Saginaw Chippewas, writing scathing letters to McCain and the *Washington Post*. The *Post* received at least a dozen letters to the editor trying to balance their attack on me, but printed none. Several of the writers then complained to the *Post*'s ombudsman that their letters were being ignored, that the stories had numerous factual errors and that the tone was hardly balanced. When the ombudsman finally took up the matter, however, she focused her writing on the legitimacy of describing me as an Orthodox Jew, ignoring completely the concerns of at least a dozen correspondents.

Chief Martin withdrew his support of me after a few weeks, but sadly it did not save him when he next had to face the tribe for election. Maynard stood steadfast in my support, even recording a YouTube video detailing the reasons he has stood firm.

In the weeks following my departure from Greenberg, I met with Gerry Cassidy, head of Cassidy Associates, the biggest non-law firm lobbying shop in Washington. Gerry had a reputation for being a tough guy, but nothing could have seemed further from the truth during our meeting. He was kind and insightful. I made an arrangement to move several of my team members to his company and to join as a consultant until the scandal passed. I still thought it would be a matter of weeks or, at worst, months before this nightmare would pass.

I leased space near the White House and tried to get myself organized to endure the ordeal. I had contacts from a score of friends who wanted to find something to do together with me, and I intended to pursue other business opportunities.

During this period, I camped out at Signatures, where I could maintain some semblance of routine and meet with friends. Among them was Ralph Reed. Our meeting was brief, but friendly as always. I thought I owed it to him to let him know that McCain had subpoenaed all my emails from Preston Gates and Greenberg Traurig—over 800,000 of them.

Ralph calmly advised I hold nothing back and be cooperative. It wasn't like me to hold anything back, but this time it wasn't even up to me. The firms were the purveyors of these emails to the Committee, not me. I reminded him that there were hundreds, if not thousands of emails between us, and that all would be available for the world to see. He didn't seem to recall just how much we communicated via email. He would soon get a bitter reminder.

Later, Ralph would run his political career aground by denying, first, that he took money from the tribes, and then asserting that the money he took had no nexus to gaming. Both assertions were ridiculous, of course, and suicidal since the media had unfettered access to the emails thanks to McCain's staff. Not only should Ralph not have denied taking the money, he should have been proud about it. Had he been the public relations guru many thought him to be, he would have held a huge press conference with a map of the southern states and a big star by every city which would have had a Vegas-style casino had it not been for his efforts. He could have chided the rest of the religious conservative groups for rejecting his numerous requests that they help fund the efforts against the massive casino expansion that he stopped. He could have said that, yes, he would prefer to shutter the tribal casinos too, and one day would try it, but in the meantime they had the resources and desire to stop the expansion and, after finding no other help, he took theirs.

In the same way that Ollie North became wildly popular by proudly proclaiming he took weapons from Israel, sold them to Iran to kill Iraqis, and then took the money to fund anti-Communists in our hemisphere, Ralph could have turned a negative into a positive. Instead he lost a primary race for Lieutenant Governor in Georgia and saw his political career set back a decade or more.

I instructed Abbe and his staff to call the Department of Justice and let them know that I wanted to cooperate. At that point, I didn't realize I had done anything of consequence wrong, at least not intentionally, and figured that the quickest way to get through all of this was to cooperate with their investigation. Abbe made the call, but Justice wasn't ready to sit with me yet.

While we waited, McCain's staff rifled through the emails they had received from Preston and Greenberg. They found a number of stupid, jocular missives I had fired off to a variety of folks, but mainly Scanlon. They promptly leaked them to the *Post*. Abbe filed a protest with the Senate Ethics Committee, after McCain's lead staffer, Pablo Carrillo, admitted being the source of the leak. No response. I soon became a poster boy for, "Don't put anything in email that you don't want to read on the front page of the *Washington Post*." Articles about my follies were published daily.

Shortly after the complaint to the Senate Ethics Committee, Abbe was attending a Washington reception honoring Columbia University. Also attending was Senator McCain. Out of cordiality, Abbe extended his hand to the senator. McCain stared him in the eyes and then suddenly thrust his face to within an inch of the astonished Abbe.

"You don't say hello to me!" he shouted at the top of his lungs, startling everyone in the room. "I know about your Ethics Committee complaint! I know what you people do!"

Abbe was shaken and sought refuge among some of his social companions. A few minutes later, he felt a slap on the shoulder. There was McCain, the man who came close to leading the free world, suddenly calm and collected once more. He looked at Abbe as if nothing very unusual had just happened and said, "Hey, how are you doing? Sorry about that, buddy."

On advice from Abbe and his team, I was hunkered down hoping to ride this out, so I didn't reply to the last minute calls I received from Schmidt of the *Post* soliciting my comments for her every slam piece. I didn't trust her, given how she had misreported my interview comments. Moreover, she was also incredibly sloppy in her reporting. She couldn't even get my birthday right. It didn't matter.

For weeks, the *Post* continued to pound me, but they weren't alone. The rest of the media pack jumped in and were competing to see who could write the most incendiary piece. The *Los Angeles Times* seared me with front-page pieces about my past. One hit me on the Hawthorne

Elementary School election, claiming that innocent loss was the start of my corrupt career. Another censured me for a violent hit I put on an opponent—when I played football in high school. Were there no journalistic standards in our nation any longer?

When the scandal started, I put each new article into a special media folder, thinking the whole thing would be over in a week or so. As my world came apart piece by piece, I found myself adhering to this morbid ritual each morning. As the summer progressed, not only did things not die down, they accelerated. I found myself on the front page of the *Post* more frequently than John Kerry, the Democratic nominee for President. When I finally quit clipping new articles, there were already almost 10,000 separate stories in that folder.

After a few months of this, Gerry Cassidy summoned me to his office. He had been warned by Senator Daniel Inouye, one of Cassidy's biggest allies on the Hill, that if I were associated with their firm, they were no longer welcome in his Senate office. It was ironic, since Inouye was the subject of a number of past scandals himself, including his earmarking American taxpayer funds for an overseas school he favored.

Cassidy had no choice but to let me go. As I walked to my car, I remembered that a few years before, when Inouye was chairman of the Indian Affairs committee, Chief Martin told me how he tried to shake down the tribe for money for the Democratic Senatorial Committee. I stopped the Chief from paying Inouye's tribute, but I was never sure if the Senator knew I was the one who stood in the way. Whether he knew it or not, he got his revenge.

From the outset, McCain had announced he would hold Senate Indian Affairs Committee hearings about the scandal in the fall. As the date approached, I received a subpoena to appear. After almost six months of non-stop blows, I was almost numb. I tried to keep my sanity, though I sunk into a fairly deep depression. There were many days when I just didn't want to get out of bed. I forced myself to stick to a routine, though it became harder and harder. I gained weight. I stopped caring.

My family was suffering as well. My beloved mother was diagnosed with liver cancer, and my father and she were pained to see their son attacked. My children didn't quite know what to think. Their father was being accused of horrific crimes, and made out to be one of the great villains in recent history. This didn't comport with their image of me. They were worried and scared. Pam tried to keep us all sane, and I pretended all would be well, even though I started to doubt it.

When I lost my job at Greenberg, and the Cassidy consultancy was cancelled, I lost my source of income. I announced to the staff at Eshkol Academy that I was no longer financially able to support the school, but that I would keep it open from February until the end of May, despite my lack of income, so the children would not be deprived of a full school year. Considering my cash position was usually tight, and I was now facing huge legal bills, keeping the school open even one more day was imprudent, but I didn't want the kids to suffer. I got my thanks when a group of teachers sued me for closing the school a month early. They had fallen into the grips of a publicity-seeking, ambulance-chasing lawyer. To add insult to injury, they took their case to the press. The *Washington Post* was more than thrilled to have another angle of attack. Thanks to Abbe's solid work, the state court eventually dismissed the case, but it was another unwelcome distraction. My faith in humanity was bolstered by the fact that only a small percentage of our teachers joined this ungracious effort. The others went to great lengths to apologize for their former colleagues.

Signatures, one of the only parts of my old life still intact, took on a funeral atmosphere. One by one, congressional offices barred their staff from eating there. The lobbyists joined the boycott immediately. We were left with the food community of Washington, D.C., but that would not enable us to stay open for long. I still clung to a sliver of hope that the storm would pass, and I could ride it out.

As the September Indian Affairs Committee hearing approached, I huddled with Abbe and Pam Marple, his top counsel at the firm. Abbe heard that the Committee had my tax returns from the past ten years and were planning on going through them with me in public, line by line. They were going to keep me there for a couple of weeks, until I admitted my depravity, or until I had so deeply perjured myself as to enable them to whisk me off to prison.

I had a choice. I could stand toe-to-toe and duke it out with them, knowing that they weren't only the opposing team, but the judge, jury, and executioner, or I could defer a confrontation by pleading my rights under the Constitution. In other words, take the Fifth. Since everyone else was incriminating me, it almost seemed silly not to try to defend myself, but I still clung to the belief that I had not intentionally committed a crime, and therefore was not going to prison. The slightest chance of landing myself in the hoosegow made my choice obvious. Everything in my life was slipping away, and I didn't want to lose the one thing I cared most deeply about: my family. Going to prison would have deprived me of them, a fate far worse than remaining silent in the face of my accusers.

The atmosphere in the room was charged before I entered, but as one senator's diatribe followed another's tirade, it got far worse. I could hear the rumblings in the crowd behind me. They booked this hearing in the main showroom, the biggest room on the Senate side of the Hill.

The rules of the Senate provide that, if one avails himself of the Fifth Amendment, he cannot answer any questions other than basic identification. Abbe was very clear on this point: no matter what lies I heard, no matter how upset I got, I could not break my discipline and answer. If I chose to plead the Fifth, I had to stay the course. Any deviation would waive that assertion, and I would have to answer everything they asked.

Before the inquisitors commenced their grilling, Abbe reminded the senators of Senate Rule No. 26-5, which discouraged committees from holding hearings open to the public, when those proceedings would "tend to charge an individual with crime or misconduct, to disgrace or injure the professional standing of an individual or otherwise to expose an individual to public contempt or obloquy." Since this hearing was not only open to the public, but also televised live and arranged to coincide with the opening of the Native American Heritage Museum in Washington, was this not a violation of the letter and spirit of that Rule? Abbe got his answer immediately: No.

As I sat in the witness chair, the senators fired question after question at me. Actually, few were real questions. Most were just insults. "How could you, as a Jewish American, do these things?" "Don't you have any shame?" "This is the worst abuse of Native Americans since Custer."

The senators had prepared materials, provided by Carrillo. As Abbe predicted, the purpose of the hearing wasn't to inquire what happened. Its purpose was to bring the evil Abramoff in for a beating. And a beating it was. The "questions" continued for twenty minutes, each more insulting and inflammatory than the last. After every question, I dutifully answered that I "respectfully had to decline in asserting my rights under the Fifth Amendment."

I wanted so much to answer these accusations, combat this derisive vilification. But I had to remain silent. I had to endure this and get it over with. Like so much of this nightmare, I just had to take it. I couldn't explain anything.

The worst part for me was the hypocrisy of the whole thing. Most of these senators had taken boatloads of cash and prizes from my team and our clients. I stared stonefaced at Campbell as he hurled invectives at me. I wondered how he'd react if I reminded him about the twenty-five thousand dollars in campaign checks I delivered to him during our breakfast meeting at posh Capitol Hill eatery La Colline the morning of April 23, 2002. I'll never forget that breakfast. After I handed him the envelope full of campaign contributions, he let me know that my clients would be treated well by his Indian Affairs Committee. That's what I wanted to hear. We left arm in arm, but neither of us paid the check. By then, I ate all my meals at my restaurants, and forgot there were such things are restaurant bills. He must have figured that the envelope full of checks also came with a free meal.

Each member of that panel had the same skeletons in their closet I did, or worse. But no one was grilling them.

I calmly plead the Fifth to every question. Over and again, I had to repeat my assertion of my rights. That seemed to infuriate them even more. Senator Kent Conrad of North Dakota, another recipient of thousands of dollars of campaign largesse, pummeled me over a series of emails regarding the Tigua tribe. He quoted my communications about closing the Alabama's casino and claimed they applied to the Tiguas. This was the Indian Affairs committee, and they didn't even know the difference between the two tribes? Or did they?

A number of senators lashed out prior to my entry into the room. Byron Dorgan railed against the "cesspool of greed" surrounding my practice. I guess it wasn't a cesspool when he had his hand out to take over $75,000 in campaign contributions from our team and clients. Senator Tim Johnson, another recipient of thousands of campaign dollars, fulminated about my "insatiable desire to line my pockets." On and on they went.

Finally McCain, of all people, warned the senators that they were on the verge of harassing the witness. Conrad just ignored him and kept going. McCain pressed the point and finally the ordeal ended. Campbell dismissed me, but warned us that I might have to come back for more.

Abbe, Pam, and I made a hasty exit. I would never step foot in a senate hearing room again.

Over the next few weeks, Abbe, Pam Marple, and I continued to pour over my emails. Eventually, it became clear that I was not as blameless as I first thought. I had broken the law. I might not have intended to do so, but as I came to understand, under federal criminal law, intentions didn't matter. I also came to understand that, once you're vilified in every newspaper in the United States, guilt and innocence are measured differently. In any event, I was faced with another difficult choice.

I had been willing to cooperate when this first started because I didn't think I did anything that was criminal. Stupid, maybe. But not criminal. Now after reviewing my emails, despite my past state of denial, it was clear I had broken laws. I had violated the gift ban and caused scores of representatives and staff to do the same. I hadn't revealed to my clients that I shared in the profits with Scanlon. I used non-profit organizations to conceal our political activities on behalf of the clients. I failed to register representations when trying to deceive our opponents.

In the end, perhaps the biggest question I should have pondered was why I thought I hadn't broken the law. In doing each of these things and more, I had intellectualized and rationalized my actions. I found—and sometimes created—loopholes and shortcuts. In my rush to do a million things simultaneously, I did some of them incorrectly and illegally. As I reviewed actions taken years before, I cringed in horror. Had I really done that? What was I thinking?

Now all of my past sins, mistakes, and, yes, crimes confronted me. Abbe was gentle: "Jack, you have a choice, and it is your choice. You can either fight or plea. If you fight, I'll be your champion. I'll be there and slug it out for you, but you need to know what might happen."

He reminded me that I would be in front of a jury in the District of Columbia and that I was a white, male, conservative, perceived to be wealthy, Orthodox Jewish lobbyist. I was the worst possible defendant. Plus,

I had been pilloried in the media, and it wouldn't take much for any able prosecutor to bring a jury to hate me. I had broken the law in several areas.

I would be indicted on fifty counts or more. The public nature of my infamy almost required it. On those fifty plus counts, I would at least be convicted on the ones where I had clearly violated the law, but by the time the jury got done with me, I'd probably be convicted on others as well. My judge would then have the option of sentencing me within the much-criticized, harsh federal sentencing guidelines, which were by then advisory, and I could easily wind up with fifty years in prison. I would be whisked away to a maximum-security penitentiary where I would spend the rest of my life among murders, rapists, and child molesters. Or I could agree to cooperate, admit what I did wrong, and hope for the best. There was no way to gauge what the sentence would be at this stage, and once I started to cooperate, I couldn't reverse course. But if I would be completely honest with the Department of Justice, I at least had a chance of being with my family again.

I was horror-struck. No matter what I chose, I was going to be taken from my children, my wife, my parents, and sent to prison. How could I endure this?

I sat staring at Abbe speechless. Pam Marple looked on sympathetically, as she always did. I felt tears welling in my eyes, and said I would discuss with my family and let him know in the morning. As I slid into my car, I saw my reflection in the mirror. I was completely pale. I had already passed to another world. My drive home felt like a funeral procession.

When my wife Pam returned from work, I embraced her and the tears flowed. I felt like my life was over. I wanted my life to be over. As usual, she tried to buck me up.

"We'll get through this. We have to be strong." I wondered if I had any strength left. I wondered where she found hers. And I wondered what I did right to deserve such a faithful, supportive wife.

Over the next few weeks, I reflected on my stupidity, my mistakes. My crimes. How could I have allowed things to get so far out of hand? My friends consoled me, reminding me that there was a bigger plan afoot, that God was in control, and I had to be patient. I knew they were right, but it was unbearable to see my entire world come apart.

McCain planned for a second hearing. Scanlon and I were supposed to appear together at the first hearing, but while they properly served the subpoena on me, the committee neglected to send him a subpoena. So he didn't show. Why should he do their job for them?

At my hearing, when the senators weren't lacerating me, they were spewing venom on Mike. They left the impression the he evaded their subpoena and had broken the law by not attending the hearing. I saw Scanlon's attorney's letters to the committee reminding them that they hadn't effected service of the subpoena, but that didn't stop them from making a side show of Mike's absence, implying they'd send federal marshals to hunt him down.

Mike's turn on the rack would come less than two months later. The committee dumped emails into the press for several weeks leading up to the big event, as they did in advance of my hearing. For his show, the focus was to be on the Tigua tribe.

After my hearing in September, the media started to show up at our home. This really rattled my children. Pam and I tried to keep them calm. I remember Ollie North telling me how horrible it was to have the press on their lawn during the Iran-Contra affair. Now I knew this pain firsthand. The CNN crews came to the front door, but I told them I wouldn't give them an interview, and they needed to go through my attorney. They left.

One day, a crew from Bill Moyers' show came to film the house. My son Alex had had enough. He was a smart kid, doing square root equations in kindergarten, but he was unusually tough, and exhibited a fearlessness which made me nervous. As he grew, he developed into a pugnacious young man. When he played hockey, invariably he would attack the biggest kids on the ice and land in the penalty box. With the press visiting our property regularly, Pam and I figured it was only a matter of time before Alex would try to take matters into his own hands. Defending our home was his passion. I had already stopped his brother Daniel and him from sneaking through the forest to pelt the CNN trucks with paintballs, but I wasn't home when the Moyers' crew arrived.

When the camera crew stepped onto our property, Alex ran out to greet them with a baseball bat. Fortunately, Pam arrived home at the same moment Alex emerged, and sent him back into the house. The crew apologized, quickly recorded their assigned shots and left. That crisis was averted, but the tension was rising.

A week later, one of my attorneys called. NBC wanted to get footage of me for a piece they were doing on the Tigua case. I told him there was no way. They could do their hit piece without my help. He responded that they were hoping to get me to cooperate, but if not, would probably send a crew to the house to capture me on film leaving one morning. I couldn't risk another incident at the house, so I agreed to be filmed.

On the day of the filming, the NBC crew set up in Abbe's conference room. They wanted to get some shots of me there and walking on the street. I hated this more than words could convey, but I had no choice. I was more concerned about my kids' sanity. As I sat in Abbe's office waiting for my cue, I told him I couldn't take these Tigua accusations. Of all the distortions, this was the worst. I watched Abbe work on his computer, nodding.

"Abbe, I want to talk to NBC about this."

"What? Sorry, what did you say?"

"I said I wanted to talk to them about this. Maybe I could explain what really happened, and they would cut this out."

I couldn't believe how naïve I sounded, but I was desperate. I was sick of being made out to be evil incarnate. This accusation, that I had been the one responsible for closing the Tigua casino just so I could get them to hire me to re-open it, was so outrageous it made me ill.

I assume Abbe understood what I must have been feeling, because he said, "Well, why don't you see if they'll speak with you off the record and give it a go?"

I couldn't believe it! Abbe was letting me off the leash we both created. I bounded down the hall into the conference room. The crew was adjusting the lighting. The first person to notice me was the producer, Sol Levine. Immediately, I saw the usual withering scowl which I got from everyone in those days.

"I'm Jack Abramoff, and I would like to speak with you off the record. Are you OK with that?"

Until then, I hadn't given any radio or television interviews. Levine jumped at the chance.

"Sure, absolutely."

I led him to another conference room, and we sat down. I said I knew they were doing the Tigua story, and I presumed they planned to run the same nonsense everyone else was peddling. He frowned, but I continued.

"I want to explain Tigua to you in detail. I have watched people misreport that representation, and I want someone to hear my side of this."

Now he perked up.

I spent an hour going through every detail of how we wound up in Texas. I showed him a map and described the three tribes involved in this matter: the Louisiana Coushattas, the Alabama Coushattas, and the Tiguas. Incredibly, when the horror story was presented in the press—and even by the Indian Affairs Committee—they left out the Alabama Coushattas. Instead of reporting our efforts to close their illegal casino outside of Houston, we were accused of closing the Tiguas. Even a cursory check of newspaper articles would have made it clear that was nonsense, but no one wanted to exonerate the evil, "disgraced former lobbyist."

When I was done, Levine sat silently for a few moments. "Can everything you have said be verified?" he asked.

"Yes, all of it. Check it out." I left him alone in the conference room, and he started making calls. I returned to Abbe's office, feeling relieved. Levine might not believe me, but at least I got to tell someone my side of things.

After a half hour, Levine emerged from the conference room.

"We have the story wrong. Would you be willing to sit for an interview on this?"

We agreed, as long as Abbe—who was not happy about this turn of events—was able to stop the conversation should it become problematic. Soon I was sitting in front of the camera. Levine asked questions, and I answered them. For the first time in months, I had hope. Maybe, somehow, the storm clouds would break. Day after day, I waited for NBC to air the story, but it was radio silence. Finally, Abbe called Levine. Not surprisingly, the story was spiked.

# 14

# DOUBLE JUDGMENT

In the next year, 2005, there were more hearings, more press hits, and more misery. Eventually, I began my meetings with the Department of Justice, hoping my cooperation would help bring some sort of closure.

That summer, I took my kids away on mini-vacations. I didn't know how long I would have with them, and I wanted every minute to be memorable. I took Levi and Alex to the rural Shenandoah Valley, while Livia and I went to Boston, Daniel and I went to New York and Sarah and I to Los Angeles.

By that time, it was quite obvious I would never be a lobbyist again, so I decided to venture back to the motion picture business. Though other filmmakers would eventually create a theatrical film and a documentary about my situation, I was hardly interested in making one about myself. The projects I started to craft were fantasy and adventure pictures, not horror stories resembling my life.

The trip to LA gave me a chance to advance my film projects, and spend some time with Sarah as I had with the other kids. At first, we had a lot of fun. We saw sights and visited family. My meetings on the film projects were yielding some positive results. But as I sat at the Beverly Hilton Hotel on the morning of August 11, 2005, in a breakfast meeting with a screenwriter, my phone rang. It was Neal Sonnett, my attorney in Florida, who had been our point man dealing with the federal investigation into Suncruz. My assumption was that I would be a witness against Kidan, who had stolen money from me and crashed the company, but Neal's voice indicated a crisis was afoot.

"Jack, the media are telling me that you're being indicted today in Miami."

"Indicted? Why? For what?"

"Suncruz."

I was being indicted, along with Kidan, for the bank fraud. Neal asked where I was. When I told him, he said I should look into flying to Miami immediately to be arraigned. Sarah was still sleeping when I returned to the hotel room. I had a meeting with a talent agency about one of the films later that morning and invited her to join me. I didn't have the heart to tell my twelve-year-old daughter that our precious time alone together would be cut short.

As the agents and I discussed possible directors for the film, my phone rang again.

"Mr. Abramoff, this is the FBI. We need you to turn yourself in at the federal building in Los Angeles immediately."

I excused myself from the meeting and called my attorneys. The U.S. Attorney in Florida wouldn't permit me to fly there to be arraigned. He wanted me to be in chains that very day, in time for his press conference. Kidan, the architect of the Florida debacle, would be allowed to fly to Miami to be arraigned at his leisure. Apparently he didn't need to turn himself in, let alone be jailed.

The only piece of good news I got that day was that the FBI lost patience with the U.S. Attorney's demands that I be perp-walked on camera to coincide with their press conference, and arranged for us to meet at a baseball field, far from the paparazzi cameras already in place at the federal building. Sarah and I met my brother Bob a block away. Her tears broke my heart. I assured her it would all be OK.

Accompanied by a local LA attorney sent by Abbe and Pam Marple, I headed to the ballpark. The FBI agents were kind and sympathetic, professional and decent, which was the best I could hope for under the circumstances. On the way to jail, they tried to put my mind at ease.

"You'll be out by tomorrow for sure. It's too late today, or they'd have you out before nightfall. You'll be fine. You'll watch TV and play ping-pong. You'll be out before you know it."

When I arrived at the Metropolitan Detention Center, I was put into the segregated housing unit, known as the "hole." I was told that, because I was all over the news, if they put me into the general population I'd be dead before morning. Some inmate would want to claim his fifteen minutes of fame by becoming my murderer. Great.

I was put into a cell with a tattooed inmate, and immediately had every bad prison movie playing in my head. He turned out to be a lapsed Mormon and not a bad guy at all. He was serving his sentence in the hole because he didn't like the inmates in the main prison. Most federal prisons permit inmates to opt for the hole over living with the general population. Few inmates would choose to live in the restrictive environment of the hole, but my new "cellie" did.

The next morning I was chained hand and foot and led to the courthouse across the street. When I emerged into the defendant's area, the place was packed. I recognized some of the media from D.C. I guess they flew out on the red eye once they got the great news that this notorious, dangerous lobbyist had finally been captured. The media alternated between smirks and sneers, but I just stared right into their faces. Quickly they looked away. I didn't take my eyes off them, and they craned their necks to avoid making eye contact. I noticed a sketch artist just to my right, furtively glancing at me and looking extremely uncomfortable. I leaned over and told him not to worry, he was only doing his job, and I knew it.

"Just see if you can make me look less fat."

The judge set bail at $2.5 million, and required my brother, my father, and me to put up our homes as collateral. Bob was in the court, and had a car ready for a quick exit, but the media was right on our heels as we left the courthouse.

By then it was Friday, and there was no way for me to return to D.C. in time for the Sabbath, so I took a room at the airport Hilton and was booked on a late Saturday night flight home. I arrived in time to attend synagogue services for the fast of Tisha B'Av, the annual commemoration of the destruction of the Temple in Jerusalem. Appropriately, it's the saddest day of the Jewish calendar.

In the final months of 2005, the Department of Justice and my attorneys worked on my plea deal. I was told that each Department of Justice division, which worked on my case, would have one count in the plea. I also had to plea in Florida, although I was promised that the Florida charges would be combined with the case in Washington, which meant I wouldn't face the longer sentence resulting from two separate felony convictions.

The entire time I was meeting with the Department of Justice, I assume my former colleagues were doing the same. Most of the people involved in my case didn't attempt to fight; like me, they pled. There were some exceptions, though. David Safavian was charged with making false statements and obstruction of justice. He fought the charges and was convicted. He appealed and won, and was re-indicted and convicted again. Kevin Ring spent about a year cooperating with the federal government and then withdrew from cooperating and was indicted on charges of conspiracy, fraud and obstruction of justice. His first trial ended in a hung jury, but his second trial led to his conviction on five counts of conspiracy to corrupt public officials.

Mike, like most of the others, was pleading and, as far as I knew cooperating. When the Justice Department decided to allow him to go to court to enter his plea first, the media speculated that his plea would put pressure on me to do the same, as if he had somehow turned on me. The press loves that kind of melodrama, but it was completely untrue. I went to Justice long before Mike and was never going to be fighting them.

The Justice Department decided I would plea in Washington first. In order to avoid the media, I planned to arrive at the courthouse in D.C. very early on Tuesday, January 3, 2006, the morning of my court appearance. It was raining, cold and still dark when I left home that winter morning. I grabbed a black raincoat and rain hat from the hall closet, and went to Abbe's office. From there, Abbe, Pam Marple, and I took a taxi to the court. We beat the press and were able to get inside the court house safely and without notice. Eventually we were taken to a conference room, and joined by Mary Butler, Leanna Saler, and the rest of the prosecution team. I had spent hours and hours with these folks, and genuinely liked them. They were never cruel or unfair to me. And they were honest public servants, who at times seemed truly saddened at my fate. As far as I could tell, they weren't the ones hoping I would land in prison for years. The

Republican higher ups in the Bush Department of Justice were in charge of that task, undoubtedly trying to prove to the world that they could punish a fellow Republican.

We sat in court waiting for the arrival of Judge Ellen Huvelle. The media packed the visitors' gallery and seemed to be having a great time, like a celebrating nineteenth century crowd at a public hanging.

The judge entered, and the hearing commenced. After the technicalities, I rose to make a statement: "Your honor, words will not be able to ever express how sorry I am for this, and I have profound regret and sorrow for the multitude of mistakes and harm I have caused. All of my remaining days, I will feel tremendous sadness and regret for my conduct and for what I have done. I only hope that I can merit forgiveness from the Almighty and from those I have wronged or caused to suffer. I will work hard to earn that redemption."

As I finished the statement, I looked up and was a bit stunned to see sadness in the faces of the prosecutors and FBI agents. They had read thousands of my emails, not just the few parsed, stupid utterances fed to the press by McCain's staff. I think they thought me foolish and impetuous, and at times reckless. But I never once felt they thought I was evil. The whole thing was just a tragedy to them. They had their job to do, and did it as professionally and gently as they could.

When the hearing ended, we returned to the conference room. I put on my coat and hat, and followed Abbe and Pam Marple out to the waiting car. It never dawned on any of us that what I was wearing would cause such an explosion. But as soon as we exited the court, the cameras set upon me. One of the nasty tricks of the paparazzi is to shout to get your attention. If you turn to them, their footage is more valuable. As soon as I emerged, I heard shouts: "What's with that hat? What, are you a mobster?"

Immediately, I knew I had a wardrobe malfunction. I had worn the hat for two reasons. First, it was raining when I left for court that morning and I didn't want to get wet. Second, I wanted to cover my head. Throughout this traumatic time in my life, as in my past, I felt highly connected with God. In our faith, men are bidden to cover their heads. I didn't wish to impugn my religion more than I had already by wearing something so obvious as a yarmulke, nor did I want to be accused of playing the religious card. My whole life I had downplayed my religious observance in the political and business world for fear of being accused of trying to use it for gain. Now I wanted to downplay it because of the shame I had brought on my fellow Jews. I figured the hat was a good way to de-emphasize my observance and yet keep my head covered. I never dreamed it would ignite such an uproar.

After that short walk in the hat, the media unloaded on me. I was again the topic of late night monologues. Leno quipped, "Jack Abramoff pled guilty to corruption and fraud charges. When they booked him, they had to empty his pockets. Tom DeLay fell out."

Conan O'Brien chimed in: "Republican lobbyist Jack Abramoff has agreed to cooperate with federal prosecutors. He could name up to twenty congressmen. When he heard this, President Bush said, 'That's amazing. I can only name three congressmen.'"

The rest of the media comments weren't so funny.

The day after I pled in D.C., I flew to Miami to offer a plea to the charges there. The charges I pled to that day were wire fraud and conspiracy to commit wire and mail fraud. The press was all over the place. As I got out of the car to enter the court, they charged, blocking my way. I just kept walking ahead and at the last minute they stepped aside to let me through, shouting all the while. This time, much to the disappointment of the paparazzi, I wore a baseball cap without a logo. The judge set my sentencing for March, and I headed back to D.C. for my meetings with the Justice Department. I had hoped that after my plea, the media attention would wane. Instead, I soon found my pensive face on the cover of *Time* magazine, with the headline, "The Man Who Bought Washington." Each day seemed to bring another dozen stories. The press was hitting me from all sides. My black hat became the most infamous chapeau in the land.

The mass circus reached its climax when George Clooney ascended the stage to accept the 2006 Golden Globe for Best Actor in a Dramatic Film a few weeks after my plea in court.

I had little interest in watching the Golden Globe awards, or anything else on television for that matter, except perhaps an occasional rerun of "Seinfeld." But that wasn't the case with my teenage daughter Sarah. Along with her schoolmates, she loved to watch America's celebrities in action. That night she tuned into the awards show from my office at home and chatted happily with her friends on the phone as they watched.

But as I walked by my office, I noticed Sarah was crying. With three elder brothers in the house, I assumed one of them drove her to tears. "Who did this? Daniel? Alex? Levi?"

She looked up and pointed to the television. "No, he did!"

I entered the office and saw George Clooney on stage. Immediately, I hit Tivo to rewind the broadcast and got a healthy dose of Hollywood wisdom. Instead of thanking the people responsible for getting him that award, Clooney decided to take a swing at me. "What kind of parents would name their kid 'Jack' when his name ends in 'off?' No wonder that guy is screwed up!"

With that obscene comment, the suave jester drove a little girl to tears. And he gave the newspapers a new angle of attack, which they used with abandon. After a few days of simmering, the street fighter in my father erupted with a caustic missive to Clooney, which he copied to the *Hollywood Reporter*: "Your glib and ridiculous attack on my son, Jack, coupled with your obscene query as to the choice his mother and I made in naming him brought shame and dishonor on you and your profession." Clooney was lucky that this confrontation hadn't taken place sixty years earlier when Dad settled altercations in the street without the benefit of stunt men.

While the press went on and on about me and my case, I spent every day for months on end trudging to the FBI offices in Virginia to meet with agents and investigators. All the meetings were tolerable, but going over hundreds of my emails each day drained me of the energy I needed to try to get some business going. Our finances were perilous. Pam was working full time, but not bringing in the kind of money needed to support five children. Dad helped as much as he could, but we were barely making it. And I couldn't get anything moving myself, as much as I tried.

At the end of March, I headed to Miami for sentencing. It was the first time I had seen Kidan since Suncruz days, and he looked older and tired. We were seated apart from each other at sentencing, and while Kidan rose to make a statement, I chose silence. I did not hate Adam. I felt badly for him. Whereas I had a loving wife, children and parents to support me through this nightmare, he had no one. I couldn't imagine how he endured, but then again, Adam had a great capacity to compartmentalize and an unlimited capacity for self-delusion. Yes, he'd do just fine.

The judge gave us each 70 months in prison, and then pronounced that we should report to prison in six weeks. My attorneys started to jump up to object, but they didn't get a chance. The Justice Department didn't want me in prison yet. They had two thousand open investigations, and they felt I could shed light on many of them. The local prosecutors in Florida didn't want Kidan in prison just yet either. He was cooperating in the case of the murder of Gus Boulis. The judge didn't seem impressed with either request, and admonished the prosecutors to hurry up. He announced his intention to revisit the matter in six weeks' time. The pressure in my head was building. This was the first time going to prison became a time-sensitive reality for me. It was a crushing moment when it really hit me that I'd be taken from my family.

Pam joined me for sentencing in Miami, even though she previously hadn't appeared in court to protect her privacy. Her presence and support was the only positive element that day. We sat in silence on the plane ride home, knowing the next few years would be the hardest of our lives.

I spent the next six months working with the Department of Justice. The entire time, I was treated with dignity and kindness. It's not that anyone did me any favors, but they were extremely kind and under-standing. That alone made a huge difference to me.

In October 2006, the judge scheduled a third conference to discuss when I would enter prison. In the past, he'd agreed to allow me more time to work with the DOJ. When Pam Marple and Abbe reached me this time, I expected more of the same. Instead, I was told I had to report to prison by November 15. I was floored. Wasn't the DOJ upset by this ruling? It didn't make sense to me. How could the DOJ allow all their political corruption cases to be compromised because their Miami U.S. Attorney decided to indict me? Why was the Florida judge so insistent on my going to prison in the midst of these investigations? I wasn't a flight risk. I wasn't a danger to society. I would never find out the cause of this inexplicable turn of events; all I knew was my days of freedom were at an end and a new chapter of my nightmare story was about to begin.

I spent the next few weeks doing my best to prepare for prison, which meant I did whatever I could to get my finances in order so my family would survive the incarceration. But there was little I could do. I had no revenue sources, and we were already long ago drained of our funds. We were living on fumes. Pam's income would have to carry us, along with help from our generous friends and family. Already in his eighties, my father helped us in every way possible. But even with the help, I knew the following years would be full of hardship. A storm tore up the roof of our home shortly after my departure. It took two years for Pam to get the money together to fix it. Daily prayer is what kept our house—and family—from collapsing.

There were few good parts in our family's story at this point in time but, worst of all, we were losing our mothers. As our lives crumpled, Pam's mother passed away. She had concealed an illness and died before we could even process what was happening. The loss of this incredible person in our lives was devastating for us all, but for Pam it was cataclysmic. Her mother was her best friend and confidante, other than me. Losing the two of us at the same time was a crushing blow.

At the same time, my mother was fighting for her life. When my collapse came, Mom was diagnosed with liver cancer. She battled the disease while watching my career end in infamy. I will never know if the stress of seeing me so publicly torn apart caused the acceleration of her illness, but Mom's suffering intensified during my final months of freedom. I visited as frequently as I could, but it wasn't often enough. I last saw her just twenty-three days before I had to report to prison. We kept trying to convince each other that she would get better and that I would get out in time to see her again. We both knew better and fought back a stream of tears. As I looked into my beloved mother's eyes for what would be the last time, she nodded as if to say all will be all right. I cried the entire way back to Washington.

On my final Sunday of freedom, Pam and I drove to see my Aunt Bea in Southern New Jersey. Aunt Bea had just celebrated her ninety-third birthday and was still going strong. The last surviving child of my inspiring great-grandmother, and sister to my mother's mother, Aunt Bea is far closer to me than any aunt could possibly be. As I held her hand, I prayed silently that God would sustain her and enable us to be together again. I am eternally grateful that prayer was answered.

In the final days leading up to Wednesday, November 15, things reached a fever pitch in our home. The kids were stressed, but put on a brave face for me. We planned to go to the prison together as a family. Since the media were still lavishing their attention on me, we anticipated a gaggle of cameras greeting us. Prisoners are required to report before 2:00 p.m., so I let leak to the media that I would arrive at noon. Then my family and I prepared to leave our house in the middle of night, so we would arrive at 6:30 a.m.

Pam Marple was kind enough to join us on the ride. She is a brave and kind soul, and I was sorry she had to witness the emotion and angst of our family that morning. As we pulled away from our house at 3:30 am, I looked back at our home longingly, wondering when or if I would ever see it again. I stopped the car, and spoke to my children. I hoped they could be brave and patient while I was gone. Like so many times in their past, I tried to link our present circumstances—happy or sad—to the Bible and our faith. In this context, I reminded the children of Psalm 126, which we sing in Hebrew each Sabbath during our grace after meals prayers. I noted that, like so many other things we do regularly in life, we sometimes miss the meaning of our utterances and actions. Embedded in King David's masterpiece Psalm 126 is the line, "Those who sow with tears will reap with joy." Now we had tears. One day soon we would have joy. I begged my five children to wait patiently for that day to come.

As I finished, my voice cracked, and my own tears flowed. I loved my family so much, and now I was about to lose them. Nothing could have been worse.

We drove for several hours and stopped at the parking lot of the Cumberland Holiday Inn for morning prayers. We shared hugs and got back into the car for the final leg of our dreaded journey.

As we rounded the bend near the facility, I saw six camera crews set up by the side of the road. They hadn't been fooled by my announced noon arrival. I was sitting in the second row of our car, surrounded by my sons so they couldn't film me, giving me but some slight comfort at that difficult moment.

We pulled into the prison parking lot and got out of the car. It was time to say goodbye. I had dreaded this moment for a long time. It was like a slow motion train crash. The kids were crying, as was I. Pam tried to maintain her equilibrium, but it was hard. I kissed and hugged each child, from youngest to eldest. Neither the children nor I wished to let go. As I released each child, they turned and burst into tears. My heart tore. Finally, it was time to say goodbye to my beloved wife. It would be a long time before we would next embrace in freedom. Neither of us could choke out a word.

Pam Marple stood by, trying to comfort the children. When I had finished saying my goodbyes, she accompanied me into the prison lobby. Just before the door closed behind me, I turned back to look at my family once more. We waved weakly, and I nodded to them, the same way my mother had nodded to me. With that nod, I entered Cumberland Federal Correctional Institution.

# 15

# CUMBERLAND CORRECTIONAL

It's hard to pinpoint the worst day in all of this. There are so many candidates. My hearing in the senate. Being fired from the firm. The day I realized I was going to prison. The day we ran out of money. But the day I reported to federal prison was when I truly hit rock bottom. Stripped of all worldly possessions, dispossessed of my family, shorn of all self-worth, I was clad in a prison uniform and sent into a strange new world.

I was assigned to the minimum-security facility, or camp, which was adjacent to a medium-high security prison. The medium, as we called it, housed some pretty tough guys. Murderers, rapists, child molesters, gangs, Mafiosi. The camp was mainly drug dealers, mixed in with a sprinkling of white collar offenders.

My difficulties at Cumberland were put in place even before arrived. The staff assumed I would come in and try to run the place and were on the defense from day one. They'd been instructed to deny me virtually every request, to ensure that I would not seduce them with my "devious personality." One staff member, a pseudo-psychologist, told his co-workers that based on what he had read in the media, I was the most manipulative person on earth, that they had never had an inmate who was so capable of bending their will. Nothing could have been further from the truth. I was a broken man. I was humbled and unsure of myself. I missed my family and only wanted to go home. They had nothing to fear from me.

Cumberland was grossly overcrowded. Built to house 150 inmates, it was home to over 300 of us. Six men shared 150 square feet of space in a cubicle, and there were eight cubicles in each wing. For six months, I was housed in a wing where the average age was considerably younger than mine. The lights never seemed to go out. The noise was incessant and disturbing. Sleeping was virtually impossible. The inmates in my cube were polite to me, but they might as well have been from another planet. The senior inmate in the cube introduced himself as "N.O." Like the other four inmates in our cube, he was a drug dealer, and like the others, his tastes in music and literature, if one can call it that, were obscene. The drug of choice among these dealers seemed to be crack cocaine. Like the rest of our wing, these guys never seemed to sleep at night. At all hours of the night, they would play dominoes or Scrabble, accompanied by loud banging. Worse than the noise was the cigarette smoke. Though smoking was banned in federal facilities years ago, there was a healthy black market in tobacco and most inmates on the wing indulged in the habit. The problem was that they smoked in the stairwell only ten feet from my bed. All night the inmates would sneak into the stairwell and puff away. When the warden finally visited the dorms, she noted the strong stench of smoke. When she failed to do anything about it and wouldn't move me away from the health hazard, I contacted my attorneys to file a second hand smoke lawsuit. Within two days I was transferred to a wing filled with older, quieter men, who slept at night, and didn't smoke. Life became a little more bearable at that point.

In almost every area of life in prison, I was stifled. Although everyone has to work in prison, there aren't enough real jobs to go around, and most men are given menial tasks to occupy their monotonous days. My first job was in the kitchen, washing dishes. For hours each day, I ran myself batty filling up utensil bins. My fellow inmates made fun of me for working so hard at something so trivial. Clearly, we had different work ethics. I was now a dishwasher, so I'd be the best dishwasher I could be. I certainly wasn't doing it for the pay. At twelve cents an hour, I wasn't even making enough in a month to park a car in downtown Washington, D.C.

After putting in my time in the kitchen, I was told a clerkship in the chapel was open. I worked hard to land that position and was able to do so thanks to the counselor in my housing unit. Working in the chapel was a choice job at Cumberland. My two co-clerks were bright and well read, and helped to fill my days with intelligent conversation. With the diversity of faiths in the prison, the chaplain had decided to hire a Christian, Muslim, and Jew to fill the three clerk positions. I was the Jew. The Christian clerk, Kehinde Oladapo, was a friendly and fervently religious Nigerian who was also there for a white-collar crime. The Muslim clerk, Ray Smith, was a member of a group called the Moorish Science Temple, which focused on connecting African Americans to Moorish roots in Africa. He was finishing a seventeen-year sentence for drug dealing. We didn't always agree on political issues—actually we never agreed on political issues—but we got along quite well nonetheless.

Because the chaplains who served the camp spent most of their time in the medium prison, we clerks more or less controlled the chapel. In the past, this power was abused with inmates actually hiding contraband pornographic materials in the chapel ceilings, but that didn't happen while the three of us worked there. We were all very serious about our faiths, and had no sympathy for the introduction of contraband into the chapel.

Despite the new job, and the fact that most of my days were free of harassment from the staff, for the first eighteen months at Cumberland I was constantly singled out. Once, I was berated by a staff member for having seven books in my locker, instead of the prison limit of five. "Yeah, that's the problem here," I thought to myself. "Too much reading!" Those inmates who did read had scores of books in their lockers, but I was the one who got in trouble for breaking the rules. At first, these scoldings were frightening. I didn't want trouble and tried to follow every rule carefully. Eventually, I realized that the main goal was just to disorient me. There would soon be bigger things to worry about than having extra books taken away.

Eight months after my arrival in prison, in June 2007, my mother's health took a final turn for the worse. I called her as frequently as I could while she withered away at the hospital, but we were limited to 300 minutes of phone time each month, and very soon my minutes for June were gone. Fortunately, our prison was the first to test a new inmate email system, which enables incarcerated men to stay in touch with their families electronically. The system is onerous, requiring email be sent to the prison authorities, who review and possibly reject it, and then sent to a Web site where family members can access the email and reply. The prison officials also filter the replies before they're sent back, so what takes a few moments outside the prison takes hours inside, but it was the best means of communication I had.

On June 26, 2007, Pam emailed me that my mother had passed away. I was devastated. I had applied to the prison to visit Mom on her deathbed, as many other inmates had been granted these final visits with their parents and immediate family, but they never replied. My last image of my mother was that compassionate nod she gave me as I left her for the final time nine months earlier.

Since I wouldn't qualify for new phone minutes until July 1, I tried to find out if I could purchase next month's minutes for immediate use. No one could answer that question. In a daze, I walked to the administration building, only to see the staff member who had castigated me for having too many books. With no confidence that he would help me, I started, "Sir, my mother just passed away and…"

"I know, Abramoff. I am very sorry."

It was the first decent thing a staff member had said to me. I asked about purchasing next months' minutes in advance, but he said that wouldn't be possible. Disappointed, I was surprised when he offered to take me to his office and let me call from there. I was grateful and relieved to speak with Pam and my kids. I tried to reach my father, but with no luck. He was probably making arrangements for Mom's funeral. The staffer told me to come back tomorrow, and he'd put me on the phone with my father. I decided to push it and ask about the funeral.

"I see that other inmates have been allowed to attend their parent's funerals, and I was wondering whether I might be able to attend my mother's?"

"Abramoff, if it were up to me, I would send you right now, but I have to be honest with you. They aren't going to allow you to go. They're scared to death of being seen as mollycoddling you, and you know that the press would be there, at your mom's funeral. You can request it, but they'll almost certainly turn you down. I'm sorry."

In the midst of utter despair, this one man's kindness meant the world to me. I was crestfallen that I couldn't go to my own mother's funeral, but at least, for the first time there, someone had shown a sense of compassion and understanding.

I returned the next morning, hoping to call my father. Unfortunately, instead of this officer who had been so kind the day before, a cold and nasty female staff member we referred to as "the Witch" was manning the administration office. (Actually, most inmates called her something which only rhymed with "witch.') We had started off on the wrong foot when I first arrived at the prison. She was the one who asked where I would like my dead body shipped. I didn't have much hope that she would help me out now, but I had to try.

"I beg your pardon, ma'am, but my mother passed away the other day…"

"Yeah, I know… And?" she glowered at me.

"Well, uh, I've used up my phone minutes this month and…"

"You should have planned ahead."

"Yes, ma'am, you're right, but I was trying to speak with my mother every occasion I had, since it was her final time …"

"You still should have planned ahead. What do you want, Abramoff?"

"I was hoping to be able to call my father. You see, yesterday I was allowed to call my wife and children and…"

"You got your calls yesterday. You can call your father when your minutes renew."

"Yes, ma'am, thank you, but I was hoping to call him before my mother's funeral and…"

"This conversation is over. Out."

"Yes, ma'am."

With that, I returned to the unit to mourn my mother alone.

Two months later, more trouble came my way. There were a small number of Jewish prisoners at Cumberland. I was the only religious Jew, but the others participated in the variety of events I organized as clerk of the chapel. I spent my time at Cumberland teaching introductory classes in Judaism to the Jewish inmates, as well as typing, public speaking, and business to the general population. Teaching gave me a sense of purpose in an environment which does little to encourage enterprise and ambition.

In Judaism, communal prayer is only possible with ten men, a minyan. Without this requisite amount, there can be no communal reading from the Torah, nor a variety of other prayers, including the mourner's prayer, kaddish. As our numbers grew to eight men, I approached the volunteer local Reform Rabbi, Steven Sniderman, who would visit us on a biweekly basis, and asked if we could borrow one of his community's Torah scrolls, should we wind up with a minyan. He agreed to provide one, if his board concurred, and asked that I just give him some advance notice.

By Labor Day 2007, another three Jews arrived at Cumberland, and we had our minyan. I approached my boss, the chaplain, and related my conversation with the rabbi to him. He was supportive of our having a Torah scroll, and told me to raise it with the rabbi when he was next visiting. I mentioned that the rabbi was coming that Thursday, but if he was unable to bring the Torah with him that day, we would not have it in time for the Jewish high holidays, which were starting that next week. I asked the chaplain to call him, but he demurred, saying he was very busy that week. Then I remembered that the rabbi was not the only visitor from the local Jewish community. Every week, two lovely elderly ladies would visit us. We had converted those sessions into Bible classes, which I led, and they were enthusiastic and regular attendees. I mentioned to the chaplain that the ladies would be at the prison the next day, on Tuesday, and that I would ask them to contact the rabbi. The chaplain agreed to the plan, and went over the steps I would need to take to get us the Torah. I jotted them down and returned to my workstation.

On Tuesday morning, before the ladies arrived, I typed up the notes from the chaplain so the instructions were clear. I didn't want anything to prevent our getting the Torah. When the ladies arrived, I mentioned the plan and gave them the typed instructions. They were enthusiastic, noting that the local synagogue had more Torahs than members. All the guys were elated at the prospect of our obtaining a Torah scroll. Most of them had never seen one before, and now we would be able to read from the Torah when we prayed.

That Thursday afternoon, the rabbi arrived for his regular biweekly session. He had nothing in hand. I asked about the Torah, and he abruptly and firmly said he couldn't bring us anything. We were all bewildered.

Why? Did his board reject it? He wouldn't answer. When he left, I called Pam and asked her to have one of our local orthodox rabbis call the chaplain, to see if we could have one of their Torahs sent to us. I knew that the prison was listening to the call, as they recorded every call made in the institution, and mine were favorites among the staff.

The next day, Friday, the assistant Chaplain came to the camp in the afternoon. That was rare since the Chaplains only visited us on the weekends and Mondays. He called me into his office. "Abramoff, what's going on with this Torah situation?"

I explained what was happening. He looked at me suspiciously.

"Then why would the associate warden be talking about shipping you to another prison?"

My eyes widened.

"What?"

"They are saying you are harassing a rabbi and that you might be shipped. This sounds very odd."

I explained what happened and asked whether I should be worried about this. He said not to worry about it, that it was likely a misunderstanding, but of course I was concerned. That evening, the guard told me I had to go to the medium prison to see the lieutenant. I was handcuffed, which he assured me was standard procedure, and taken to the lieutenant's office. There sat a dour faced, middle-aged officer.

"You are under investigation for violation of prison rules," he said, "and are going to be placed in the Segregated Housing Unit."

The hole.

"You're accused of sending a letter to volunteers outside the normal prison mail system. This is a serious violation of security," he continued.

"Do you mean the letter to the rabbi about the Torah?"

"Correct."

He picked up a piece of paper—my letter. The rabbi ratted me out!

I was stripped of my clothing, given a tightly fitting jump suit, and put into the hole. It was cold. The lights were on all the time. The noise from the other inmates in that unit never stopped. There was no view from the window, so you wouldn't know if it were day or night, let alone what time it is. The guards shine a light in your face every two hours to see if you are still there. Or alive. One can pace the entire cell with no more than five steps. Five small steps. There was nothing to read. Nothing to hear except the shouting of the other inmates. Months later I read that after more than three days in the hole, one can lose one's sanity. Three days? More like three hours.

The witch showed up to pay me a visit, just when I thought it couldn't get worse. "Abramoff," she started, "I am here to check to see if you need anything. Do you?"

I was thrown off by her humane tone. "Yes, thank you so much. I need my prayer book and my religious items. They are in my locker at the camp. If you could arrange to have them provided, I would be most grateful."

"OK, I'll see what I can do."

The next morning, I received a visit from one of my conservative movement friends. They chained me and brought me to the visiting room. My visitor was aghast, having previously visited me in the relatively pleasant visiting room of the camp. Now I was in the medium prison and obviously under tremendous duress. I asked him to let Pam know about this turn of events. Maybe she could call my attorney.

Soon after I was returned to my cell, the witch showed up again. And again she said, "Abramoff, I am here to check to see if you need anything. Do you?"

"Yes, please, I need my prayer book and other religious items in my locker," I repeated the request from her previous visit.

"I'll see what I can do."

The next day, Sunday, I was still in the hole when Pam arrived to the visiting room with another friend. She had called my attorneys, and they were working on getting me back to the camp. We tried to have a pleasant visit, but I was nervous about being shipped to another prison, and didn't do a great job hiding that fear.

Upon arrival back at my cell, I heard the unmistakable footsteps of the witch yet again. By now I knew the drill. "Abramoff, I am here to check to see if you need anything. Do you?"

"No. I am fine." I finally got the joke.

I had spent every waking moment since I arrived at Cumberland praying to God to get me out of the camp. As soon as I was put in the hole, I spent every moment praying to get back into the camp. The next day, I finally got my wish, with no explanation. But the matter wasn't over.

I was brought before a small panel of officials, led by the witch herself.

"Abramoff, now that you have been found guilty of circumventing the mail system, we have to administer your punishment."

Wasn't the three days in the hole punishment? Apparently not.

"We are going to recommend that you lose thirty days of your good time, thirty days of your access to the commissary, and thirty days of phone use."

"Good time" was the days by which your sentence is reduced for good behavior. I didn't want to stay in that place one more minute than necessary, but it wasn't the good time that bothered me.

"Ma'am, my mother passed away two months ago," I started, as she rolled her eyes. "And, well, I have been calling my father as often as possible, since he is now alone, and I want to comfort him. Please don't take my phone use away."

Ignoring me, she continued.

"Since we can't take your good time away on our own, we have to refer the matter to the Disciplinary Hearing Officer, who will decide."

The DHO is not part of the prison chain of command, but rather an outside arbiter of fairness. I didn't care about the good time. It was a badge of honor to me to endure another month in prison for having tried to secure a Torah scroll for prayer. But the phone restriction depressed me. I had let my father down by not being there for Mom and him, and now I couldn't even call him. I knew he'd understand, but I couldn't get around this. Plus, I would now be cut off from calling my children and Pam. This couldn't possibly get any worse, I thought. And yet it did. A few days later, I got the verdict.

"Abramoff, the DHO refuses to allow us to take away your good time."

Of course not, I thought. He probably read this so called "case" and tossed it out. I had no ill intent. I didn't know that you can't give a volunteer a note. Plus, this note was about getting a Torah scroll with the chaplain's instructions. Harmless.

But she wasn't finished.

"Since we can't take away your good time, we've decided that your punishment is to lose your phone privileges ... for ninety days."

What an idiot I was. I should have begged her not to take my commissary use. As soon as I mentioned the phone, I cut my own throat. And that was that.

Two months into the ninety-day phone suspension, my Nigerian co-worker Kehinde asked me for a favor.

"Jack, I saw on the television a most beautiful Bible called the Rainbow Bible. I want to order this Bible, but to do so I would need the address and phone number of a bookstore that carries it. I don't have any friends or family in this area, since they are all back home in Nigeria. Could you ask one of your friends to get me this information so I can have the prison issue a check from my commissary account?"

I sent an email to my old pal Paul Erickson. I knew he'd come through. But, instead of sending the Bible ordering information, Paul did what any decent person would do: he just went out and bought a Rainbow Bible and sent it in. In our email exchange, I thanked Paul, but cautioned him that prison rules forbade me from giving the book to another inmate. It would have to be Paul's gift. Naturally, he agreed.

A week later, the Bible arrived. I didn't suspect anything when I was called to the front to receive the package, but I should have. All the other packages were distributed through the regular mail system. Inmates would place mail on beds at night, but this time I had to sign for it. The guard made some excuse, and I didn't think anything about it.

As I walked to the chapel, I opened the packet and saw the Rainbow Bible inside. As I entered the clerk's office, Kehinde was seated at the desk reading. I cautiously placed the Bible on the shelf and withdrew from the office to another chapel room. All of a sudden I heard an exclamation of delight, "The Bible!"

He took the Bible back with him to the housing unit and read until he fell asleep. Our cubicles were across from each other. At 10:00 pm, I heard the guards coming into our wing. You could always hear them at a distance, their key chains echoed like Jacob Marley's chains in A Christmas Carol. Kehinde never broke the rules—he was a model inmate—so when the guards roused him from bed and took him away, I was shocked. Usually, when the guards came to arrest an inmate from bed, it was because of contraband, and we would never see that inmate again. But around midnight, Kehinde walked back into the wing.

"Jack, we're in trouble," he whispered from his cubical. "They accused me of receiving the Bible from you and are going to be questioning you tomorrow. They wanted to throw me in the hole, but since I wouldn't admit you gave it to me, they couldn't do anything, yet."

"But I didn't give it to you! I put it on the shelf, and you just took it."

"Yes, I know. I told them that, but they don't believe me. They said that they wouldn't care about it, but you're involved. Are you in their bad graces?"

That was the understatement of the year. "Yes, they seem to think that they need to keep me under their yoke. I am sure we'll be OK."

That wasn't an understatement. That was a lie. I thought we were both in trouble, but why worry the guy?

The next day, I was called to the administration building. An investigator from the medium security prison was in the conference room ready to see me.

"Abramoff," she began, "You are accused of a Series 328 violation, giving something of value to another inmate. From what we can determine, you received a book in the mail and gave it to one Kehinde Oladapo. Is this correct?"

"No, it is not. I received the book—a Bible—in the mail and put it on the shelf in the chapel. Mr. Oladapo retrieved it from there, as inmates do all the time. I work in the chapel, and whenever an inmate wants a Bible, they get it from that shelf in our office."

"Well, that's what Oladapo said as well. But we don't believe you. And, in any case, why would you give away the Bible. Why not just keep it and use it yourself?"

"I'm Jewish and that's not our Bible."

"Jews don't believe in the Bible?"

"Yes, but we don't have the Christian scriptures in ours."

"You don't believe in the New Testament?"

"No, ma'am, just what you call the Old Testament."

"You mean you don't believe in Jesus?"

This was the investigator assigned to ferret out the truth in Bible-gate. My fate was in her hands.

"I find you guilty," she pronounced. Why was I not surprised?

The punishment phase would be administered by another panel of officers. Fortunately, the witch was not among them, or it might have been worse. They took away my commissary and email for sixty days.

I pleaded with them.

"You've already taken away my phone use. Removing email will cut me off from the outside world entirely. I have two sons studying in Jerusalem, where there are terrorist incidents regularly. Without any form of contact, I won't be able to know if they're safe."

They stared at me in silence. They didn't even blink. For the first and last time in the prison, I lost my temper with the staff.

"You know, the last time I was involved in an incident where someone got punished for giving someone else a Bible was twenty-five years ago." They perked up. Was I about to admit to another infraction? "It happened in a place that reminds me of this one: The Soviet Union."

With that, I excused myself and stormed back to the chapel to calm down.

I was utterly cut off from the world. Except for Sunday visits, I had no contact with anyone other than through unreliable and slow snail mail. One day, an inmate came running to tell me he had just watched a report about a terrorist attack in Jerusalem. Arabs had shot and killed a number of young boys studying in a yeshiva. My heart sank. I was in a panic. There was no way to find out what happened. I ran to the administration building, praying there would be a staff member there willing to help me. Fortunately, I encountered a guard willing to find the name of the attacked yeshiva on his computer. It wasn't where Alex and Daniel were studying. I was grieved for the other families, but relieved that at least my two boys were not among them.

After about eighteen months at Cumberland, the harassment stopped. I don't know why exactly. Maybe they realized I wasn't trying to run the prison. Maybe they decided I wasn't the arrogant jerk they thought I'd be.

When I entered prison, I had high hopes that I wouldn't have to stay for more than a couple of years. Based on a sentence of seventy months, I anticipated a reduction based on my cooperation. Plus, I took part in the programs that provided for early release. Those hopes, like so many others before them, were dashed when I was finally sentenced in the D.C. Court.

The Florida judge moved the Suncruz case at record speed, including sentencing and incarceration. The judge in Washington was more sensitive to the scheduling requests of the Department of Justice, since those cases were likely to be brought in her court. As a result, my sentencing in D.C. didn't occur until I had already been in prison for almost two years. After months of preparation and the submission of a brilliant sentencing memo crafted by Chris Man at Abbe's firm, I was taken by the authorities to the federal court in Washington on the day of sentencing, September 4, 2008. The Department of Justice requested a sentence of sixty-four months, with credit for the twenty-two months I had already served. Abbe proposed a sentence of forty-four months. I was hoping the judge would just send me home that day.

Pam and the kids all attended the sentencing, and we were all hopeful that the nightmare might soon come to an end. I tried to glance at them, sitting bravely in the first row, but the marshal behind me admonished me to keep my eyes on the judge. I knew there was trouble when the judge incorrectly—or so I thought—declared that my base sentence range started at 120 months. I had always been told it was ninety one months. Where did 120 come from?

After Abbe did a masterful job in pleading my case for a reduced sentence, the court heard testimony from several tribal members, including the provocateurs from Saginaw Chippewa and Coushatta. As one can imagine, they were not arguing for a reduced sentence. My hope rose as the judge seemed to castigate the Saginaw Chippewa member, noting that his tribe was not in complete agreement with his harsh comments about me.

The final witness the court heard was Delores Jackson, former council member of the Saginaw Chippewa tribe. Delores had been a constant supporter of mine. She came to the senate hearings to protest what she felt was unfair treatment at the hands of the committee, and she came to visit me in prison. She wrote strong letters attacking those who she felt brought this destruction to my life. Although wracked with an illness which would soon end her life, this angel and friend came to defend me in the court, recounting how much I had done to help the tribe, and how the accusations against me were totally unfair. I wanted to hug Delores, but since the marshal wouldn't even permit me to look at my family, I might have been shot had I tried to embrace my dear friend from the tribe.

Finally, I was given a moment to speak before the judge. I was so overcome with emotion that I could barely articulate my thoughts. I told the judge that I was a broken man and that additional lengthy incarceration would serve no purpose other than to cause my family to continue to suffer. I had difficulty holding back my tears as I expressed my deep regret for what had become of my life. When I finished, I prayed to God that He would move her heart and soon put an end to the terror of these past few years.

The judge then proceeded to read her sentence. My knees started to weaken as the judge continued to address me. "You've impacted seriously the public confidence in the integrity of the government," she said. "These activities corrupted the political process and deprived the public of the honest services of their own public officials, both in the legislature and executive branch."

Then the judge declared that she was going to give me forty-eight months, starting that day. At first, all I heard was "forty-eight months." I had already served twenty-two. This was good news, wasn't it? Then I realized that the forty-eight months would be in addition to the twenty-two I had already spent in prison. My total sentence was to be seventy months, eight months more than Justice had requested. I was discouraged and confused.

Before I had a chance to ask Abbe what this all meant, and with no chance to communicate with my family, I was whisked out the side door of the courtroom, into a holding cell. I was then transported immediately to the car that returned me to Cumberland.

# CONCLUSION

# PATH TO REFORM

I tried to make the best of the rest of my time at Cumberland, enduring life in such a coarse and isolating place. I worked in the chapel, exercised, read, taught, and wrote. I continued to worry about my children and Pam, but, other than pray and offer love and encouragement, there was little I could do to make their lives easier from prison.

Friends and family made my stay in prison tolerable. I was blessed to have regular visits from almost 150 friends and relatives during my incarceration. The sacrifice of these steadfast supporters in making the long drive to the western tip of Maryland was appreciated more than I could ever express. I was in the prison for 185 weekends, and had visits for all but one of them. Being able to leave the environment of the prison to spend time with loved ones in the visiting room kept me sane and focused on getting through the ordeal. No one visited me more than my beloved wife, who frequently made the hours-long drive alone.

I was fortunate to have some intrepid public officials make the trek to Cumberland, including Congressman Dana Rohrabacher, his wife Rhonda, and their adorable triplets, but the visit which sparked the most interest among the inmates took place in in the spring of 2009.

In March of that year, the former managing partner of Preston Gates, and my long-time racquetball partner, Larry Latourette, came for a visit. Larry was kind enough to make the trip to the prison several times during my incarceration, but this time he had a mission. Through a mutual friend, Larry had become acquainted with George Hickenlooper, a motion picture director. Hickenlooper was making a feature film called "Casino Jack", about my lobbying activities. He very much wanted to meet and introduce me to the actor playing my part in the film—Kevin Spacey. I told Larry I would agree to the meeting, but only after I had read the screenplay, which I received a few days later.

I read the screenplay twice and was not impressed. It was disjointed and boring. It was hard for me to believe that Spacey—one of the world's great actors—had signed onto this project. I communicated with Larry that I would see Hickenlooper, but he should come alone. The last thing a director wants is for his actor to hear that the screenplay stinks.

Larry brought Hickenlooper to see me that next weekend. As I entered the visiting room in the prison, I saw Larry sitting with the large, bearded George Hickenlooper. He could barely contain his enthusiasm that he was meeting with me in a prison—a real Hollywood moment, I guess. The visiting room at Cumberland was normally a bustle of activity, with small children running about and inmates loudly conversing with their visitors. We sat in the midst of this ruckus, talking about George's film and comparing notes on our various entertainment acquaintances. Finally, George asked how I liked the screenplay.

"Frankly, George, it stinks."

"But Jack, you have to understand. We can't make you out to be a hero."

"I get that, and don't expect to be made a hero. I'm not a hero. But even if I am to be a villain, why must I be a boring villain? You have to have a main character that audiences will want to spend two hours with. I don't want to spend two hours with him, and he's me!"

Hickenlooper stared at me, perplexed.

"George, a screenplay must have three acts. This has one act and then a jumbled bunch of scenes. Your set up in the first act is clumsy and you don't pay off even the awkwardly set up premises in the end. The main character—my character!—is not only boring, but there is no character arc. There is no danger. There is no redemption. There is nothing. It's a flat line screenplay which wouldn't get made at any studio. Right?"

His eyes widened. He wasn't expecting a critique like this from me. I reminded him that I'm not without experience in film, and that, in prison, I had been reading every filmmaking book I could get my hands on. It was always a topic that fascinated me. George stammered that they were still working on the screenplay and that perhaps I read an early draft.

I interrupted him, "George, perhaps the worst thing, from a film maker's point of view, is that your screenwriter made up things which were far more boring than reality. He obviously did almost no real research in putting this film together, other than trolling the Internet, but even there he could have found some better scenes."

George asked if I would be willing to help them, to give them some scenes which would really work. I explained that it was their film, not mine. I was a prisoner, and was not permitted to work on their film with them, but even if I did wish to work on a film, it wouldn't be this one. George was disappointed. I told him that I wanted to see him alone, because I could not imagine he wanted his actor to hear these things, and I had no reason not to be honest about it. George insisted that he did not want to shield Spacey from my opinion and asked if I would meet him. We agreed to meet that next Friday evening, when visiting would resume. I told George that the condition of my meeting was that the meeting could not be leaked to the press. He had revealed they were not yet fully funded, and I didn't want them using a meeting with me for their fundraising purposes.

When I was called to the visiting room late Friday afternoon, April 24, 2009, I was redirected into the administrative offices of the prison instead of the visiting room. There I was greeted by the Camp Administrator Duwayne Hendrix, who told me that my visitors were moved to his conference room to avoid any situations in the visiting room. He feared the other visitors, not used to seeing a Hollywood star in their midst, might cause a disturbance by asking for a photo or autograph from Spacey, so we were moved to his offices.

In my days as a lobbyist, I would give tremendous thought to the location of meetings. I always wanted an advantage in the discussions or negotiations, and would often place meetings in locations where I could dominate, such as Signatures. As I walked to the conference room to meet Spacey, I thought about my old ways. Obviously I was now a prisoner, not in command of much, let alone meeting locations, but had I the choice and need for advantage, I would have put the meeting in the visiting room. That room was disorienting for visitors. I was used to it. It didn't matter, though, since I had no agenda for this meeting, or much else at that point.

As I entered the room, I saw Larry and George, and turned to see Kevin Spacey. He was wearing a baseball cap and casually dressed. He greeted me with a handshake and a wry comment, "I am to play you."

"Well, I guess that's the end of your career," I responded with a smile. He laughed, and I knew we'd get along fine. Our conversation was wide ranging. He struck me as incredibly bright and kind. His questions were sensitive and uninvasive, but he clearly wanted to know more than the media had portrayed. He asked what it was like to go through my situation. I tried to tell him, though how can one really describe all of this properly? We talked about Reagan and Clinton—and exchanged impressions of the presidents we held in the highest esteem. Finally, he asked about the screenplay. Did I like it?

"I only have one question, Kevin. Why are you doing this?"

"Well, I think your story is interesting and…"

"I guess my story might be interesting, but that wasn't my question. Why are you doing this screenplay?" With that darted probe, I saw George's face turn white. I had warned him this would happen.

Spacey stared at me perplexed. I launched into the same screenwriting 101 speech, and watched Kevin smile.

"Jack, these are good points. George?"

Hickenlooper's started bumbling, but I intervened with another question: "When are you planning to commence filming?"

Hickenlooper estimated filming would commence in six weeks. With that response, I realized they had no intention of fixing the film. They had to be deeply into the pre-production phase of their project, and major alterations to the shooting schedule were unlikely at this point. Politely, but without enthusiasm, I said that they should keep me posted. Hickenlooper asked whether I could help promote the film when I was released. I reminded them that I was more than a year away from leaving the prison, and, if they were filming in June of 2009, the film would be in the theatres prior to my exit from the prison. Even I didn't count on the subsequent delays because no major distributor wanted the project. In fact, I was released before the film, but still I was not involved in helping their efforts.

Before they left, Hendrix reminded them that the condition of the visit was that no publicity about their trip to the prison would be allowed.

George enthusiastically nodded his assent. Spacey affirmed they had no intention of violating that pledge. Little did he know that Hickenlooper had already violated the pledge before they arrived. His interviews about the visit to the prison were updated as he sped away from the gates of Cumberland. Hendrix and I were furious, but there was nothing we could do at that point. Spacey sent an apology for George's perfidious conduct. Hickenlooper denied he broke his promise. He might have been more adept in the lobbying world than he realized.

There was a second film called Casino Jack released about my case—a documentary—but it, too, was poorly done and grossed even less than the Spacey film. In fact, the combined box office grosses of these two pathetic efforts paled even in comparison to the box office receipts of *Red Scorpion*. Spacey turned in a stellar performance, as did Jon Lovitz, who played Adam Kidan. Barry Pepper, a fine actor, played Mike Scanlon, though the character concocted by the screenwriter and director had little resemblance to the real Scanlon. The film benefitted from the Golden Globes nomination given to Spacey, but his defeat meant I wouldn't witness a second actor ascending the platform to thank me at that awards ceremony.

Spacey continued his graciousness in the interviews attending the film's release. After enduring the feckless Clooney, my daughter Sarah—and our entire family—had an actor we could admire and a friend to whom we were grateful in Spacey.

Often I would sit alone by the prison camp ball field, or walk the uneven and unpaved perimeter track in solitude. I had a lot of thinking to do. How had I wound up in this place? Why had I not seen where I was headed? After I crashed, I began to see the road signs that might have warned me of the dangerous cliff I eventually drove off, but why was I so blind at the time?

I believe in the Almighty, yet my arrogance led me to try to play God. In order to get the outcomes I desired, I found myself ignoring the rules—the laws—and rationalizing away my offenses. I couldn't accept defeat. Raised on the inane cliché that the only real loser is a good loser, I set out to win everything. In doing so, I won many battles for my clients, for my firm, and for myself, but I lost the war.

My mantra during the go-go years of my lobbying life was, "If it's worth doing, it's worth overdoing." That, too, was immature, selfish, and foolish. Human beings have limits, but I refused to recognize mine and, instead, used my creativity, intellect, work ethic, and the power of manipulation to get what I wanted. It didn't matter that I believed my actions were for the good of my clients; they were wrong—I was wrong. Moreover, not only were some of my actions illegal, many of them were corrupt despite their legality.

The lobbying business isn't very popular in America. That was true even before I walked out of court one rainy day, wearing a black hat. But I wasn't the only villain in Washington. If that had been the case, all political corruption would have disappeared when I walked through the gates of Cumberland.

For at least eighty years, the most consistent urge in Washington has been to accumulate power and sanctimoniously proclaim you are doing so for the good of the nation. Sometimes it's true. More often it's not. But regardless of whether one is using power for good or ill, the potential for corruption is always present, as I painfully learned.

Americans rail against the special interests. They decry the number of lobbyists in Washington. But are the lobbyists really the only problem? Are they the only ones with special interests?

Think about it this way. Say you own a small factory in the Midwest that makes picture frames. The company has been in business for one hundred years. It was started by your great grandparents, and handed down generation after generation. You take pride in what you do and have built the company into an international competitor.

One day, a U.S. Senator from New England goes to Target and buys a picture frame. While hanging it on the wall, his frame breaks, falls, and crushes his big toe. That representative shows up on Capitol Hill with a bandaged foot and a distinguished cane. But he also arrives with something far more destructive: legislation. He's not going to let the picture frame industry get away with this indignity. No sir. He informs his staff that he wants a bill drafted, before the end of the day, regulating the picture frame industry and imposing federal construction standards. Senator Yankee's legislation is born in secret, but eventually starts to leak out.

As you stroll through your factory, the phone rings. Your uncle tells you that his bowling buddy's cousin's daughter's college roommate knows a guy who works on Capitol Hill, and he told her about the Omnibus Picture Frame Act, which you best look into. You rush to the Internet and pull up the proposed legislation. If passed, it will force regulations on your company, which will make it economically impossible to continue doing business.

Now you have a few options: 1) You could rummage through your attic to find your lucky rabbit's foot, ignore the legislation, and hope it goes away; 2) You could convene a meeting of your family, friends, and employees and tell them that it has been a pleasure making picture frames all these years, but you are going out of business; 3) You could pack your bags, move to Washington, D.C., and rush about Capitol Hill full time telling anyone who will listen that this bill is a bad idea; or 4) You could hire a lobbyist to make sure the bill never becomes law.

Obviously, your best choice is to hire a lobbyist. No one is likely to give up on his or her cherished business, and moving to Washington is not practical or wise.

Once you decide on the lobbying route, you have to decide which lobbyist to hire: The lobbyist who knows about picture frames, or the lobbyist who is golfing buddies with Senator Yankee. If you're being honest with yourself, you know the right choice is the golfer who will have the best chance of influencing the Senator whose legislation threatens your business.

Who is the immoral one in the above scenario? You, the owner of the picture frame factory, for bringing in a lobbyist and pushing your special interest? The lobbyist because he plays golf with the Senator and can presumably stop the bill before it becomes law? Or is it Senator Yankee, who yields far more power than the Founders of this nation ever intended?

No one in their right mind would blame you for doing everything you could to stop the destruction of your company. Few would think Senator Yankee was using his governmental power properly. But the lobbyist confuses us. We resent that there is someone with such a strong connection to those with power, but without him, the picture frame factory would most certainly be shuttered.

The fundamental problem in this scenario, and in too many similar and far more egregious cases in Washington, is that Congress has the power to destroy the picture frame company in the first place. Hundreds of members and thousands of staff, along with thousands more in the executive branch of our government, have too much power over our lives. Our wise Founders created a limited federal government, restrained by a thoughtful system of checks and balances. Their successors replaced it with an all-encompassing state. The reason there are tens of thousands of lobbyists is because the ever-expanding federal government creates ever-increasing opportunities for abuse.

There is no way to eliminate corruption in human endeavors, but the removal of temptation is always a good place to start. In the case of the federal government, that means paring back the size and scope of its activities. The more the federal government does, the more lobbyists there will be to protect special interests at the expense of the common interest. A federal government actually limited to the functions set out in the Constitution would offer far fewer opportunities for special interest chicanery. But that's not going to happen any time soon.

In poll after poll, Americans express their exasperation with unconstitutional federal spending and infringement of our liberties. Yet when the time comes to cut back, Americans are irresolute. They want someone else's program cut, not theirs. They want the federal government to defund someone, just not them. As the late 18th Century historian Alexis DeToqueville foretold, our Republic would be doomed once the "voters discover that they can vote themselves largesse from the public treasury." It seems we have long passed that threshold.

If our society is unwilling to return to a limited, Constitutional government, what can be done to diminish the corruption tarnishing our nation? The usual answer is reform.

But reform can be an illusion.

Each year, the congressional high priests offer a sacrifice to the idols of change. They pass reform bills or change the rules in Congress. These alterations are supposedly done to fix the system, yet nothing seems fixed. Is corruption in Washington really ended by forbidding representatives from accepting free meals and, instead, permitting them to gorge to their heart's content, as long as it's at a fundraising event—where they'll also pocket thousands of dollars in contributions? This is the kind of reform Congress proposes, passes, and then congratulates itself about?

What if Congress were forced to enact real reforms? What would those be?

As I paced the track at Cumberland, day after day, this topic consumed me. I relived my career, recalled those of others, and slowly assembled a list of changes that would bring real reform to our political system. This list might not seem remarkable to the average American, who would in fact be surprised that most of its elements weren't already in place, but the necessary changes aren't always the most showy.

Inevitably, I decided those who rail against the connection between money and politics were right. But in order to fix the problem, they brought an axe to do the job a scalpel would have done more efficiently. Instead of limiting the size of every American's political contribution, we need to entirely eliminate any contribution by those lobbying the government, participating in a federal contract, or otherwise financially benefiting from public funds. If you get money or perks from elected officials—be "you" a company, a union, an association, a law firm, or an individual—you shouldn't be permitted to give them so much as one dollar. It does no good to ban Jack Abramoff from giving $2,000 to Congressman Badenov, but allow the members of his law firm to pick up the slack. If you choose to lobby, if you choose to take money from our nation, if you choose to perform federal contracts, or if you draw your compensation from any entity which does, you need to abstain from giving campaign contributions. It's your choice either way. But you have to choose one, not both.

Not only should lobbyists be banned from contributing to officials' organizations and campaign funds, they should be banned from gift-giving as well. Instead of limiting the amount of money a lobbyist may spend on wining and dining congressional members and staff, eliminate it entirely. No finger food, no snacks, no hot dogs. Nothing. If you are going to lobby the federal government, take from the treasury, or work as a contractor, you shouldn't be permitted to give one penny to any elected official or staff, including the executive branch. Remove all temptations. Eradicate even the scent of impropriety.

Next, the lure of post-public service lobbying employment needs to be eliminated. The revolving door is one of the greatest sources of corruption in government. If you choose to serve in Congress or on a congressional staff, you should be barred for life from working for any company, organization, or association which lobbies the federal government. That may seem harsh—and it is. But there's a reason. Congressmen know better than anyone how to get around a ban on lobbying. They "consult." What's the difference? If you lobby, you officially try to persuade a representative or staff. If you consult, you call the representative to say hello and ask that representative to meet with your new partner at the law firm. You don't lobby. Your partner lobbies. Does anyone believe the representative doesn't get that joke?

If you choose public service, choose it to serve the public, not your bank account. When you're done serving, go home. Get a real job. Washington is not a safe place to live.

When I was a lobbyist, I opposed term limits for representatives. I truly believed it was wrong for the voters to be limited in their choices. But that wasn't the only reason I opposed them. Like almost every lobbyist I knew, I didn't want to have to build relationships with new members constantly. A representative who stayed in Washington for decades, and was a friend, was worth his weight in gold. But permitting people to rule for decades is a recipe for disaster. Is there really a difference between a permanent Congress and a president for life? Representatives should be allowed to serve for three terms of two years, senators for two terms of six years. Then they should get out of town.

Another bullet point on my wish list is to do away with what we call "bringing home the bacon." For most representatives, the metric of success is how many federal tax dollars they can bring back home beyond what their district contributes. One need not be a certified public accountant to see how dangerous that is. Many times the federal funds are directed to companies, unions, and organizations close to the representative. Furthermore, the so-called "horse trading," which stains the congressional appropriations process, only serves to increase the federal budget. It's not uncommon to hear, "If you support my train station, I'll support your research experiment." Or, "Congressman Obi Wan asked for funding for a new federal recreation center in his district so he can win re-election." Multiply that by almost 435 representatives and one hundred senators, and you can see how things can quickly spiral out of control.

But what if representatives were barred from proposing, lobbying for, and perhaps even voting on projects in their districts and states? This may sound crazy, but is it any crazier than the system currently destroying our economy?

Here's a simple idea: Apply every federal law enacted by Congress to the Congress itself. Currently, Congress exempts itself from a myriad of strictures they blithely place on all the rest of us. Let's see them live under the very same laws they create. That should help stop more of the nonsense.

Less than a hundred years ago, U.S. senators were elected by their state's legislature. They represented the interests of their state in Washington, and provided a nice balance to the directly elected representatives. With their representatives in Washington, the states were able to preserve some of their powers and prerogatives. In 1913, that changed. From then until now, senators have been elected directly. Instead of having to secure the support of other elected officials with a specific interest—their state— they were now open for business nationwide, seeking votes and funds from every party with an interest. Repealing the 17th Amendment to the Constitution would restore the election of senators to the state houses, and probably ensure that some of the jokesters who can marshal funds and media will not join the most exclusive club in the world.

The conclusions I came to in prison will not be popular with my former colleagues in the lobbying world, or with the Congress. I might dream, but I am no dreamer. I know that, barring a torch and pitchfork uprising, no real changes will occur. Still, as I sat in prison, the world changed and the seeds of uprising took root. The rebellion coalesced into the Tea Party. Among the hundreds of letters I received while in prison, many were from citizen-activists who helped form this indigenous movement. In the last election, these citizens rose up and threw the bums out, again. But will these new reformers stay the course? Will they enact the kind of real reform noted above? For the sake of our nation, I can only hope they do, before the next man in a black hat emerges.

But what steps can Americans take, today, to get a real reform process going? In my view, only the creation of a new organization dedicated to a serious agenda of reform can push the legislative changes which must be enacted to clean up our system. The organization should be modeled like the effective and powerful group Grover built, Americans for Tax Reform, and hold Congressional feet to the fire in the same, forceful way ATR does it. Candidates seeking federal office should be asked to sign a pledge to clean up government—and that pledge should include a promise to resign their position should they fail to do their part.

It won't be easy to clean up the swamp we call our nation's capital, but if America is serious about change and reform, the effort must start now. It is a mistake to view the financial and debt crises striking our nation as disconnected from the corruption epidemic plaguing Washington. Our debt crisis was created by a spending crisis, and the spending crisis results from a federal government trying to do too many things. Each spending program has a champion in the Congress, and often these champions are created and nurtured by special interests and lobbyists. The only permanent way to stop the special interests and lobbyists who control so much of our federal government and budget—and who exacerbate, if not cause, the crises which threaten to bring down this great Republic—is to return the federal government to its constitutional boundaries. That is a long and difficult fight, but the only way to guarantee this nation endures. In the meantime, though, even the most ardent defenders of state spending and control would have a hard time rebuffing the reforms enumerated above.

On June 8, 2010, I was released from Cumberland Federal Correctional Institution. In those forty-three months behind bars and the years since my career as a lobbyist ended, I had endured more unpleasantness than I could have ever imagined possible, but as a result I had come to a new approach for my life.

When the day of my release arrived, my family came to bring me home. They arrived in the same car and parked in the same space as they had that horrible day in November 2006, when we had to say goodbye at the prison gate. Our separation was hard on all of us. Our children were fatherless during critical years of their development. They suffered from financial, emotional, and spiritual deprivation. My beloved wife endured loneliness for 185 weeks. I lived for 1,299 nights in misery and pain. And all because of my decisions.

Waiting to be discharged, I sat in the same holding cell I occupied on the day I was admitted to Cumberland. With my head bowed, I thought about my journey, and the lessons I learned. I pondered how a person with every opportunity in life—unlike so many of my fellow inmates in the prison—could have veered off course so dramatically. Life is always complicated, and mine was probably more complex than most, but, ultimately, I was the cause of my difficulties. Regardless of my rationalizations, I was the one who didn't disclose to my clients that there was a conflict of interest in the arrangement I had with my partner to split the profits from the programs they funded. I was the one who lavished contributions, meals, event tickets, travel, golf, and jobs on innumerable federal public officials with the expectation or understanding that they would take official actions on my behalf or on behalf of my clients. I was the one who diverted income from those activities to non-profits and other entities thereby evading federal income taxes. These activities added to the corruption which engulfs our nation's capital, and I'm not proud of my part in it. Sure, I did a lot of good during my years as a lobbyist—for my clients, my firms, and many needy people—but I also broke the law, for which my family and I paid a dear price. I continue to pay that price every day of my life.

In prison, I had an epiphany. Languishing at rock bottom, I was finally able to look up and examine myself. I wasn't the devil that the media were so quick to create, but neither was I the saint I always hoped to become. I was somewhere in the middle, but no where near where I wanted to be. I decided that, in order to move myself closer to the angels, I would take what happened in my life, try to learn from it, and use it to educate others. My long journey is not over and it will continue to be arduous for a long time, but it is the journey I must take and this book is an important part of that voyage.

After what seemed to be an eternity, I was brought to the front door of the prison and allowed to leave. I restrained my instinct to run to the waiting arms of my family, and my feet were only outpaced by my beating heart. I fell into the arms of my beloved wife and children and we cried and hugged and kissed.

Thanks to the grace of the Almighty, we had somehow survived the ordeal.

Now it was time to rebuild our lives.

# ACKNOWLEDGMENTS

In the Hebrew language, the word gratitude is rendered hakaras hatov, the literal translation of which is the recognition of the good. Our lives are made meaningful in this world by acts of kindness and by recognizing the acts of kindness of others. For my family and me, there is so much kindness to recognize and acknowledge.

With gratitude for the inestimable assistance in preparing this work for publication, I thank my brilliant and sensitive editor, Alys Yablon Wylen, as well as her most patient family. I thank my publisher, WND Books— Joseph and Elizabeth Farah, the incomparable Megan Byrd, Mark Karis, and my dear friend, Janet Fallon. I thank my e-book team, including my lifelong friend and partner Ben Waldman. I also thank Monty Warner, Paul Rosengard, Ralph Benko, Vicki Herson, David Altschuler, Jeff Schechter, Chris Man, and our dear friend Augusten Burroughs for valuable input and suggestions. I thank David, Giliah, Moshe and Maury Litwack, one of the world's most creative families and dearest friends.

With gratitude for the unbounded generosity and assistance our family received during the years of privation and travail, I thank our dear friends Stanley and Joyce Black, Steve Markoff, Neil Sunkin, Ronnie Rosenbluth, Mike Herson, Vincent Vanni, Jerry Wachs, Hyam Singer, Jimmy and Ita Mond, Ellen and Leon Taksel, Ian Goldman, Jared and Livia Dunkin, Dennis Berman, Jeffrey Cohen and our beloved friends from the Woodside, Kemp Mill, Potomac and White Oak communities.

With gratitude for the boundless and everlasting kindnesses that kept my family and me believing better days were just ahead, I thank Rowena Akana, the Aleph Institute, Bill Anderson, Dave Barron, Rabbi Moshe Bleich, Paddy Bowie, Rabbi Yitzchak and Sally Breitowitz, David Brog, Harry Brown, David Butler, Rabbi Raphael Butler, Rabbi Yitzchak Charner, David Cohen, Ed and Ginny Cook, Freddy deFreitas, Roger Engone, Paul Erickson, Governor Ben Fitial, Kevin Fowler, Allan Franco, Vic Frazer, Adina Gewirtz, Rabbi Jonah and Blanche Gewirtz, Rabbi Zvi Gluck, Ohran and Ashira Gobrin, Michael Goland, Eitan Gorlin, Yossi Green, Josh Gross, Father John Guiliani, Shoshanna Hannah, Jason Hickox, Lior and Janet Hod, Adonis Hoffman, Dov and Fraidy Hook,

Dave Jackson, Gil Kapen, Jay Kaplan, Rabbi Mendy Katz, Rabbi Zev Katz, Shraga Kawior, Eric and Peggy Kerbel, Uri Kerbel, Becky and Al Kotz, Rabbi Hertzl Kranz, Rocky Lang, Uri Landesman, Rabbi Yehudah Lapian, Rabbi Daniel Lapin, Larry Latourette, Fred and Dina Leeds, Buddy Lichter, Nachman Lichter, Larry Loigman, Jim Lucier, Jodi and Fred Mailman, Dick Morris, Evelyn Scruggs-Murray, Stephen Nemeth, Jason Osborne, Dave Parent, Howard and Peggy Phillips, Elie and Judith Pieprz, Jim and Barbie Prince, Adam Rishe, Congressman Dana and Rhonda Rohrabacher, Avi Rosenbluth, Desi Rosenfeld, Allen Rothenberg, Brian and Chaya Rozen, Howard Sabrin, Sue Sabrin, Jerry Saunders, Rabbi Mayer Schiller, Rabbi Shmuel Spritzer, Ken Sragg, Chris Stahl, Rabbi Yossi Stern, Robert Stroud-Hinton, Mary and Lee Swaboda, Rabbi Zvi Teitlebaum, Christine and Sea Thomas, Jeremy Vallerand, Philip and Laura Vallerand, Michael Waldman, Lance Waller, Donn Weinberg, Jack Wheeler, Rabbi Kalman and Rivka Winter, Adam Zagorin, Mike Zapolin, Richard Zaremba, Eli Zicherman and Frank Ziezeula.

With gratitude for unimaginable courage and unflinching allegiance, I bless the memory of my good friend Delores Jackson, may she rest in peace, and thank Chief Maynard Kahgegab, Velma Kyser, Anne Peters, Gary Sprague, and all those members of the Saginaw Chippewa tribe who risked everything to stand by me in the darkest of hours, as well as the many Native Americans who have written expressing their support and faith in me. Few things have ever meant more.

With gratitude for the years of hard work and dedicated effort to getting me through the crucible years, I thank my sagacious and venerable teacher, Rabbi David Lapin, and my sapient, generous and dependable attorneys, accountants, advisors, doctors, and representatives. I thank Abbe Lowell, Pam Marple, Chris Man, and Peggy Creason for leading me through the confusing maze that had become my life. I thank the brilliant and patient Lou Ruebelmann for his guidance. I thank Fred Adams, Roy Bank, Dr. Tim Brown, Dr. Kenneth Friedman, Bill Gladstone, Dr. James Gilbert, Scott Goldschein, Bruce Goldstein, Dr. Steve Horwitz, Dr. David Jacobs, Dr. Alan Kermaier, Barry Krost, Rabbi Avrom Landesman, Marc Levin, Judith Regan, Dr. Ira Reiz, Herman Rush, Steve Sadicario, Christopher Schelling, Bill Sheinberg, Dr. Paul Silver, Neal Sonnett and Jon van Horne.

With gratitude for a life made more complete thanks to a loving family, I thank my beloved Aunt Bea Reisman. I thank my Aunt Bernice Abramoff, as well as my cousins Steven and Jeri Abramoff; Janet and Abe Gol; Shirley Milgrim, Joyce and Bob Lempert; and Ruth and Ron Mutchnik. I thank my dear in-laws Tom Olsen; James and Liz Alexander; and their children Morgan, Marie, and James, as well as Patty Alexander and her children Meg and Andy. I thank my sister Linda Rosenblatt, her husband Mike, and sons Matt, Jordan, Zack, and Dillon. I thank my faithful brother Bob, his wife Rene, and their daughters Hayley and Melanie.

With gratitude for sustaining and nurturing me from the day I was born until this day, I thank and bless my dear father, Frank Abramoff, and his new wife, partner, and beloved friend, Barbara Miller Abramoff. My gratitude to my dear mother, Jane Abramoff, may she rest in the Lord's abode, knows no earthly bounds. I miss her every waking moment.

With gratitude and unlimited love and devotion, I thank the children who have given my life purpose and meaning. Levi, Alex, Daniel, Livia, and Sarah—you mean more to me than it's possible to express. Thank you for being my inspiration and light in these dark days.

With gratitude to my partner and wife, with whom I have laughed and cried for over twenty-five years, I thank my sweetheart, best friend, and most beloved of all, Pam Abramoff.

And finally, with full recognition of my shortcomings and failings, and with hope for redemption, mercy and salvation, I express my gratitude to the Master of the Universe for blessing us and sustaining us and permitting us to reach this season of renewal.

I pray that those steadfast friends whose names should have been included above but were not will attribute these omissions to my memory lapses and not to my lack of gratitude for their kindnesses.

# APPENDIX A: WHERE ARE THEY NOW?

**Todd Boulanger** left Greenberg Traurig to join Cassidy & Associates, a rival lobbying firm, after the scandal commenced and proceeded to rebuild his lobbying career. He resigned from Cassidy November 21, 2008 and pleaded guilty to bribing public officials.

**Ben Nighthorse Campbell** left the United States Senate in January 2005 and became a lobbyist with the firm Holland and Knight.

**Tom DeLay** was indicted in Travis County, Texas and resigned as Majority Leader of the Congress on September 28, 2005. Tom was convicted of money laundering and conspiracy on November 24, 2010 and remains free while he appeals what are widely seen as politically motivated convictions. When interviewed by Brian Ross of ABC News in August 2010, DeLay reaffirmed our friendship.

**Christopher Dodd** left the United States Senate when polls showed he was heading to certain defeat in the 2010 elections. He is one of Washington's highest paid lobbyists at the Motion Picture Association of America.

**Ben Fitial** became governor of the Northern Marianas on November 6, 2005 and was re-elected for a second five-year term in 2009.

Since resigning from the Congress, **Newt Gingrich** has made a fortune as an author and political contributor for Fox News. In 2010, he published his seventeenth book, and on May 11, 2011, he announced his bid for the Republican nomination for the Presidency.

**Bob Goodlatte** still represents the sixth Congressional district of Virginia and is now chairman of the Judiciary subcommittee on Intellectual Property, Competition and the Internet in the House of Representatives. After I went to prison, Goodlatte was finally able to sneak his anti-Internet gaming legislation through the Congress in a midnight session, crushing the market value of virtually every company engaged in that enterprise. He had by then labeled his bill the "anti-Jack Abramoff measure."

**Richard Gordon** served for forty-one years as one of Georgetown Law Center's most popular and distinguished professors before succumbing to cancer in 2003.

**Steve Griles** resigned as Deputy Secretary of the Interior December 7, 2004. He pleaded guilty to charges of obstruction of justice on March 23, 2007, and was sentenced to ten months imprisonment. He served his time at the federal prison camp in Petersburg, Virginia.

**George Hickenlooper** died on October 29, 2011, before his *opus magnus* directorial project *Casino Jack* could be released into theatres.

**Adam Kidan** was indicted in 2005 on bank fraud and conspiracy to commit bank fraud in connection with his Suncruz activities. He pleaded guilty and was sentenced to seventy months in federal prison, but saw his sentenced reduced to thirty-five months. After Suncruz, Kidan continued to pursue the cruise casino business in New England, but his entrees were rebuffed. He remains a witness in the investigation into the murder of Gus Boulis. The production team of *Casino Jack,* starring Kevin Spacey, reported receiving numerous importuning phone calls from Kidan that his character in the film did not convey the dignity and grandeur that the real-life Kidan possesses.

**Dolph Lundgren** continued his acting career after making *Red Scorpion*, starring in almost fifty motion pictures. He is also a celebrated author and fitness and nutrition expert.

**Imelda Marcos** continues to live free in the Philippines, where she continues in her efforts to have her husband's remains returned home to be buried with military honors.

**Chief Phillip Martin** served the Choctaw nation for over fifty years before being defeated for re-election in 2007. He died on February 4, 2010, after suffering from a stroke. Since the Chief lost his position, the Choctaws have suffered from internal political scandal and economic difficulties, leading many in the tribe to question the wisdom of removing one of the greatest leaders in American Indian history from his position as Chief.

**John McCain** continues to serve as U.S. Senator from Arizona, though a serious party nomination challenge confronted him in 2010. On September 4, 2008, the day I was sentenced in federal court for the charges related to the lobbying scandal, John McCain accepted the nomination for president at the Republican National Convention in St. Paul, Minnesota. He continued to milk the scandal he helped ignite, even interjecting into his speech that night the self-congratulatory encomium, "I've fought lobbyists who stole from Indian tribes."

**Lloyd Meeds** retired from Preston Gates Ellis & Rouvelas Meeds after a long career and passed away at the age of seventy-seven on August 18, 2005.

**Bob Ney** resigned from Congress on November 3, 2006, several weeks after pleading guilty to federal corruption charges. On January 19, 2007, he was sentenced to thirty months in prison, but served less than a year before being released. In April 2009, Bob began broadcasting the "Bob Ney Radio Show" in West Virginia. In 2010, it was reported that Bob had moved to India to study meditation techniques with exiled Tibetan monks.

**Grover Norquist** weathered a barrage of media attacks over his ties to my scandal but has emerged more powerful than ever and was never charged with any crime or improper action. As politicians grapple with the debt crisis, some have tried to renege on the Tax Payer Protection Pledge, but Grover isn't allowing these members to easily break their promise to their constituents. Americans for Tax Reform continues to grow and Grover continues to organize conservative voters and organizations – always cheerfully making strides to the goal of drowning the remnants of the federal government in a bathtub.

**Howard Phillips** was the Taxpayer Party's presidential nominee in 1992 and 1996. Today, he continues to lead the Conservative Caucus and is a prolific writer and publisher.

**Kevin Ring** was arrested on September 8, 2008, on conspiracy, fraud, and obstruction of justice charges. On October 15, 2009, a mistrial was declared in federal court when jurors could not agree on a verdict. He was convicted in a second trial on November 15, 2010, of five counts of conspiracy to corrupt public officials. In their sentencing request, prosecutors asked the judge to imprison Ring for seventeen to twenty-four years, far in excess of anyone else involved in these cases.

**Ralph Reed** lost his bid to secure the Republican nomination for Lieutenant Governor of Georgia in the 2006 primary elections. He has recently re-entered public life by creating a new Christian political organization, the Faith and Freedom Coalition. He was never indicted on any charge related to his involvement with the tribes or me.

**Scott Reed** benefitted from the scandal to secure a representation of the Saginaw Chippewa Indian tribe, but never became the "king of Indian gaming" as he hoped.

**Dana Rohrabacher** continues to serve the people of the 46th Congressional district of California and the American people as chairman of the House Foreign Affairs subcommittee on Oversight and Investigations. Dana has championed the average citizen with his efforts to control the size of the federal government and his focus on patent reform.

**Karl Rove** resigned from the Bush White House on August 31, 2007, and has since worked as a contributor for *Newsweek*, the *Wall Street Journal*, and Fox News. Through his organization American Crossroads, Karl raised more money and had a more powerful impact on the 2010 Congressional elections than any political consultant in America.

**Tony Rudy** left Greenberg Traurig on August 1, 2002, to join Ed Buckham, DeLay's former Chief of Staff, at Alexander Strategy Group. In the wake of the lobbying scandal, the company folded, and Tony plead guilty to one count of conspiracy related to his participation in my facilitating the hiring of his wife to consult for a non-profit, funded by my clients.

**David Safavian** resigned as chief of staff of the General Services Administration and was indicted October 5, 2005, on charges of making false statements to federal investigators and obstructing investigations. David was one of the few defendants in the scandal to go to trial. On June 20, 2006, the jury convicted him of three of five charges, but David appealed and successfully overturned all convictions on June 17, 2008. He was retried and convicted a second time on October 16, 2009. Sentenced to serve a year in prison, David reported to Devins Federal Medical Center, a minimum security prison in August 2011.

**Mike Scanlon** kept a low profile in the wake of the scandal which destroyed our political careers, quietly cooperating with the investigation. On November 21, 2005, Mike pleaded guilty to one count of conspiracy and, on February 11, 2011, was sentenced to twenty months in federal prison. Mike commenced serving his sentence at the Pensacola Federal Prison Camp in March 30, 2011.

**Froilan Tenorio** continued to run for governor after his defeat at the hands of Pedro P. Tenorio in 1998, but was unable to retake the position. In 2009, he switched his life-long affiliation with the Democratic Party to join the Covenant Party. With the support of former rival Governor Ben Fitial, Froilan won a seat in the legislature and was subsequently elected Speaker of the House in the CNMI.

**William Worfel**, having escaped the threat of violence from rebels who took power at the Coushatta tribal council, disappeared from the public eye, only to emerge during the McCain hearings. Notwithstanding his public condemnation of McCain and his methods, at the hearing he was effusive in his praise of the senator and his role in the scandal. His rivals at the tribe thanked him for joining their side by banning him from ever running for tribal office again. He currently lives in proximity to the Coushatta reservation.

# APPENDIX B: TIMELINE

| | |
|---|---|
| February 1959 | Jack Abramoff born in Atlantic City, NJ to Frank and Jane Abramoff |
| July 1969 | Abramoff family moves from Margate, NJ to Beverly Hills California |
| September 1971 | Jack Abramoff enters Hawthorne Elementary School, Beverly Hills, California |
| September 1974 | Jack Abramoff enters Beverly Hills High School |
| June 1975 | Jack Abramoff hired at Beverly Theatre, Beverly Hills |
| December 1976 | Jack Abramoff named all-West Side Los Angeles football offensive lineman |
| June 1977 | Jack Abramoff graduates Beverly Hills High School |
| July 1977 | Beverly Theatre closes |
| August 1977 | Jack Abramoff enters Brandeis University, Waltham, MA |
| May 1980 | Jack Abramoff elected Chairman Massachusetts College Republican Union |
| July 1980 | Jack Abramoff attends Reagan Youth Training Seminar in Los Angeles |
| September 1980 | Jack Abramoff meets Grover Norquist, student at Harvard Business School |
| Fall 1980 | Jack Abramoff organizes over 40 chapters for College Republicans of Massachusetts |

| | |
|---|---|
| November 1980 | Ronald Reagan elected 40th president of the United States |
| | Jack Abramoff and college republicans credited with winning Massachusetts |
| May 1981 | Jack Abramoff graduates Brandeis magna cum laude with degree in English and American Literature |
| June 1981 | Jack Abramoff elected Chairman, College Republican National Committee |
| | Meets Ralph Reed |
| September 1981 | First Fieldman Program for CRNC launched |
| | Poland Will Be Free petition drive launched |
| December 1981 | Jack Abramoff and Grover Norquist brief Ronald Reagan in Oval Office |
| January 1981 | White House dinner and movie about Polish Solidarity Union |
| January 1982 | Second CRNC Fieldman program launched |
| July 1982 | CRNC 90th Anniversary conference |
| June 1983 | Jack Abramoff re-elected CRNC Chairman |
| September 1983 | Jack Abramoff hires Adam Kidan to produce student radio program, "Fall Out" |
| July 1984 | Fritzbusters campaign launched |
| August 1984 | Jack Abramoff speaker at Republican National Convention, Dallas, TX |
| November 1984 | Ronald Reagan re-elected to second presidential term |

| January 1985 | Jack Abramoff hired as executive director Citizens for America, President Reagan's grassroots lobbying organization |
| March 1985 | MX Missile Vote in House of Representatives |
| May 1985 | Jamba meeting of anti-Soviet freedom fighters |
| July 1985 | Jack Abramoff leaves Citizens for America |
| May 1986 | Jack Abramoff graduates Georgetown Law Center with a juris doctorate |
| June 1986 | Jack Abramoff marries the former Pamela Alexander in Washington, DC |
| September 1987 | Levi Abramoff, first child of Jack and Pam Abramoff, born in Silver Spring, MD |
| December 1987 | Commence filming *Red Scorpion* in Namibia |
| February 1988 | Complete filming *Red Scorpion* |
| April 1989 | Alexander Abramoff, the second child of Jack and Pam Abramoff, born in Silver Spring, MD |
| April 1989 | *Red Scorpion* released in theatres |
| August 1991 | Daniel Abramoff, the third child of Jack and Pam Abramoff, born in Silver Spring, MD |
| April 1993 | Livia and Sarah Abramoff, the fourth and fifth children of Jack and Pam Abramoff, born in Silver Spring, MD |
| September 1994 | Torah School of Greater Washington opens |
| November 1994 | Republicans capture control of Congress |
| December 1994 | Jack Abramoff starts as lobbyist at Preston Gates |

| | |
|---|---|
| March 1995 | Dennis Stephens starts at Preston Gates |
| March 1995 | Jack Abramoff meets with governor's staff from the Commonwealth of the Northern Mariana Islands |
| April 1995 | *Red Scorpion 2* released on HBO and video. |
| July 1995 | Jack Abramoff hired by CNMI to stop federal takeover of economy |
| August 1995 | Trip to CNMI with Lloyd Meeds |
| October 1995 | Jack Abramoff hired by Mississippi Band of Choctaw Indians |
| December 1995 | Jack Abramoff and his Preston Gates team stops massive tax on Indian tribal gaming revenues |
| December 1995 | Jack Abramoff and his Preston Gates team stop CNMI takeover bill |
| March 1996 | Pat Pizzella starts work at Preston Gates |
| April 1996 | Start of Congressional staff and members trips to Saipan |
| May 1996 | Indian Child Welfare Act legislative effort in Congress |
| November 1996 | Jack Abramoff reconnects with Adam Kidan |
| July 1997 | Jack Abramoff first meeting with Imelda Marcos |
| Summer 1997 | Congressional coup against Speaker Newt Gingrich |
| Summer 1997 | Tom DeLay trip to Russia |

November 1997      Governor Froilan Tenorio loses re-election bid in CNMI

December 1997      Tom DeLay trip to Saipan

January 1998      Jack Abramoff helps save Imelda Marcos from prison term

March 1998      Jack Abramoff's CNMI memo leaked to media

May 1998      Manny Rouvelas predicts Jack Abramoff will be "dead, disgraced or in jail in five years"

August 1998      Choctaw National Indian Gaming Commission fee battle

September 1998      Jack Abramoff meets Michael Scanlon

October 1998      Guam gubernatorial election: "Typhoon DeLay" evens race

November 1998      Jack Abramoff Hired by Primedia to help "Channel One" network

November 1998      First threat emerges to Choctaw gaming market in Alabama

January 1999      Chief Martin proposes Choctaw "Land in Trust" project

July 1999      Congressman George Miller late night attack on CNMI from floor of House

July 1999      Office of Insular Affairs staff caught breaking law by House Resources Committee, computers seized

August 1999      Jack Abramoff first golf trip to Scotland for National Republican Senatorial Committee, with Adam Kidan

| | |
|---|---|
| August 1999 | Todd Boulanger joins Team Abramoff at Preston Gates |
| October 1999 | Landmark Choctaw "Land in Trust" legislation passed |
| November 1999 | Ben Fitial wins seat in CNMI legislature |
| November 1999 | Jack Abramoff invests in Riverjet |
| November 1999 | Art Dimopolous proposes Suncruz purchase to Jack Abramoff |
| November 1999 | Kevin Ring joins Team Abramoff at Preston Gates |
| January 2000 | Ben Fitial elected Speaker of the House in CNMI |
| February 2000 | South Carolina Republican Presidential Primary Election |
| March 2000 | Michael Scanlon joins Team Abramoff at Preston Gates |
| March 2000 | Rep. Bob Ney enters attack on Gus Boulis into Congressional Record |
| April 2000 | Jack Abramoff hired by e-lottery to defeat Internet Gaming Prohibition Act |
| May 2000 | Jack Abramoff meets with Avery Ellis, executive recruiter representing Greenberg Traurig |
| July 2000 | House Resources Committee holds hearing on OIA Scandal |
| August 2000 | Tom DeLay trip to Scotland |

| | |
|---|---|
| Sept 2000 | Jack Abramoff and Adam Kidan buy Suncruz Casinos for $150 million |
| September 2000 | House votes on Internet Gambling Prohibition Act |
| November 2000 | George W. Bush elected 43rd president of the United States |
| December 2000 | Jack Abramoff becomes president of Yeshiva of Greater Washington |
| January 2001 | Jack Abramoff and Team Abramoff commence work at Greenberg Traurig |
| January 2001 | Tony Rudy joins Team Abramoff at Greenberg Traurig |
| January 2001 | George W. Bush inaugurated president |
| February 2001 | Susan Ralston leaves Team Abramoff to join Karl Rove in White House |
| February 2001 | Gus Boulis murdered in gangland-style slaying |
| March 2001 | Coushatta Tribe hires Team Abramoff |
| May 2001 | Adam Kidan admits under oath that he cheated Jack Abramoff during purchase of Suncruz |
| June 2001 | Jack Abramoff sells entire interest in Suncruz back to Boulis estate |
| September 2001 | Mississippi State Senator Jack Gordon proposes massive tax on Choctaws; Scanlon unleashes grassroots response; Gordon relents |
| October 2001 | Ralph Reed, Michael Scanlon and Jack Abramoff fight Texas casino legislation |

| | |
|---|---|
| November 2001 | Ben Fitial loses gubernatorial election to Juan Babauta |
| December 2001 | Jack Abramoff dubbed "Casino Jack" by Ralph Nader activist fighting Channel One |
| December 2001 | Saginaw Chippewa Tribe of Michigan hires Team Abramoff |
| January 2002 | Jena Tribe tries to obtain Louisiana casino— first effort |
| February 2002 | Jack Abramoff opens Signatures Restaurant across from National Archives in Washington, DC |
| February 2002 | Neil Volz joins Team Abramoff |
| February 2002 | Jack Abramoff contacts Tigua Indians, El Paso, Texas |
| March 2002 | Congressman Bob Ney signs on to help Tigua tribe |
| March 2002 | Duane Gibson, from House Resources Committee, joins Team Abramoff |
| March 2002 | Eddie Ayoob, from Senator Harry Reid's office, joins Team Abramoff |
| April 2002 | Deputy Assistant Secretary of Interior Wayne Smith discloses Scott Reed's plan to be "King of Indian gaming" |
| August 2002 | Congressman Bob Ney golf trip to Scotland |
| July 2002 | Agua Caliente Tribe of California hires Team Abramoff |
| September 2002 | Eshkol Academy opens doors |

| | |
|---|---|
| November 2002 | Jack Abramoff opens Stacks Kosher Delicatessen on Pennsylvania Avenue, Washington, DC |
| April 2003 | Tyco Corporation hires Team Abramoff |
| May 2003 | Iowa Sac and Fox Indian tribe hires Team Abramoff |
| November 2003 | Jack Abramoff gets Tyco out of General Services Administration debarment |
| December 2003 | Saginaw Chippewa Tribe of Michigan fires Team Abramoff |
| December 2003 | Jena tribe tries to obtain Louisiana casino— second effort |
| February 2004 | Armed takeover of Coushatta Tribal offices |
| February 2004 | Jack Abramoff interview with Susan Schmidt, *Washington Post* |
| February 2004 | Washington Post hit piece published |
| March 2004 | Jack Abramoff fired by Greenberg Traurig |
| March 2004 | Jack Abramoff commences consulting relationship with Cassidy & Associates |
| April 2004 | Stacks Kosher Delicatessen closes |
| April 2004 | Abbe Lowell files complaint with Senate Ethics Committee over McCain staff tactics |
| July 2004 | Jack Abramoff ends consulting relationship with Cassidy & Associates |
| July 2004 | Ralph Reed loses Georgia Lieutenant Governor's race |

| | |
|---|---|
| September 2004 | First United State Senate hearing: Jack Abramoff |
| November 2004 | Second United States Senate hearing: Mike Scanlon and Tigua |
| November 2004 | NBC News interview on Tigua; story not run |
| May 2005 | Jack Abramoff settles civil litigation from Foothill Capital regarding Suncruz Casinos loan |
| June 2005 | Third United States Senate Hearing: Kevin Ring and Choctaw tribe |
| August 2005 | Jack Abramoff indicted for conspiracy and bank fraud in Suncruz case; |
| | Jack Abramoff incarcerated in Los Angeles |
| November 2005 | Signatures Restaurant Closes |
| November 2005 | Fourth United States Senate Hearing: Coushatta tribe and Steven Griles |
| November 2005 | Fifth United States Senate Hearing: Italia Federici |
| Jan 2006 | Jack Abramoff enters guilty plea at federal courts in Washington, D.C. and Miami, FL |
| January 2006 | Actor George Clooney attacks Jack Abramoff at Golden Globe Award ceremony in Los Angeles |
| March 2006 | Jack Abramoff sentenced to 70 months in the Florida Suncruz case |
| June 2007 | Jane Abramoff, Jack Abramoff's mother, passes away |

| November 2006 | Jack Abramoff enters Cumberland Federal Correctional Institution |
| September 2007 | Jack Abramoff placed into segregated housing unit ("hole") for "Torah incident" |
| December 2007 | Jack Abramoff punished for giving Bible to another inmate |
| September 2008 | Jack Abramoff sentenced to serve an additional 48 months for honest services fraud, tax fraud and mail fraud at federal court in Washington, D.C. |
| March 2009 | Actor Kevin Spacey visits Jack Abramoff in prison |
| June 2010 | Jack Abramoff released from Cumberland |

# INDEX

# AMERICA
# DISARMED

## INSIDE THE U.N. & OBAMA'S SCHEME TO DESTROY THE SECOND AMENDMENT

## WAYNE LAPIERRE

# WND Books

WND Books   •   a WND Company   •   Washington, DC   •   www.wndbooks.com

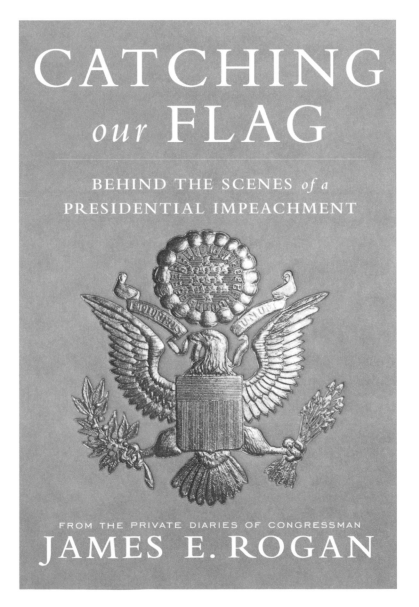

# CATCHING
## *our* FLAG

### BEHIND THE SCENES *of a* PRESIDENTIAL IMPEACHMENT

FROM THE PRIVATE DIARIES OF CONGRESSMAN

# JAMES E. ROGAN

## WND Books

WND Books • a WND Company • Washington, DC • www.wndbooks.com